JUN 2 2

# Exploring American Healthcare through 50 Historic Treasures

**About the Organization**

TThe American Association for State and Local History (AASLH) is a national history membership association headquartered in Nashville, Tennessee, that provides leadership and support for its members who preserve and interpret state and local history in order to make the past more meaningful to all people. AASLH members are leaders in preserving, researching, and interpreting traces of the American past to connect the people, thoughts, and events of yesterday with the creative memories and abiding concerns of people, communities, and our nation today. In addition to sponsorship of this book series, AASLH publishes the *History News* magazine, a newsletter, technical leaflets and reports, and other materials; confers prizes and awards in recognition of outstanding achievement in the field; supports a broad education program and other activities designed to help members work more effectively; and advocates on behalf of the discipline of history. To join AASLH, go to www.aaslh.org or contact Membership Services, AASLH, 2021 21st Ave. South, Suite 320, Nashville, TN 37212.

**About the Series**

The American Association for State and Local History publishes the Exploring America's Historic Treasures series to bring to life topics and themes from American history through objects from museums and other history organizations. Produced with full-color photographs of historic objects, books in this series investigate the past through the interpretation of material culture.

# Exploring American Healthcare through 50 Historic Treasures

TEGAN KEHOE

ROWMAN & LITTLEFIELD
Lanham • Boulder • New York • London

Published by Rowman & Littlefield
A wholly owned subsidiary of The Rowman & Littlefield Publishing Group, Inc.
4501 Forbes Boulevard, Suite 200, Lanham, Maryland 20706
www.rowman.com

6 Tinworth Street, London SE11 5AL, United Kingdom

British Library Cataloguing in Publication Information Available

**Library of Congress Cataloging-in-Publication Data**

Names: Kehoe, Tegan, author.
Title: Exploring American healthcare through 50 historic treasures / Tegan Kehoe.
Description: Lanham : Rowman & Littlefield Publishers, [2021] | Series: Aaslh exploring
    america's historic treasures | Includes bibliographical references and index.
Identifiers: LCCN 2021021610 (print) | LCCN 2021021611 (ebook) | ISBN
    9781538135464 (cloth) | ISBN 9781538135471 (ebook)
Subjects: LCSH: Medical policy—History. | Medical policy—United States. | Medical
    care—United States. | Health care reform.
Classification: LCC RA395.A3 K45 2021  (print) | LCC RA395.A3  (ebook) | DDC
    362.10973—dc23
LC record available at https://lccn.loc.gov/2021021610
LC ebook record available at https://lccn.loc.gov/2021021611

# Contents

# Acknowledgments

Any work of history relies heavily on archivists and librarians, and sometimes curators and collections managers, and that's especially true for this one. Thank you to Sarah Alger, Annie Anderson, Virginia Bones, Dawn Bonner, Emily Bowden, Alan Chilton, Lauren Clontz, Kay Coats, Emily Crumpton, Anna Dhody, Linda Drew, David Driscoll, Edward Dzierzak, Lowell Flanders, Brian Fors, Morgan Gieringer, Amanda Granek, Dominic Hall, Alan Hawk, Mary Hilpertshauser, Sara Hume, Polina Illieva, Beth Ann Koelsch, Megan Lallier-Barron, Jared Leighton, Donald Merritt, Marty Miller, Chessie Monks-Kelly, Jessica Murphy, Jennifer Nieves, Melissa Peña, Stacie Petersen, Kay Peterson, Doug Platt, Eileen Price, Nan Prince, Sondra Reierson, Terry Reimer, Molly Sampson, Anna Schuldt, Trenton Streck-Havill, Matthew Toland, Laura Travis, Lisa Verwys, and Sofia Yalouris. I'd like to give an especially big thank-you to Nona Bixler, Gary Bowen, Stephanie Crumpton, Adrian Fischer, Daryn Glassbrook, Stephen Hall, Adam Johnson, Scott McLaughlin, Cassie Nespor, Shannon O'Dell, Jamie Rees, Elizabeth Schexnyder, Trenton Streck-Havill, and Paula Summerly, who were particularly helpful with thorny problems or with tracking down information or images.

Several museum professionals and historians helped me along the way although they were not my point of contact regarding a particular artifact, including Tara Backhouse, Elizabeth Barrett-Sullivan, Tessa Campbell, Judy Chelnick, David Favloro, Terese Greene, Amanda K. Gustin, Zerah Jakub, Jori Johnson, Adriene Katz, K. LaSpruce, Kevin Levin, Lea McChesney, Lynda McLellan, Cathy Notarnicola, Rebecca Ortenberg, Barbara Rathburne,

Cameron Saffell, Katy Schmidt, Anton Sohn, Eliseo Torres, Ken Turino, and Rebecca West.

This book would not be what it is without my peer editors and sensitivity readers, Julie Bracker, Dominic Bradley, Marcella Lopez, Irene Vazquez, and Vickie Wu, my peer reviewers, or my editor Charles Harmon. I'd also like to thank the Librarians, Archivists, and Museum Professionals in the History of the Health Sciences (LAMPHHS); even those of you I didn't speak with directly about the book have been helpful in making it happen.

It's cliché for a writer to say their spouse is their best editor and greatest source of support, but Matt, I don't know how people write without a partner like you, and there's no one like you. A heartfelt thank-you goes out to my parents and the friends, loved ones, mentors, and colleagues, near and far, who have supported and inspired me during this project. I hope you know how much it means to me.

# Timeline of Objects

**c. 1925**
Midwife kit, page 126

**1936**
Schlitz "Sunshine Vitamin D beer" can,
page 130

**1938**
Infant incubator, page 134
Blood transfusion kit for house calls,
page 142

**c. 1940s**
Container for producing penicillin,
page 138

**1942**
Insurance card, page 147

**1945**
Army Nurse Corps seersucker dress,
page 150

**c. 1930s–1950s**
Protective mask, page 156

**c. mid-twentieth century**
DDT canister, page 164

**1952**
Emerson respirator, page 168

**1955**
Upjohn Disney collection, page 172

**c. 1960**
Straitjacket, page 177

**1960**
Model 4990 fiber optic gastroscope,
page 182

**c 1960**
Enovid birth control pill pack, page 187

**c. 1961**
Insulin syringe, page 122

**c. mid- or late twentieth
century**
Machine smoking filter pads, page 190

**c. 1960s**
Wheelchair, page 194

**1970s**
Heart-lung machine, page 198

# Introduction

A young couple watches their preterm baby, not three pounds and seemingly too small to be alive; her frail chest rises and falls steadily inside her incubator. A team of researchers scrambles to make enough of a miracle drug to be clinically useful. A doctor steps onto the front porch of her newly completed hospital, her community's first. Healthcare history is full of drama, yet also full of the routines of daily life. In this book, museum artifacts are windows into both famous and ordinary people's experiences with healthcare throughout American history, from patent medicines and faith healing to laboratory science.

This book showcases little-known objects that illustrate the complexities of our relationship with health, such as a bottle from the short period when the Schlitz beer company sold lager that was supposed to be high in vitamin D. It also highlights famous moments in medicine, such as the discovery of penicillin. The book looks at the artifacts and historic sites as individual things or places with their own stories, and as keys to larger trends. It samples topics spanning the late eighteenth through early twenty-first centuries, but omits topics ranging from chemotherapy for cancer, statins for cholesterol, and the influence of ayurvedic medicine; readers should not assume a topic is unimportant if it is not included here. The chapters are arranged chronologically, and while each one can stand on its own, reading them in order can provide a deeper sense of how they relate to one another and to larger trends in history.

Some of the artifacts in this book are truly treasured, while a few are vital connections to shameful events and currents of thought. For the sake of focusing on the objects and their own stories, some information that may be surprising is presented without detailed explanation. The fact that Nazi Germany based its sterilization program on one developed by an organization in New York State sounds like the stuff of rumor, but it is true. The bibliography includes sources that cover these assertions and the data supporting them in more depth.

A popular impression is that medical history is a tidy story about progress and the march of science, in which one discovery builds on another while incorrect ideas get discarded and forgotten. In some other tellings, science veered off of the path of what humans need and now progresses further away. At the same time, the popular imagination paints medical history as a gruesome spectacle, filled with the macabre and not for the faint of heart. The artifacts in this book show that both the "inevitable march forward" and the "macabre" templates are partially true, and both have flaws.

Behind the ghastly reality of surgeons operating without cleaning their bone saws between patients, there were people doing their best with what they knew. The same is true for patients buying nostrums, and the same is true of doctors and public health officials debating the safety of raw milk in the 1880s or of DDT in the 1960s. Rather than solely looking at advances in healthcare, it is useful to examine trends in how people have answered some fundamental questions with what they knew. Each artifact tells some piece of the story of how its users approached or answered one or more of these questions.

Perhaps the most basic of these questions is this: What causes sickness, and what causes health? Mainstream scientific understanding has not only changed over time, but has gone through periods of expansion and contraction, supporting either one underlying cause of disease such as unbalanced humors or invading microorganisms, or diverse causes including vitamin deficiency and pollutants. Meanwhile, cultural and religious practices, home remedies, and sales pitches provided alternative theories, many of which appeared to their adherents to counterbalance the flaws of mainstream science. A related question is this: How do we solve health problems that have been identified, when knowing what causes them isn't enough? Often it becomes an engineering problem—literally, in the sense of creating new technologies, or figuratively in creating new surgical techniques to address a known issue. The field of healthcare has developed clearer, more helpful, and more accurate answers to these questions over time, and yet there is still much to learn.

Broadening the scope from how to treat diseases to how to treat patients, another fundamental question is how care should be organized within care facilities and within professions. Something as simple as a nurse's uniform is actually part of the complex evolution of the role of the nurse from an informal, untrained caregiver, to a member of an emerging trade (with clothing resembling that of a maid), to a trained professional. Organizing care involves challenges when money, physical space, and practitioners' time are all finite. These questions become urgent when conditions like war or epidemics create the need for decisions that affect who lives or dies.

Another core question is this: To what extent can everyone know and master the principles of health, and to what extent do people need to rely on outside authorities? Relatedly, how can a patient determine whether a provider truly wants to help, or only wants to exert control or make money? The decades of the late nineteenth and early twentieth centuries are well-represented in this book because of a large number of developments in scientific medicine. The germ theory revolution, x-rays, antibiotics, and other developments greatly increased many people's willingness to trust science. However, both alternative health trends and unscrupulous practitioners persisted, creating the need for a trend toward greater accountability in the twentieth century, including FDA regulations and the requirement that research abide by institutional review boards.

When not everyone agrees on who has authority in health, how much should doctors and governments provide for the health of the populace? When there is a risk-benefit judgment to be made, who makes it? People often care about factors that science ignores, such as whether a treatment is affordable, and whether it's in line with their understanding of the world and their attitude towards outside authority and systems of power. This is clear in the diverse public attitudes toward masks and vaccines in the coronavirus pandemic, which is an evolving story as this book is being written.

These questions may be cerebral, but healthcare is inherently visceral. Think of the cool feel of nitrile gloves, the goopy strep throat medicine you took as a child, or the closeness of a mask. At a given moment in the past, the physicality of healthcare might be the soft worn edges of the toys the visiting nurse brought with her, the grasp of the metal calipers measuring your head, or the tarry stink of carbolic acid, a precursor to today's much gentler antiseptic hospital smell. The physical stuff of healthcare makes abstract concepts like trust, prejudice, and persuasion tangible.

Historian and museum curator Daniel Neff has remarked on a powerful phenomenon he observed when giving tours on both "Weapons of the American Revolution" and "Medicine of the American Revolution" at the same museum. Visitors were excited by visceral, gory content on the weapons tour—a bayonet makes a triangular wound that heals poorly—but fearful or disgusted by similar content on the medical history tour. It soon became clear that visitors imagined themselves inflicting the damage when taking the weapons tour, but imagined themselves as the victim or patient when taking the medicine tour. The history of healthcare can inspire deep empathy. I invite you to look for opportunities for empathy with the patients, caretakers, researchers, and victims and survivors of the complex stories that these historic treasures tell.

# Unwashed Groins and Child Labor: Cancer in the Early Industrial Age

Six- or seven-year-old children were the main defense against fires in eighteenth-century towns. A soot-filled chimney can easily catch fire, and many chimneys were constructed either too narrow or with too many turns and tight corners for an adult to sweep out. Master chimney sweeps used "climbing boys" (and rarely girls) who climbed into chimneys. They loosened the soot with a brush, and to an extent, with their own bodies. They were at risk of falling, suffocating, or getting stuck. Difficult, dangerous, and much-derided, the task of chimney sweeping was left to some of the poorest classes, which in the American colonies were enslaved and free Black workers. Sweeps were at high risk for lung diseases, often mistaken for tuberculosis. They also faced one risk almost no one else did: cancer of the scrotum.[1]

## CHIMNEY SWEEP'S CANCER

Decades after his climbing-boy days, a chimney sweep might notice ulcerous sores in the folds of his scrotum where soot had gotten lodged. These sores hardened into lumps, known among sweeps as soot wart. Sweeps often tried to remove the warts themselves with a knife, but if they had become cancerous, it was too late. The only cure was surgical removal of part or all of the scrotum. The disease most affected sweeps who had begun as children. Climbing boys occasionally went into chimneys naked, to avoid getting their clothing caught. A blanket over the fireplace collected soot, which the master sweep sold for fertilizer. Climbing boys often slept on bags of soot under these same blankets. To top it off, it was not unusual for a climbing boy to go two months without a bath.[2]

Soot wart or chimney sweep's cancer is a squamous cell carcinoma. Untreated, it spreads into the abdomen, where it is fatal. The disease was known to science since at least 1740, but English surgeon Percivall Pott connected it to soot in 1775. He was the first to link cancer with an environmental carcinogen, and the first to effectively describe a type of cancer as an occupational health issue.[3]

## WORKPLACE DANGERS

Pott's discovery came early in the Industrial Revolution, when there was a determined workers' rights movement. England passed the Chimney Sweepers Act in 1788, which banned apprenticeships for children under eight and required appropriate clothing and living conditions. An 1811 bill in New York would have done the same, but it died in committee.[4] In 1836, Massachusetts mandated that workers under fifteen be given at least three months of schooling a year. It was the nation's first child labor law.

Gradually, both stronger child labor laws and new machines to sweep a chimney's nooks reduced the number of climbing boys. Starting in the 1860s, doctors noted a decline in soot wart. But starting in the 1870s, doctors noticed this same cancer increasing among "mule spinners"—textile workers exposed to shale oil in factories. It became known as "mule spinners' cancer."[5]

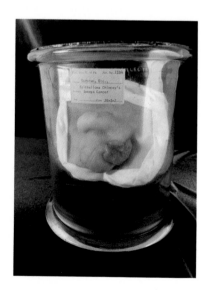

Wax model of scrotum, chimney sweep's cancer, undated.

WAX MODEL OF SCROTUM, CHIMNEY SWEEP'S CANCER, UNDATED. MÜTTER MUSEUM, PHILADELPHIA, PENNSYLVANIA. THE IMAGE IS USED BY PERMISSION OF THE COLLEGE OF PHYSICIANS OF PHILADELPHIA. PHOTOGRAPH BY LOWELL FLANDERS, 2020

This wax model of a scrotum with cancer is typical of the models doctors and medical students used to study a variety of diseases in the eighteenth century. The Dickensian image of a child chimney-sweep is equally obsolete, but occupational exposure to carcinogens is still a leading cause of scrotal cancer, and workplace health hazards continue to be relevant to health and medicine.[6]

## 2

# George Washington's Toothbrush

When George Washington was inaugurated as the first President of the United States in April 1789, people of all social classes came out to see him. Many of them had brushed their teeth that morning with a twig and some salt. Others used a sponge or rag, and still others a toothbrush, which had been gaining in popularity since about the 1750s. Some hadn't brushed their teeth all week, because dental hygiene and the causes of tooth decay were not yet well understood.

Despite his best efforts, Washington suffered serious dental disease throughout his life. He had lost all but one tooth by his inauguration. He wore five sets of dentures over the course of his life, none of which sat quite right in his mouth. While an oft-repeated myth says they were wooden, his false teeth actually included horse or cow teeth whittled to size; teeth made of elephant, walrus, or hippopotamus ivory; and human teeth. The latter could come from cadavers or living people who sold the teeth out of their own mouths for money. His household's ledger book noted that "Negroes" were paid for nine teeth, although at a much lower price than what denture-makers typically paid. It is possible that he bought them from some of the three hundred-plus Africans and African Americans he held in slavery, who did not have the right to refuse him.[1]

### THE PRESIDENT'S TOOTHBRUSH

Washington and his contemporaries subscribed to a vague notion that an unclean mouth caused bad breath and that brushing the teeth could prevent disease. Plagued by tooth decay, Washington took fastidious care of his teeth. To care for his own and false teeth while on the road, he used a travel dental set. Inside the stylish leather case, the set included a five-inch-long tooth-brush, a tooth powder box, and a tongue scraper. Each was silver—favored because unlike some metals, it is flavorless. The toothbrush has an ivory head and animal hair bristles. The tongue scraper is a flat silver strip, slightly flared at each end, thin enough to bend into a bowed shape.[2]

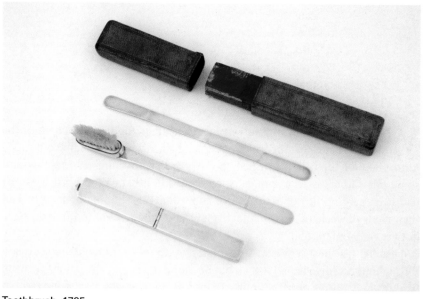

Toothbrush, 1795.
GEORGE WASINGHTON'S MOUNT VERNON, MOUNT VERNON, VIRGINIA. COURTESY OF THE MOUNT VERNON LADIES' ASSOCIATION.

Some dentists recommended that people brush their teeth with salt or baking soda, but many recommended tooth powders made of cream of tar-tar, ground bricks, charcoal, powdered crab shells, or other abrasives. Tooth powders were somewhat expensive, so not everyone used them. Not everyone brushed daily, either. Some dentists recommended tooth powder a few times a week.[3] Tooth*paste*, rather than powder, would become increasingly available in the nineteenth century.

## THE FIELD OF DENTAL HEALTH

Washington lived in the century when dentistry started coming into its own. The first comprehensive book on dental care came out in 1723; it laid to rest the medieval idea that cavities were caused by tiny worms. One of Washington's own dentists, John Greenwood, created the first foot-powered dental drill in 1790 by adapting a spinning wheel. It was not until a century later that it was understood why teeth decay (and thus why toothbrushing can prevent or slow the process). In 1890, Willoughby Miller, an American dentist working in Germany, applied the recent germ theory of disease and demonstrated that tooth decay is caused by microbes.[4]

As Washington took attentive care of his teeth, he probably would have liked to know that later on, some dentists tried to merge with other forms of healthcare. In 1840, a pair of dentists approached the University of Maryland School of Medicine about adding dentistry to the curriculum. The faculty dismissed the idea and sneered at dentistry as a profession. The moment confirmed that dentistry and medicine would stay separate, an episode dentists called "the historic rebuff." Even today, the fields are quite separate, although it's understood that oral health is essential to overall health. As Washington wrote, "Disorders oftentimes are easier prevented than cured."[5]

# The Age of the Vaccine

"It will be a great service indeed rendered to human nature to strike off from the catalogue of its evils so great a one as the small pox. I know of no one discovery in medicine equally valuable," wrote President Thomas Jefferson to Dr. Benjamin Waterhouse.[1] Smallpox was recognizable by the foul-smelling pustules that covered a person's body, but it killed by causing internal bleeding and damaging the heart, lungs, and liver. In different outbreaks, the disease killed 10 to 50 percent of its victims. It was also the first disease to have a vaccine. Doctors understood that the vaccine worked nearly a century before they understood precisely *why* it worked, but it took effort to convince colleagues, government, and the public that the vaccine was as revolutionary as it was.[2]

## THE AGE OF INOCULATION

Smallpox, caused by the *variola* virus, had been with humans for at least three thousand years. The earliest known prevention practices began in the twelfth century. People in Asia, Africa, and the Mediterranean protected themselves by deliberately catching a mild case of the disease that left them immune. They inhaled powdered material from smallpox patients' scabs, or inoculated themselves by inserting the scab material under their skin. When smallpox spread to Europe around the fifteenth century, knowledge of these practices did not spread with it. Soon afterwards, Europeans spread smallpox to the Americas.[3]

In 1717, Lady Mary Wortley Montagu had her son inoculated while living in Turkey, then brought the practice to doctors in her home country of England. Around the same time, New England minister Cotton Mather learned how to inoculate from Onesimus, a West African man he was holding in slavery. Mather started an aggressive campaign for inoculation, also called variolation after the *variola* virus that causes smallpox. However, he was met with equally aggressive resistance. English colonists believed that the practice was dirty or that it subverted God's will. Their prejudice against the peoples of Africa and Asia also led them to be suspicious of a health practice from these continents.[4]

It is part of several Native American cultures' oral traditions that European settler-colonists spread smallpox to them intentionally. Recent scholarly analysis of the letters and log books written by those involved has corroborated the oral tradition. In one instance in 1763, English soldiers presented Lenape messengers with a "diplomatic gift" of smallpox-carrying blankets, thus gaining the military advantage in the region. The European settler-colonists had some immunity to smallpox, so outbreaks did not have the same devastating, depopulating effect on them as on Native groups. However, the disease was still deadly and still feared, and it hit the continent in a series of epidemics spaced a decade or two apart throughout the eighteenth century.[5]

Few people were enthusiastic about inoculation unless the threat of smallpox was imminent, because it was a risky procedure. Inoculation guaranteed the patient would get the disease, but with a high probability it would be mild. With no inoculation, the patient ran the risk of getting smallpox naturally, with no guarantee it would be mild, but there was a chance they wouldn't get it at all. This tradeoff was hotly debated during the epidemic that swept North America during the Revolutionary War. Individuals and families weighed their options, and military strategists discussed the risks of inoculating the troops. Patients had to recover for about two weeks after inoculation, and they were contagious during that time. Mass inoculation meant leaving armies vulnerable to enemy attack.[6]

## FROM VARIOLATION TO VACCINATION

In 1796, English doctor Edward Jenner began a new era when he inoculated eight-year-old James Phipps not with smallpox, but with a milder, related disease called cowpox. Jenner wanted to scientifically test a phenomenon that a number of people had noticed: milkmaids who had contracted cowpox seemed to be immune to smallpox. After inoculating Phipps with cowpox, he tried to inoculate him with smallpox, but the boy did not contract the latter disease. Jenner began testing more people and writing up his results. He called his process vaccination, after the cowpox virus *vaccinia*.[7]

Dr. Benjamin Waterhouse, a founding faculty member of Harvard Medical School, read Jenner's report. Intrigued, he wrote to Jenner and asked for cowpox material to do his own experiments with. One of Waterhouse's first study subjects was his own five-year-old son. Experiments related to vaccination were often done on children because they had not had smallpox yet. Three more of his children and two household servants followed. Waterhouse became the first proponent of vaccination in the United States. He regularly purchased cowpox material from England, shipped in poultry feather quills. In a shipment in 1802, Jenner packed the quills inside a gift for Waterhouse: a small finely made silver snuffbox with a gold inlay.[8]

Waterhouse passionately supported public oversight of vaccines. It gave him a chance to be an exclusive supplier of vaccine material, and he also feared the consequences of unregulated vaccination. In Marblehead, Massachusetts, in 1801, a smallpox outbreak that killed sixty-eight people was attributed to the cowpox-based vaccine. Waterhouse was concerned some

Snuffbox that contained cowpox quills, 1802.
IMAGE BY THE AUTHOR. COLLECTION OF THE WARREN ANATOMICAL MUSEUM, CENTER FOR THE HISTORY OF MEDICINE IN THE FRANCIS A. COUNTWAY LIBRARY OF MEDICINE BOSTON, MASSACHUSETTS.

doctors had used smallpox rather than cowpox. Additionally, the vaccine was made from fluid taken from the pustules of cowpox patients, so failure to vaccinate correctly threatened the vaccine stock in the near future. "The enemies of vaccination wax strong owing to a few spurious cases under the care of some country practitioners," Waterhouse wrote. "I know not how large a gap our opponents will make in our practice." Later, the Massachusetts Medical Society held the position that the smallpox outbreak happening right after vaccination had been a coincidence. This was fully possible as smallpox was still regularly circulating.[9]

Waterhouse persuaded Boston's Board of Health to conduct their own trial of vaccination, and they came out strongly in favor of the vaccine. He also tried to persuade them to vaccinate the poor for free. When England created a national vaccination program in 1808, Waterhouse campaigned for Congress to do the same. While the young United States was beginning to embrace vaccination, Waterhouse's ideas about government-led widespread vaccination did not catch on. Meanwhile, many people on both sides of the Atlantic resisted the vaccine, wary of introducing a disease they personally knew little about into their bodies. A cartoon lampooning both the vaccine and popular fears showed people turning into half-human, half-cow monstrosities.[10]

Vaccination was often carried out in response to a current or potential outbreak. Smallpox continued to spread over the continent through trade, warfare, and migration. Representatives of the US government offered vaccination to a number of Native groups, but withheld it from Native groups who did not cooperate with forced removal from their land. Rates of vaccination and of the disease varied by race and socioeconomic status; in the American Civil War, case rates of smallpox were more than six times higher among Black soldiers than among white soldiers. In the late nineteenth century, the United States finally did get serious about mandatory vaccination as Waterhouse had wanted. Public health authorities targeted the poor, minorities, and immigrants. They saw these communities as reservoirs which could spread disease to the rest of the population.[11]

In the mid-twentieth century as vaccines for more diseases became available, states began requiring several vaccines in childhood. This era also saw a level of confidence in science which was not yet present in Waterhouse's time. At last, following over a decade of massive vaccination efforts worldwide, the World Health Organization declared victory over smallpox in 1980. It was the first, and so far only, human disease to be eradicated.[12]

Even an advance as important as vaccination did not become ubiquitous immediately after successful tests. Doctors like Waterhouse took up Jenner's work and continued both the studies on safety and efficacy, and the equally formidable task of convincing doctors and the public to accept the small cost of vaccination in exchange for the great benefit of "striking off" smallpox for good.

# 4

# No Wrong Way to Eat

Food has historically been a major logistical hurdle for people whose digestive systems do not work well. In this case, the essential question for patients and providers is not what causes poor health, but what tools and techniques can address or work around the problem. Most famously, after President James Garfield was shot in 1881, his doctors inserted a mixture of whiskey and enzyme-treated beef into his rectum, following a practice used since the ancient Egyptians. He ate that way for two and a half months until his death.[1] Thankfully for the nearly half a million people who use a feeding tube in this country today, alternative feeding methods have improved.

## BOATS AND STRAWS

The simplest solution for people who can't chew or sit up is food mush. Since antiquity, the main formulas were "pap," made of flour or breadcrumbs and water or milk, and "panada," made of bread, milk or broth, and other ingredients like eggs, beans, oil, or butter. Feeding vessels are often called pap boats after the style popular from the Renaissance through the nineteenth century, resembling a small gravy boat. They ranged from simple clay or metal vessels to ornate pieces of dishware.[2] Pap boats were also used as infant feeders until baby bottles overtook them in popularity.

People with disabilities that interfered with drinking from a cup popularized the drinking straw, first commercially produced in the mid-nineteenth century after years of straws made of actual straw. In the 1880s, a new design for a disposable paper straw, combined with the recent popularity of soda

Pap boat, undated.
COURTESY OF THE TOUMA MUSEUM OF MEDICINE, JOAN C. EDWARDS SCHOOL OF MEDICINE, MARSHALL
UNIVERSITY, HUNTINGTON, WEST VIRGINIA

fountains, made straws popular for nondisabled people too. In the 1930s, an inventor created a bendable plastic drinking straw for his daughter. The new design made it easier for children, disabled people, and sick people to drink. Hospitals were among the first to buy these straws.[3]

### TUBES AND PUMPS

Pap boats and straws helped many people, but only those who could swallow. In the late sixteenth and early seventeenth centuries, some doctors fed patients broth or mush with a metal or leather tube down the throat or nose. A more practical and comfortable soft rubber feeding tube was invented in 1874. Today, most tube feeding is done through a surgically-created hole called a stoma. Gastrostomy (creating a stoma in the stomach) had been tried in the nineteenth century with little success, but surgeons performed gastrostomies reliably beginning in the 1910s.[4]

If a person's stomach doesn't tolerate a tube, they might vomit or just not absorb nutrients well. In 1910, Max Einhorn pioneered inserting a feeding tube through a patient's nose all the way down into the duodenum, the first part of the intestine. Another way around the stomach is intravenous sugar solutions, which were developed in the 1930s. By the 1960s, both tube feeding (called enteral nutrition) and intravenous nutrition (parenteral) had kept people alive, and doctors debated their merits. Evidence that has been accumulated since then supports enteral feeding in most cases.[5]

Pharmaceutical and infant formula companies began selling premade tube-feeding food in the 1950s. Tube feeding was becoming a recognized niche of needs. However, people who were medically fragile in certain ways were usually turned away for gastrostomies before 1980 because of the risks of major surgery. That year, minimally invasive surgery to create a stoma debuted. This technique, percutaneous endoscopic gastrostomy (PEG), greatly increased the availability of tube feeding. In the late 1980s came tubes that do not stick out from the body. The low-profile tube connects to an extender while people take their meals, and lies flat under clothing the rest of the time.

Today, some patients use feeding tubes temporarily while in intensive care in a hospital, and some people with disabilities use a feeding tube for decades while leading active lives. Pap boats, on the other hand, have become museum pieces only. For people who need help eating but don't need tube feeding, spoons and straws are enough.

# A Pioneering Operation

Jane Todd Crawford needed help. Her abdomen was painfully swollen and somewhat misshapen. Several doctors had agreed that she was suffering from a pregnancy gone wrong, perhaps well past term, but she had had five children, so she may have known this felt different. Her doctors called a surgeon to assist with the delivery, but feeling her abdomen, the surgeon declared the swelling was an ovarian tumor. It was 1809 and no one had removed a tumor in a patient's abdomen before, but Ephraim McDowell thought he could do it.[1]

## SURGERY ON THE FRONTIER

Some of McDowell's colleagues tried to dissuade him from this ambitious, dangerous procedure. Many doctors still believed tumors were caused by a whole-body imbalance of the "humors" that governed health. An excess of the humor "black bile" was thought to make a patient melancholy and cause cancer. An untreated tumor can produce a mass of dead tissue with dark fluids, and doctors interpreted the fluids as black bile. It was not clear that Crawford's tumor was cancerous, but most of the medical profession believed that removing a tumor was hopeless.[2]

Moreover, the state of surgery itself was only questionably ready. European and American surgeons were still evolving from medieval barber-surgeons, who would shave one person, extract another's tooth, then perform an amputation all as part of their trade. By McDowell's day, surgeons went to medical school, but amputation was still the most common form of surgery, and post-surgical infections were expected. Some procedures on the skull and genital area had been developed, but this was as close to the core of the body as the scalpel went. Operations on the chest and abdomen were considered too dangerous, at least in the West. There were even some who said attempting a risky surgery like this was murder.[3]

McDowell took on not-insignificant professional risk in attempting the operation, but Jane Crawford had to take on personal risk. McDowell told Crawford her condition was dangerous, and the surgery he proposed would be an experiment. He was willing to try if she would come to his home office in Danville, Kentucky. It was sixty miles away, and even in his case report he noted that this journey seemed impracticable. While this may seem unnecessarily cruel, it's possible he had her come to him to prove she was committed to having the procedure done.[4]

Crawford did come to him, making a several-day journey on horseback. McDowell noted bruising on her abdominal wall, probably caused by resting her tumorous belly on the horn of her saddle. On Christmas morning, he operated. The procedure was done without anesthesia, as all operations were at the time. McDowell reported that he and assistants "took out fifteen pounds of a dirty, gelatinous-looking substance, after which we cut through the Fallopian tube and extracted the sack, which weighed seven and one-half pounds."[5] Twenty-five days later, Crawford rode home, again on horseback. She lived for thirty-two more years, outliving her surgeon.

## MCDOWELL'S LEGACY

McDowell is sometimes called "the father of abdominal surgery." Abdominal surgery was pioneered centuries earlier in the Middle East, and Cesarean sections for emergency childbirth had been performed even earlier, although they were not done regularly until the twentieth century.[6] McDowell's story is an example of how history that is complicated is often portrayed as tidy and heroic.

After operating on Crawford, McDowell continued to hone his techniques, mostly by operating on enslaved women. These women may well have been just as courageous as Crawford, but they did not have a say in the decision to make them into subjects for experimental surgery. Historian Harriet Washington writes that "their health, intrinsically, didn't need to matter to him" because they had no legal right to refuse.[7] McDowell's colleagues did not question him because many of them had honed their techniques on enslaved people too. These women were rarely remembered by his biographers and admirers, and it is difficult to learn anything about them because he did not record their names.

The operation on Crawford became the focal point of McDowell's legacy. However, it was not until the 1910s that August Schachner, a historian and biographer of McDowell, observed that Jane Todd Crawford herself was barely mentioned in other accounts. He researched her family and the five children she had before the operation. Schachner joined forces with several local history groups and local chapters of national groups, such as the Colonial Dames, to turn McDowell's home into a museum and furnish it with period-appropriate pieces.[8]

Historic house museums and local historical societies are a cornerstone of American public history efforts and are among the most common types of museum. One of their greatest strengths is the fact that they are often founded, funded, and run by people who want to celebrate their subject. However, this can also be a serious flaw when these enthusiasts—who may

"Traveler's Room" at Ephraim McDowell House, nineteenth century.
COURTESY OF THE MCDOWELL HOUSE MUSEUM, DANVILLE, KENTUCKY.

be professionals, descendants of the person being honored, or community members moved by civic pride—mythologize and eulogize a historic figure. For example, one potential source of information on McDowell is a biography of over four hundred pages written by his granddaughter, but it was largely fabricated, and the modern-day McDowell House Museum does not rely on this inaccurate text.[9]

Retellings of McDowell's story introduced the idea that he was working on the literal frontier. His two-story home with a formal parlor was certainly not rustic. Legend says McDowell operated on his kitchen table, but today, the McDowell House Museum presents the more likely scenario that saw patients in a dedicated space, the "Traveler's Room." While doctors of his era typically visited patients in their own homes, an arrangement like this was not unheard of either.

McDowell did make lasting contributions to abdominal surgery. His work on ovariotomy emboldened other surgeons to explore similar work, although the field remained (rightly) hesitant until sterile surgery in the late nineteenth century reduced the risks. McDowell was also known for his skill at lithotomy—removing kidney stones, gallstones, and so on. He removed bladder stones from seventeen-year-old future president James Polk.[10] Lithotomy was not at all new, having been practiced in ancient Greece and India and throughout the Renaissance, but it still required an adept surgeon.

McDowell's choice to practice on unconsenting patients is an example of the deeply unheroic in medical history, but his and Crawford's story is an early American example of how surgery advances: the surgeon diligently uses the knowledge available at the time, while both surgeon and patient take risks.

# 6

# Healing by a Higher Power

A ccording to the story handed down for generations, a man once asked a prophet for help because his five-month-old twins were sick. The prophet turned to one of his followers and gave him this handkerchief, instructing him to wipe the babies' faces with it, and they were healed. The Church of Jesus Christ of Latter-day Saints believes that prophets and miracles are not exclusive to an ancient biblical past, but part of modern life. The handkerchief belonged to the religion's founder, Joseph Smith, and it is now displayed in their Church History Museum.[1]

Faith healing is as diverse as faith itself. The tenet that a higher power can cure illness or injury is so central in some religions that believers reject all other approaches to healing, but it's much more moderate in other religions. Most of these ideas are well outside of scientific medicine, but they're significant to many people's experiences of healthcare.

## HEALTH IN THE CHURCH OF JESUS CHRIST OF LATTER-DAY SAINTS

The Church of Jesus Christ of Latter-day Saints, whose adherents are nicknamed Mormons, was formed amid the religious revivals of the early nineteenth century. Wilford Woodruff, the man to whom Smith gave the handkerchief in 1839, described having healed over a thousand people through the power of God. The Church view on health and medicine is influenced by the teaching that God takes interest in regular people's lives.[2]

In their first decades as a church, Latter-day Saints moved en masse several times to escape controversy and persecution. They wanted their communi-

Handkerchief, 1839.

"THE CHURCH OF JESUS CHRIST OF LATTER-DAY SAINTS CHURCH HISTORY MUSEUM, SALT LAKE CITY, UTAH. PHOTOGRAPH OF JOSEPH SMITH'S RED HANDKERCHIEF © BY INTELLECTUAL RESERVE, INC."

ties to be largely self-sufficient, and greatly appreciated that a skilled midwife could reduce the need for doctors. Stories from the era describe Church leaders performing faith healing through prayer, laying of hands, and consecrated oils. The Church doctrine on health forbids tobacco, alcohol, hot drinks, and misusing drugs, and recommends eating little meat and favoring healthy foods. The teachings are similar to "clean living" movements in the early to mid-nineteenth century, which questioned medical doctrines of the day, favored prevention over treatment, and warned against substances deemed too "stimulating."[3]

Initially, the Church recommended that people favor natural and herbal remedies if their faith was not enough to heal them. In the twentieth century, when medicine had advanced well beyond the bloodletting and mercury of the era the Church was founded, Church leaders embraced modern medicine. Most Church members followed, but a significant segment stayed attached to herbal medicine in addition to or instead of conventional cures.[4]

## THE ROLE OF FAITH IN HEALING

Religion and medicine mixed freely in Western society until around the seventeenth century. However, some religions oppose medicine, teaching that all disease is illusory or caused by lack of faith. Christian Science, founded by Mary Baker Eddy in 1875, teaches that using medicine harms a patient by further demonstrating a lack of faith. Today, people turn to faith healing in numerous religious traditions for a variety of reasons. Some patients feel other treatments have failed them. Some find faith practices more affordable or culturally sensitive than mainstream care. Within their religion, people can look for help from authorities they already trust. Some parents from insular anti-medicine religious communities have gone to the press after losing a child, explaining that they had believed that their faith healer was a real, if alternative, healthcare provider. Faith healing is far too often implicated in the medical neglect of children.[5]

Present-day surveys say that over one-third of Americans pray for specific health outcomes. Research from the late twentieth century through the present has suggested that prayer can have a measurable, positive effect on health. Whether related to a particular religious denomination or not, for people of faith prayer can bring hope, comfort, and strength, which are correlated with good health outcomes. However, research has discredited the idea that people can affect a patient's health by praying from a distance.[6] Each religion and each religious person has their own journey reconciling faith and science when they seem to conflict. For Latter-day Saints, the handkerchief and its associated lesson about miraculous healing remain meaningful across the centuries, independent of whether it's medically plausible.

# Morton's Ether Inhaler and the Advent of Anesthesia

A young man with an aching growth on his neck sat waiting for the surgeon's knife. It was 1846, and surgery was excruciating. As early as ancient Sumeria, both alcohol and opium were used to dull pain, but they were not general anesthetics and large doses could be fatal. Another option was "mesmerism" or hypnotism, which many doctors scoffed at. However, this operation was supposed to be different. The surgeon, John Collins Warren, had allowed a dentist to offer a public demonstration of a drug that promised to conquer pain.

## DOUBTS

The drama of anesthesia revolved around one big question: Is this new idea trustworthy? One reason for doubt was that the Connecticut dentist William T. G. Morton was an outsider. Doctors at the time did not see dentists as fellow medical professionals. While the doctors who watched the young man's surgery may not have known it at the time, Morton had a bit of a history of hopping from one entrepreneurial idea to the next. He hoped to patent his new discovery, something that was quite unusual for medicines at the time. The drug was diethyl ether, which had been known since the mid-fourteenth century but not used for medical purposes until the eighteenth. Then, it was used for breathing difficulty, nausea, or to sober up a drunk person. Morton mixed it with essential oil and called it a formula of his own invention, which he dubbed "Letheon."[1]

In private experiments, Morton had poured ether on a handkerchief and held it up to the patient's mouth and nose. He was often the patient. For the public demonstration, he wanted something patentable. He commissioned a custom inhaler, a glass globe with an ether-soaked sponge inside. Inhalers date from the late eighteenth century and were used to deliver medication or to use steam to clear a cough. The inhalers we know for asthma today came much later, in the mid-twentieth century.[2]

Ether Inhaler, 1847.
ON DISPLAY AT THE PAUL S. RUSSELL, MD MUSEUM OF MEDICAL HISTORY AND INNOVATION AT MASSA-
CHUSETTS GENERAL HOSPITAL, BOSTON, MASSACHUSETTS. COLLECTION OF THE WARREN ANATOMICAL
MUSEUM, CENTER FOR THE HISTORY OF MEDICINE IN THE FRANCIS A. COUNTWAY LIBRARY OF MEDICINE.

There was some reason to doubt anesthesia would work. A year earlier, in 1845, dentist Horace Wells used nitrous oxide to anesthetize a patient in front of a room full of Harvard Medical School students. Also called laughing gas, the gas was already known for causing a high. It's used as a mild anesthetic to this day, but in this demonstration, the patient groaned and appeared to be in considerable pain. The students jeered and called Wells' demonstration "a humbug." In fact, Wells was not the first to try. Japanese surgeon Seishū Hanaoka is credited with creating the first modern anesthetic in 1804 while trying to re-create a legendary lost formula from second-century Chinese surgeon Hua Tuo, but the news did not spread beyond Japan. In the United States, surgeon Crawford Long used diethyl ether to induce anesthesia in 1842, but did not publicize his results until 1849.[3]

If the mystery drug worked, doctors and patients would want to know that it was safe. Some doctors were wary of drug-induced unconsciousness. Others believed pain acts as a life-preserving stimulant during the stresses of surgery. Meanwhile, some felt that people who were claiming to have solved the problem of pain were playing god. Some clergy warned that God had chosen for people to feel pain. The religious question was never cleanly resolved, but as anesthesia became more popular and more mainstream it faded into the background.[4]

With these questions swirling around the semicircular operating theater, Morton arrived at his demonstration quite late. The patient, Gilbert Abbott, sat waiting in the operating chair, while a crowd of surgeons waited to see whether the operation would be noteworthy. Morton held the inhaler up to Abbott's face, and the patient breathed the mystery vapor for several minutes. It smelled like oranges and something sickly sweet: that was the ether. Abbott drifted off, and when he awoke, he recalled only a dull scraping—the surgeon making a three-inch incision in his neck. The drug had worked, and the patient was in fine condition.[5]

## ANESTHESIA'S LEGACY

After the demonstration, news spread around the world in newspapers and medical journals. Soon, the question of trustworthiness was joined by the question of who should get the credit for the transformative new practice.

Anesthesia had a bumpy road to popularity. Dr. W. Clay Wallace of New York called ether anesthesia a "boon" but also cautioned, "It is dangerous to be made dead drunk, by any cause." A pair of doctors in Philadelphia are reported to have quickly stopped administering ether during an operation. The patient had fallen unconscious and they panicked, not understanding that this was a known effect. The actual risks of ether anesthesia included patients becoming excited and manic. Others were difficult to rouse, and some vomited copiously, while other patients had an easy experience. Dr. James Simpson of Edinburgh tested a number of volatile chemicals to find something else that could work on pain, arriving at chloroform in 1847. Chloroform damaged anesthesia's reputation because of a number of fatal accidents. However, anesthesia became particularly fashionable in 1853 after Dr. John Snow administered chloroform to Queen Victoria for the birth of Leopold, her eighth child.[6]

William Morton believed that the discovery of anesthesia was his and his alone, but not everyone agreed. Horace Wells and Crawford Long both felt they had an earlier claim. In addition, physician and geologist Charles Thomas Jackson announced that he had discovered ether anesthesia first. Morton had been nominally studying medicine under him, although the arrangement was a loose one. Jackson made a reasonably well-supported claim that he had suggested to Morton that ether might work as an anesthetic, and a hotly contested claim that he should get the credit above Morton for its discovery. They soon became bitter rivals.[7]

Morton and Jackson were jointly awarded a patent in November 1846, but far from settling the debate, this gave a greater number of people reason to be angry. In the 1840s, respected members of the medical profession did not seek patents on their discoveries; the philosophy was that one should not profit off of anything that could alleviate human suffering. Many dentists and doctors ignored the patent, and it was rendered unenforceable when even United States Army surgeons etherized patients without a license in the Mexican-American War (1846–1848). Meanwhile, the credit controversy continued, and the French Academy of Sciences fanned the flames by awarding the extremely prestigious Prix Montyon to both Morton and Jackson in 1850.[8]

Historians and writers took up the question of credit for who discovered anesthesia. Crawford Long's 1842 experiments are honored at the Crawford W. Long Museum in Jefferson, Georgia. The operating room at Massachusetts General Hospital became known as the Ether Dome. Some accounts say that the original ether inhaler broke; the one on display at the Russell Museum at the hospital is likely from the following year.[9] Those loyal to Mass General are fond of recounting that when Abbott's surgery was over, Dr. Warren turned to the onlookers, victorious, and proclaimed, "Gentlemen, this is no humbug!"

# 8

# Bitters and Irregulars: Alternative Healing in the Nineteenth Century

Bilious complaints,—those tedious ills,
Ne'er conquered yet by drastic pills;
Dread Diarrhea, that cannot be
Cured by destructive Mercury.[1]

So goes part of a many-stanza poem circulated by the Hostetter's Bitters company in 1867, mocking "regular" medicine. Today, regular medicine is called mainstream, biomedical, or scientific medicine, but it wasn't very scientific yet. Doctors raised blisters, used bloodletting, and gave laxatives and emetics. The popular drug calomel or "blue mass," often given for dysentery and a host of other complaints, could indeed cause mercury poisoning (and, ironically, diarrhea). There were two types of alternative to mainstream treatments in the nineteenth century: patent medicines like Hostetter's, and the various schools of thought that were lumped under the name "irregular medicine."

### "CELEBRATED STOMACH BITTERS"
Advertisements claimed that "Hostetter's Celebrated Stomach Bitters" cured and prevented nearly infinite ills, from gastrointestinal distress to "nervous prostration," "mental gloom," and general lack of vigor. This was a hallmark of advertisements for drugs with a proprietary formula, often called patent medicines. Most of them did nothing except make the consumer feel good briefly with alcohol, morphine, or other substances. Patent medicine sellers

professed to cure ailments from coughs (such as Ayer's Cherry Pectoral) to menstrual symptoms (such as Lydia Pinkham's Vegetable Compound). Many claimed they could cure anything and replace doctors. However, people also used patent medicines in addition to regular medicine, the way one might buy over-the-counter cough syrup today. Patent medicines came in several forms—tablets, oils, elixirs, and bitters, which are blended plant extracts usually prepared with alcohol.

Hostetter's Celebrated Stomach Bitters bottle, 1889.
COURTESY OF THE MUSEUM OF THE ROCKIES, BOZEMAN, MONTANA.

Many medicines doctors prescribed in the early nineteenth century were as poisonous as the patent medicine advertisers made them out to be. However, such advertisements painted with a very broad brush, claiming all medicines that were "mineral" in origin were catastrophic for consumers' health. The emphasis on the naturalness of their cures was something that the sellers of patent medicines and alternative healers with a range of profit motives had in common.[2]

Calomel was an easy target for patent medicine makers' jabs. Another remedy in the regular doctor's repertoire at the time was hard liquor, which was used for pain relief but also supposed to revive a weak patient or invigorate a stable one. However, since the late eighteenth century there had been increasing concern about heavy drinking. Many patent medicines positioned themselves as healthy alternatives to liquor, despite being high proof as well. Hostetter's was even served by the glass in some saloons. Some bitters makers falsely claimed their product contained no alcohol to appeal to temperance supporters, while Hostetter's and others claimed that alcohol preserved the medicinal qualities of herbs. The bitters brands that survived past the patent medicine days became cocktail ingredients, such as Angostura.[3]

Hostetter's was specifically marketed to travelers and people moving to territory unknown to them during the US conquest of the people and land to the west. Advertisements highlighted the likelihood of gastrointestinal distress on these journeys. At the time, both regular medicine and popular understanding believed that putrid smells or air caused disease. "Woe to him who encounters the malaria of a tropical seaboard, or the miasma of a Western swamp, with a stomach untoned and nerves unbraced!" This warning was in an essay in the 1868 edition of Hostetter's almanac, which the company published annually between 1861 and 1909. The proposed solution, naturally, was Hostetter's bitters as a daily preventative.[4]

Hostetter's Bitters were wildly popular, bringing in over a million dollars annually at the company's peak between 1862 and 1883. Far from being a fringe, alternative healing in the nineteenth century reflected people's desire to manage their own health.[5] Both patent and irregular medicine had broad appeal for patients who felt their "regular" doctors didn't listen to them, or who didn't want a drug that they correctly guessed was making them sicker.

## BY THEIR OWN REGULATIONS

While patent medicine companies capitalized on the public's distrust of harsh and ineffective drugs by selling them different concoctions, a number of doctors (and self-styled doctors) rejected mainstream medicine altogether and invented new schools of thought. In the late eighteenth century, German Samuel Hahnemann claimed that medicines should provoke symptoms mimicking a disease, the way high doses of the malaria drug quinine cause a fever. He also believed the body is more sensitive when sick and proposed using infinitesimal doses. Hahnemann coined the term "allopathy" for regular medicine. His system, homeopathy, survives to this day despite failing the tests of modern science.[6]

From the 1790s through the 1830s, medical societies made up of regular doctors had successfully lobbied for laws in many states requiring doctors to be licensed. Critics of the medical establishment pointed out that these medical societies were insular and elitist, granting credentials to only those who thought like them. Over the next several decades, many of these regulations were repealed or ignored. It was easy for irregulars to set up their own schools, promulgating their ideas and granting certifications in their theories.[7]

Often stressing preventive care, irregular doctors positioned themselves in opposition to the authoritative medical establishment. They appealed to people who wanted to be self-reliant or wanted medicine to seem gentle and natural. In the early nineteenth century, Samuel Thomson took the herbal medicine of folk healing traditions and home remedies and turned it into a movement. He and his followers wrote poems instructing consumers on how to use the six medicines he sold. Ideas like Thomson's were bolstered by political and cultural movements supporting "the common man" rather than hierarchy, elitism, or special expertise, such as the era of Jacksonian democracy from the 1820s to the 1850s.[8]

Some of these schools of prevention were inspired by religious beliefs, and some included driven asceticism. A number of irregular medical philosophies preached that health of the body and spirit could be attained by abstaining from alcohol, eating a specific diet (often vegetarian), or following similar rules. John Harvey Kellogg, the director of a health retreat and maker of corn flakes, believed the cereal suppressed the libido, which he saw as a health benefit. Other nineteenth-century irregular trends included naturopathy, the power of positive thinking, chiropractic, and mesmerism, which purported to manipulate the flow of magnetic life-forces in the body. The founders and most enthusiastic adherents of these trends considered them holistic approaches to health. There were also "eclectic" doctors who sampled a variety of different irregular trends. Patients whose health eluded easy answers tried anything that seemed promising.[9]

Irregular doctors included people practicing medicine from their own culture and borrowing from others, including Chinese and Latin American medicines, Ayurvedic medicine from India, and various African traditions. Some irregular practices were more open to women and non-white practitioners than regular medicine. This meant a wider range of patients could find doctors they could relate to.[10]

In the twentieth century, new standards for accreditation and licensing deepened the divide between allopathic medical schools and schools of alternative medicine. In 1910, Abraham Flexner wrote a report exposing the deficiencies of medical schools in the United States and Canada. The schools that survived the sweeping reforms that followed were supported by philanthropy and university and hospital affiliation. It was no longer the case that anyone who could find paying students could call themselves a medical school. The same generation saw a series of new regulations on medications. The patent medicine companies that survived dodged FDA review by labeling their products nutritional supplements. This is the guise that Hostetter's Celebrated Stomach Bitters was sold under until the 1960s when it ceased production.[11]

Germ theory, antibiotics, more rigorous methodologies such as randomized controlled trials, and diagnostic technologies from x-rays to MRIs have made regular medicine into scientific medicine with a body of evidence behind it. However, people continue to seek regimes they believe will allow the body to heal itself and alternatives to medicines they worry are harmful. While the presence of regulations makes a difference in how patients and consumers choose their care, the echoes of both patent medicines and irregular medicine are clearly heard today.

# Blood Shed after the Battle: Bleeding Cups

It was August 10, 1861, and neither army was prepared for the medical toll of war. The Battle of Wilson's Creek was the first major American Civil War battle west of the Mississippi River. Missouri had citizens supporting both the Union and the Confederacy, and in a sense it belonged to both North and South, and to neither. The Civil War took place at a "both and neither" time in the history of healthcare: many ideas and practices were brand-new or only a generation old, but many of the older practices had not died out yet.

During the Battle of Wilson's Creek, confederate surgeons raised a yellow flag on a house on the battlefield, signifying a field hospital. Even as bullets flew, doctors from the two sides coordinated care. The family who lived there emerged from the basement after the battle. The children fetched water and the adults helped the medics as best they could. Most of the wounded were transported to larger makeshift hospitals the next day. Some of them would lose still more blood, at their surgeon's hands.[1]

## BLEEDING AND BLISTERING

Among the treatments a soldier might receive was cupping, often used for inflammation. The surgeon made a grid of small cuts in the patient's skin using a multi-bladed tool called a scarificator, then placed a cup over them. Cups could be horn, metal, or glass, and were a couple of inches in diameter. The surgeon created suction by heating the cup or using a small pump to draw air out of a hole, raising a welt.[2]

Bleeding cup, 1860s
COURTESY OF WILSON'S CREEK NATIONAL BATTLEFIELD, REPUBLIC, MISSOURI.

The soldier sat for some minutes with several cups tugging around the area of his infected wound. The surgeon broke the suction and removed the cups, wiping away a teaspoon or two of blood. The tools were wiped down, but not truly cleaned before the next patient. The soldier may have felt a bit better because cupping acted as a counterirritant, distracting him from the pain. In time, his welts would turn into bruises, which would heal in a few days or weeks.

This process is wet cupping; without cuts, it's called dry cupping. The welt was seen as evidence that toxins were being brought to the surface. Wet cupping was often used for localized issues that were thought to be caused by too much blood, such as inflammation. A civilian doctor might have used a leech instead of the blade and cup, but leeches were hard to keep in field conditions. For systemic issues like fever, doctors tended to prefer venesection, cutting into a vein in the arm. Contrary to medical thought at the time, cupping and bleeding did nothing to aid the healing process.

## HUMORS AND HEROICS

These practices originated in the humoral theory of medicine, dating back to the ancient Greeks. In this theory, the body and personality are governed by four humors: blood, black bile, yellow bile, and phlegm. Fevers, dysentery, and inflammation were supposedly caused by an excess of blood, because they were considered hot and wet diseases and blood was the hot, wet humor. Miasma theory, a competitor to humoral theory, suggested that illness was due to bad air or noxious odors. Some doctors saw use in both theories, believing that out-of-balance humors made people more susceptible to miasmas.[3]

In the 1790s, the influential doctor Benjamin Rush streamlined the humoral theory. He believed all disease was caused by an excess of blood. He recommended bleeding, blistering with hot poultices, and "purging" by inducing vomiting or diarrhea with drugs like the toxic calomel. While he had detractors, Rush was widely influential in American medicine. He coined the term "heroic dose," meaning a very aggressive course of treatment, and his ideas became known as heroic medicine.

Bloodletting waned as medicine was influenced by new understandings of physiology. The boom of irregular medicine in the 1830s was in part a push for medicine to be gentler, in reaction to heroic medicine. Meanwhile, researchers applying statistical analysis to medicine started seriously questioning cupping and bloodletting in the 1830s. Physicians had begun to observe that bloodletting was not effective in treating fevers. Some doctors believed that humoral theory had been right but that fevers had changed, and that feverish patients now needed stimulation (alcohol and hearty food).[4]

Much of this research happened in Europe, but during the Civil War, American physicians began more actively participating in research as well. In the 1830s through 1860s, the wealthiest American medical students studied in Paris after earning their degree, where they had access to patients to practice on, bodies to dissect, and instruction from leaders in medical science. The Union Army Medical Department created the country's first national standards for licensing physicians, and required that they have a degree from a regular school, excluding homeopaths, naturopaths, and other irregulars. Meanwhile, the Confederacy faced shortages in food, medicines, and medical supplies, and they accepted homeopaths and other irregular doctors. By the end of the war, Union Army hospitals had surpassed the Paris model by incorporating rudimentary clinical trials and increased specialization of practice.[5]

During the war, many physicians raised challenges to older theories of disease, asking whether different types of disease might have their own "germ" (in the sense of seed or origin). They also debated whether disease was a product of something in the patient's physical constitution, or a localized process. Some proposed that disease matter was produced in the bodies of sick people and transmitted by their breath. Work being done in Europe would later confirm the germ theory, making it clear that inflammation was not caused by superfluous blood, nor by localized toxins. Cupping saw a revival in Western alternative medicine, influenced by Traditional Chinese Medicine and other schools of thought, starting in the late twentieth century. However, the Civil War marked the last years cupping was in fashion in conventional Western medicine.[6]

# Under the Surgeon's Tent: The Physician in the Civil War

John Wiley looked up. Two of his assistants were carrying a wounded man through the rain into the damp canvas tent. The patient was neither the first nor the last. Wiley's tenure as a Union Army surgeon would see twenty-eight battles, including the Second Battle of Bull Run, the Battle of Chancellorsville, and the Battle of Gettysburg.[1] All army physicians were called "surgeon," performing operations and tending to the sick. Working in a variety of conditions, from muddy tents to state-of-the art hospitals, they adapted to rapid changes; the decline of bloodletting is just one example. During the war, Union surgeons saw their field transform as they developed new techniques for amputations and began to learn from their colleagues in unprecedented ways. Meanwhile, surgeons, nurses, and administrators developed new systems for ensuring that patients could access care beyond the surgeon's tent, given the overwhelming need and limited resources.

## MANAGING A MEDICAL CRISIS

For the first year of the Civil War, neither side had an organized system for getting the wounded to medical care. Company musicians and assistant surgeons served as stretcher-bearers, but often, a wounded soldier's comrades would carry him away from the fighting. By 1862, both armies had organized ambulance corps, with a medical supply cart, horse-drawn ambulances, and dedicated personnel. During battle, the surgeon stayed back from the lines while assistant surgeons ran first aid or triage stations just behind the lines. Surgeons like Wiley decided which patients just needed some rest, whiskey,

Army Surgeon's Tent, 1862.
COURTESY OF THE NATIONAL MUSEUM OF CIVIL WAR MEDICINE, FREDERICK, MARYLAND.

and beef tea before heading back into the fighting, and which needed to recover at a convalescent hospital. [2]

During the war, hospitals were built on the pavilion model, with each ward
as its own well-ventilated single-story building. This was heavily influenced
by the theory that bad air or miasma causes disease, and became the standard
for new hospitals until a generation later when germ theory demonstrated
that keeping environments sterile was at least as important as keeping them
ventilated. Receiving and distributing hospitals provided short-term care
while doctors assigned the patients to other hospitals for longer care. This
organized network of triage and tiered care was a lasting effect of Civil War
medicine. Hospitals transformed from places for the poor into places where
a wide swath of society received care. Nurses went from untrained aides to a

body of caregivers who served as hospital administrators and enforced good sanitation and nutrition as well as providing treatment.[3]

## FIELD AMPUTATION

"Doc, will I walk again?" Wiley pursed his lips and probed the bullet wound in the young man's leg with his fingers. Most of a surgeon's work after a battle was removing bullets, but sometimes musket balls mutilated tissue and shattered bones, their soft lead spreading on contact rather than tearing cleanly through the body. Wiley's options were to amputate the leg above the injury, to try to excise just the part of the bone that had shattered and hope that the leg healed, or do what he could to patch up the leg without surgery. Many surgeons had preferences for one approach or another, but the right course was also dependent on the specific injury.[4]

"You'll walk better on a wooden leg than dragging what's left of your shin." Wiley knew that amputating within the first two days of the injury would increase his patient's chances of survival. This was largely due to the risk of gangrene and erysipelas, which are now understood to be streptococcal infections that grow in wounds. He nodded to one of the three assistant surgeons, who poured some ether onto a sponge and held it under the soldier's nose. The liquid's fumes put him out. They all worked together under the nine-by-thirteen-foot tent.[5]

Wiley used a different knife or saw for each part of the body he cut through. First, he cut the skin and muscle in two long flaps. An assistant held the main artery closed—perhaps Redford Sharp, who would soon be promoted to head surgeon in another regiment. A third man supported the patient's leg. Wiley sawed through the bone below the knee. Sharp tied the arteries off and Wiley sewed the flaps closed over the end of the bone. An assistant dressed the wound with bandages. The men did their best to keep their tools clean, but in the field this was not always possible. A few hospitals were testing an abrasive solution of bromine as a treatment and preventative for gangrene, but this was still experimental, and Wiley's patients probably saw no antiseptics. When the man woke, the surgeons would give him opiates or whiskey for the pain. As he recovered, he would be in a nurse's care.[6]

Wiley stood up, assessing the patients who were next. During a slow moment, he might sit down with his portable writing desk and record the nature of this man's injury and the decisions he made in treatment. The recently established Army Medical Museum collected these case histories along with embalmed specimens from interesting cases, ranging from amputated limbs to diseased tissues. Wiley and his colleagues were accountable to an outside authority in a way that they had not been before, and the printed catalog of the museum's contents helped physicians advance their knowledge. With so many patients, they honed their skills in the Civil War in a way they never had a chance to in civilian life. As a result, more surgeons chose specialties, and the war saw improvements in plastic surgery and the birth of orthopedics and neurology.[7]

At the beginning of the war, "surgeons saw wounds of such destructive nature that they had no frame of reference for the care and treatment of the patients," writes historian Shauna Devine. In just a few years, between improvements in technique, triage, and hospital care, Union Army surgeons and nurses routinely saved the lives of their amputation patients. Nearly three-quarters of amputees survived their wounds, a better track record than some of the most medically advanced countries in the world.[8]

# "Inflammatory Mischief" Meets Antiseptic Techniques

In the eighteenth and much of the nineteenth centuries, doctors commonly went straight from dissecting cadavers to delivering babies without washing their hands. In the 1840s, a few doctors suggested that doctors were transmitting diseases and causing post-childbirth infections, but the idea was widely ridiculed. By the end of the nineteenth century, science would look at contagious disease differently, in part because of English doctor Joseph Lister. The carbolic acid sprayer was one of his attempts at preventing post-surgical infection.

## THE LONG ROAD TO STERILE SURGERY

When Lister was born in 1827, it was so common for hospital patients to fall ill during their stay that their illness was often termed "hospitalism" rather than diagnosed as a specific disease. Microorganisms were first seen under microscopes about 150 years earlier, but few people connected them to disease. In the 1850s and 60s, both Florence Nightingale and nurses in the American Civil War helped make cleanliness a priority in hospitals, but they were concerned with visible filth, not microscopic germs. In 1854, London surgeon John Snow made a case against miasma theory. He mapped the victims of a cholera outbreak and traced it to a particular water pump, correctly surmising that something in the water caused the disease.

By mid-century, Lister and a few contemporaries questioned the long-held belief that pus in a wound indicated healing. They were part of the development of germ theory, the idea that pathogens such as bacteria and viruses cause disease. Lister examined pus under a microscope and saw bodies he thought might be a living thing causing the infection. Lister tried a number of possible antiseptic solutions to kill microorganisms on wounds without luck. He tested carbolic acid (also called phenol) on a child's broken leg in 1865. At the time, a badly broken leg was liable to get so infected that it had to be amputated to save the patient's life. With daily changes of carbolic acid-infused bandages, the boy's wound healed well, and he walked out of the hospital on two legs. Lister then created a comprehensive system to fight germs, using carbolic acid for handwashing and preparing bandages and sutures.[1]

Lister wrote, "All the local inflammatory mischief and general febrile [feverish] disturbance which follow severe injuries are due to the irritating and poisoning influence of decomposing blood or sloughs." That is, infection is caused by the same thing that causes food to spoil: microorganisms. "Inflammatory mischief" could have been an insult from a colleague rather than a description of infection. Among the many naysayers, some had competing theories about disease, and others felt Lister's techniques distracted doctors from their real work. Despite a growing interest in germ theory, several American hospitals banned his techniques. Doctors continued to wipe bloody tools on their unwashed coats. Despite evidence for Lister's methods, the field was slow to change until some of the old guard retired.[2]

## ANTISEPTIC SPRAY

In 1871, Lister was inspired to try to disinfect the air itself after reading that bacteria had been found in airborne dust. He developed a carbolic acid sprayer, operated by a hand pump which a surgical assistant had to constantly work. Within a few years, these sprayers were replaced by models like this one, which use steam to propel the acid continuously. This handheld sprayer, about ten inches tall, belonged to surgeon Charles Brooks Brigham. Graduating from medical school in 1870, Brigham entered the field when germ theory did, and he adopted Lister's methods, including the sprayer.[3] Brigham didn't use a sprayer for long, however. Even Lister abandoned it within a decade, as it became clear that disinfecting the air was not very effective, and his earlier idea to disinfect wounds themselves was more useful.

Perhaps it's good the sprayer didn't last. In 1871, Lister operated on an abscess on a high-profile patient. The patient's physician, William Jenner, operated the sprayer, an early model that used a hand pump. Every pump of the handle released a cloud of vapor that smelled like coal tar. Jenner accidentally sprayed his patient in the face—a fumble made worse by the fact that the patient was Queen Victoria.[4]

Pasteurizing milk had critics because it wasn't the farm-fresh milk people were used to, and they worried that both the taste and health benefits were diminished. However, "certified" pure milk was not affordable to the working class, because the testing added to the cost of selling milk. Many people in rural areas preferred to get their milk the way they always had, no certification or pasteurization.

Both certification and pasteurization were medically sound, but pasteurization rose to prominence as a public health measure. The distinction here is not just that medical decisions often focus on the individual and public health focuses on society. Faced with the decision of whether and how to regulate milk, by the early twentieth century almost all state government health agencies had chosen to require pasteurization because the low cost made it scalable as well as safe.[4]

# 13

# Skull Shape and Scientific Racism

The meaning that a tool carries is shaped by how it has been used. This Budin craniometer was created for measuring infants' skulls. It's a tool of anthropometry, or measurements of the human body. Today, anthropometric norms are used in ergonomic design, sizing medical devices, and forensics, and for years they've been used in charting children's growth. However, craniometers and other anthropometric tools also have a darker set of meanings: they were widely used in scientific racism. This school of thought aimed to classify people into "superior" and "inferior" racial categories. For much of the nineteenth and twentieth centuries, racism was codified into medical and social scientific understandings of the body.

## MEASURING SKULLS

In the nineteenth century, mainstream doctors and anthropologists began using the tools of medicine to divide people into races. Craniometers were invented for use in phrenology, which was most popular from the 1810s through the 1840s. This now-discredited practice supposedly revealed personality traits based on the bumps on a person's skull. In 1840, Swedish anatomist Anders Retzius published a system called the "cephalic index" that relied on craniometry. In this system, people and racial groups were categorized based on whether their heads were more round or tall. He and other scientific racists claimed that this index quantified how "civilized" a racial group was.[1]

Scientists carried out some of this research on living people from cultures they considered "primitive," such as Saartje Baartman of the Khoi people

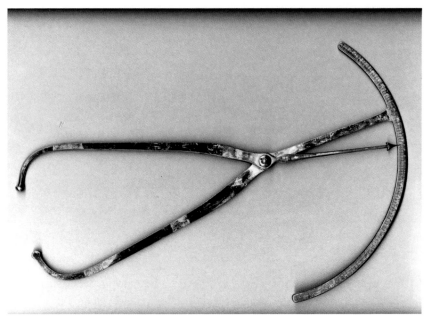

Budin Craniometer, 1885
COLLECTION OF THE NATIONAL MUSEUM OF HEALTH AND MEDICINE.

of South Africa, who was dubbed the "Hottentot Venus" and subjected to invasive medical examinations. They also performed research on specimen collections, consisting of dead bodies which were often stolen from their communities. The Army Medical Museum (now the National Museum of Health and Medicine) and several other museums amassed large collections of bodies used for actual clinical study and for anthropometry. They particularly prized samples from "vanishing" groups—often indigenous peoples whom American and European groups were killing, assimilating, and erasing. Some doctors and government officials turned the lens of scientific racism onto Native American groups struggling with tuberculosis epidemics, claiming that the outbreaks were evidence that Natives are constitutionally weak and that "stronger races" would inevitably replace them.[2]

### THE LEGACY OF RACIAL CLASSIFICATION

Scientific racism was used to justify all kinds of racist behaviors and systems, including slavery. A hallmark of the line of thought that included scientific racism was using several routes, not just race, to dehumanize people. White women were compared to non-white women. The Irish (who were not considered white at the time) were compared to Black people, who were compared to animals. Scientists made many spurious connections between race and disability, especially intellectual disabilities. People with disabilities were even more routinely dehumanized than today. These connections lasted into the late twentieth century with terms like "Mongoloid," which referred both to Asian and Pacific Islander people and people with Down syndrome.[3]

Scientific racism also provided a false theoretical backing for racism within healthcare. Medicine has a long history of using society's most vulnerable for testing. This was easier to justify when these same groups were literally considered less human. One of the better-known examples is the work of J. Marion Sims, although institutions have been just as guilty as independent doctors. When Sims used enslaved Black women for experimental surgeries, his physician colleagues refused to hold the women down because they didn't want to be in the room with their tortured screams. So, he made his test subjects restrain one another. He was hailed as the father of gynecology.[4]

Beginning in the late nineteenth century, the tide began to shift. Numerous studies disproved the theories behind scientific racism. Anthropologist Franz Boas found that the children of immigrants differ greatly from their parents in a number of characteristics that were previously thought to be genetic, including cephalic index. This was particularly important in an era when the United States had passed a number of laws restricting immigration, particularly from Asia and Eastern Europe. However, the belief that racial divides were scientifically proven continued to influence immigration policy. At immigration inspection stations in this era, the rate of recommended rejections was particularly high for Asian immigrants. Immigration officers baselessly spoke of Europeans being "a much higher sanitary type" than Asians, replacing the older language of round heads and tall heads with equally incorrect language that reflected the priorities of the day.[5]

Modern research has made it increasingly clear that "race" is not an inherent quality. It's a loose group of characteristics that varies person to person. In science, race is most usefully described as a set of statistical models—groupings that can show trends if analyzed appropriately, or be wildly misleading if used inappropriately. However, race has significant cultural meanings that can affect whether good health and medicine are within reach. In the United States, Black and Latine patients are less likely to have health insurance and to be able to pay for health services than their white counterparts. Those who do have access to services are still less likely than white patients to receive appropriate basic clinical services, cardiac care, or several other types of treatment. A persistent myth that Black people have a higher pain tolerance than white people continues to affect medical practitioners' assessment and treatment of Black patients' pain. Scientific racism casts a long shadow into the present.[6]

# "Health and Comfort of Body, with Grace and Beauty of Form"

Probably no undergarment has been more controversial. Some doctors said corsets protected women's health, while others said they violently exerted more than twenty pounds of pressure on women's insides.[1] The debate about what corsets do to the wearers was especially heated in the nineteenth and early twentieth centuries, when fashionable corsets squeezed the waist to exaggerate an hourglass shape. With medicine and social norms exerting pressure on one another, "health corsets" were designed as a less dangerous alternative to rigid corsets made of whalebone or steel.

## HEALTH AND COMFORT OF BODY

Beginning in the 1820s, when the laces that cinched corsets closed were first threaded through metal rather than stitched eyelets, it became possible to "tight-lace" a corset, compressing the body even further than the corset was designed to. Women in a too-tight corset often experienced gastrointestinal distress as well as weakness and shortness of breath. The latter two were considered elegant, feminine traits for much of the nineteenth century, when being waiflike and just slightly consumptive was heavily romanticized. Long-term tight-lacing could bend or fracture the ribs, and displace the liver and uterus. Newspapers and magazines in the nineteenth century ran cartoons about tight-lacing, perhaps partly out of genuine health concern, but also to satirize women's supposed vanity and to scold women for fashions that were considered overly sexual.[2]

In 1873, Dr. Lucien Warner responded to concerns about the negative health effects of a tight corset. He used coraline, a flexible new material made from a fibrous plant, in place of whalebone or steel to give his "health corset" its shape. Advertisements proclaimed that it offered "Health and comfort of body, with grace and beauty of form." Another brand of "health corset" was "Ferris' Good Sense Corset Waist," with the tagline "Sensible mothers wear Good Sense. Beautiful children wear Good Sense." Corsets were made for children and adults, and advertisers encouraged the already-entrenched belief that a well-fitting corset would train a growing girl's body to develop correct posture.[3]

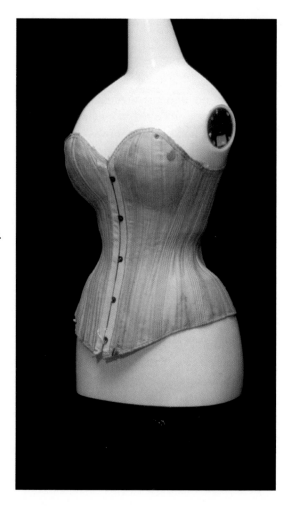

Warner's Health Corset, 1885.
PHOTO COURTESY OF THE KENT STATE UNIVERSITY MUSEUM, KENT, OHIO.

A few other trends helped flexible corsets catch on. In the second half of the nineteenth century, women were increasingly involved in sports and exercise, which made flexible corsets more appealing. Osteopaths, chiropractors, and practitioners of other health trends of the day taught that the alignment of the body was central to good health. Astute marketers sold their corsets as back braces as well as undergarments, and some companies sold corsets for men and women to use while recovering from surgery.[4]

## GRACE AND BEAUTY OF FORM

Nineteenth-century doctors loved to critique how women conformed to gender roles, including how they carried themselves. Scientists were fascinated with medically categorizing people by sex, and considered both intersex people and anyone deviating from the narrow parameters of gender norms to be freaks. For example, scientists began describing homosexuality and bisexuality as pathological, and incorrectly attributed these "flaws" to patients having physical characteristics of the "wrong" sex. The first significant body of scientific research viewing differences in sexuality and gender identity as diversity to be understood, rather than pathology to be corrected, began in the early twentieth century, headed by the physician Magnus Hirschfeld. However, the Nazis burned his work in 1933.[5]

Victorian doctors assumed that a "normal" woman's uterus and ovaries controlled both her physical and mental health, "As if the Almighty . . . had taken the uterus and built up a woman around it," wrote a doctor in 1870.[6] Doctors believed that women's nerves were literally, physically more delicate than men's. They also believed the body had a limited amount of "vital force" and argued that frail men could regain vital force, but women should not spend their force on anything but reproduction. This distinction was also racialized: doctors claimed hard labor was beneficial to Black women's health.[7]

Medical views of women's bodies created arguments both for and against the corset. Some doctors, especially women, argued that if women were weak, corsets were partly to blame. Others argued that as the "weaker sex," women needed a corset's support. Worried that the wrong amount of abdominal muscle tone could disrupt pregnancy and childbirth, some doctors cautioned against exercise that could augment muscle tone, while others cautioned against corsets that they believed caused these muscles to atrophy. Noted orthopedic surgeon Adolf Lorenz said in 1922, "A corset gives a woman the sense of being completely dressed and thus contributes to her peace of mind."[8]

The health corset allowed women to trade some degree of support for more freedom to move. Health corsets were particularly meaningful in the late nineteenth century when going corset-free was a daring statement for a middle- or upper-class woman to make. However, starting in the 1920s, corsets were no longer a staple undergarment. A variety of factors likely contributed to the change: flappers, the feminist dress reform movement, and a wartime shift away from having household staff to help with dressing.[9]

In the century since the corset debates died down, societal concepts of gender have continued to be fed through and reinforced by scientific and medical thought. Women continue to be underrepresented in medical studies, especially on medication efficacy and adverse drug reactions, and both intersex and transgender people are even more underrepresented. When sex differences are studied, they are usually studied in aggregate, although it is now understood that hormones, sex chromosomes, and sex differences in various parts of the body (reproductive and not) all play separate, interacting roles. Advertisers and sometimes doctors still conflate beauty standards with health or allow perceptions of gender to color health advice.[10] The concept of a "health corset" faded as corsets went out of fashion. The relationship between medical and social understandings of women's bodies and health, however, has remained complex.

# East Meets West in the Medicine Cabinet: A Chinese Doctor in America

The historic site Kam Wah Chung, once a bustling apothecary and multi-purpose space for Chinese immigrants, now seems incongruous in John Day, Oregon. By the time the store closed in 1948, the city no longer had a sizable Chinese population, and most patients were white. Many non-Chinese people throughout American history have seen Chinese medicine as "exotic," but Chinese medicine has always played a role in the array of American healthcare options. Kam Wah Chung was an anchor for local Chinese Americans, while its doctor Ing Hay navigated conflicting attitudes toward his validity as a healthcare practitioner.

## IMPORTATION AND IMMIGRATION

Before about 1850, Chinese immigration to the United States was rare, and Chinese medicine existed here in piecemeal influences. Colonists before the American Revolution used imported Chinese herbs like ginseng, rhubarb, cardamom, and camphor in their home remedies. In the early nineteenth century, American medical missionaries criticized Chinese medical practices but adopted certain elements at the same time. The Opium Wars, in which Britain attacked China to try to gain the upper hand in trade in the mid-nineteenth century, destabilized the Chinese economy and popularized opium as a recreational drug. In the cultural upheavals that followed, many people in China began studying Western medicine, although traditional medicine was still practiced. These upheavals also created the conditions for substantial emigration from China.[1]

In 1849 with the start of the gold rush in California, large numbers of people began making the three-month ocean voyage from China to find work. Almost everywhere there were Chinese immigrants, at least one practiced medicine and herbalism. While some Chinese doctors touted a real or imagined lineage from generations of doctors to inspire their patients' confidence, the medicine they practiced was of their time. Chinese medicine is not a unified set of traditions from an ancient source, as it is sometimes portrayed. For example, these immigrants rarely practiced acupuncture, which was a low-status treatment in China in the nineteenth century.[2]

### THE GOLDEN FLOWER OF PROSPERITY

Ing Hay settled in John Day, Oregon, in 1887, where he met his future business partner Lung On, also from Guangdong Province in China (their names would be written Hay Ing and On Lung in Western convention). This part of Oregon was populated by the Warm Springs, Wasco, Paiute, and other Native tribes until an 1855 treaty. In 1885, hundreds of Chinese moved to John Day after nearby Canyon City's Chinatown burned down and local authorities forbid its residents from rebuilding. Kam Wah Chung, or "Golden Flower of Prosperity," was a center for the Chinese community. It served as a doctor's office, general store, bunkhouse, place of worship, and unofficial post office.[3]

Ing's medicines were largely imported from China. Newspaper accounts and even Chinese doctors' own advertisements often took an Orientalist bent, playing up the bear claws, tiger bones, and other medications white audiences found exotic. However, the medicine Ing practiced was predominantly plant-based, not unlike American folk medicine. As Ing's patient base grew, people began buying prescriptions by mail, writing to him to describe their symptoms. He was credited with saving a road crew that was building a highway when the whole crew was stricken with flu. He also had a reputation for being skillful at managing infections that had entered the bloodstream. His Chinese and Chinese-American patients appreciated sharing a language and culture with their healer.[4]

Non-Chinese Americans, particularly middle-class and wealthy white people, were fascinated with Chinese medicine despite considerable animosity toward Chinese immigrants. Advertisements for Chinese medicine portrayed it as gentler and more natural than Western medicine. Ing was known for his skill at pulsology, making a diagnosis by feeling the patient's pulse at the wrist. Many women preferred pulsology over Western medicine's invasive touch, especially in an era when doctors were often authoritarian and condescend-

Kam Wah Chung pharmacy, 1880s-1940s.
COURTESY OF KAM WAH CHUNG STATE HERITAGE SITE, OREGON STATE PARKS, JOHN DAY, OREGON

ing toward women. While abortions were illegal in Oregon at the time, Ing offered them. His method included rubbing the patient with a coin, which is part of folk medicine for a variety of ailments in much of Asia, and prescribing an herbal tea for the patient to drink at home. The medical establishment saw Chinese doctors as an ideological and competitive threat. Ing was charged with practicing medicine without a license three times, but the charges were dismissed each time.[5]

When Ing retired in 1948, Kam Wah Chung sat idle for years. Stringent limits on Chinese immigration that began with the 1882 Chinese Exclusion Act had been eased in 1943, but Chinese medicine would not be in fashion again until the 1970s. The older generation of doctors who had immigrated from China before the immigration ban were retired or dead. After WWII, while biomedicine was seeing a surge of public trust, Chinese-Americans entered Western medical schools in greater numbers than before, facing prejudice but less of it than in prior decades. In the early years of Maoism in the 1950s, the Chinese government codified a variety of traditional healing practices into what's called "Traditional Chinese Medicine" in English. In part because of these changes, while Chinese medicine has seen a resurgence in the past fifty years, practitioners today (in the United States, China, and elsewhere) do not practice the same Chinese medicine that Ing Hay did.[6]

Kam Wah Chung opened as a museum in 1975 with most of its contents undisturbed. Despite their important presence in the landscape of American health practices, only two historic Chinese pharmacies in the United States are preserved as museums; the other is the Chew Kee Store in Fiddletown, California. Researchers at the Oregon College of Oriental Medicine are translating prescriptions in Kam Wah Chung's archives from Cantonese to English, expanding understanding of this piece of the past.[7]

## 16

# The "Cure" That Wasn't

Resting in a lounge chair on a porch in a bucolic village while a nurse brings you fresh milk, and scientists strive to better understand your disease in a laboratory next door, was probably as pleasant a way to be sick as any, but tuberculosis was anything but pleasant. Also called consumption, phthisis, or the white death, it is a lung disease that can be fatal without treatment. For centuries, the standard prescription was the "rest cure," meaning minimal activity and plentiful fresh air. In the late nineteenth century, sanatoriums made the rest cure available to a broader swath of society, but "cure" was a misnomer.

### "CURING" AT SARANAC LAKE

Until that time, there were few hospitals for tuberculosis. Patients who couldn't afford to travel for fresh air often tried to conceal their symptoms including fevers, weight loss, and coughing up blood. Those who could, took to the mountains. The village of Saranac Lake is in the Adirondack Park, which had become a beloved wilderness retreat for white vacationers. Dr. Edward Livingston Trudeau stayed there while recovering from his own tuberculosis, then built a laboratory to study the disease. In 1885, Trudeau opened the Adirondack Cottage Sanatorium to care for working-class people with tuberculosis. Historian Katherine Ott has asserted that people thought of consumption and tuberculosis as two different diseases, the former refined, the latter dirty. It affected all social classes, but poor tuberculosis patients died ten to twenty years younger than rich ones.[1]

Laboratory, 1894.
IMAGE BY THE AUTHOR. SARANAC LABORATORY MUSEUM, SARANAC LAKE, NEW YORK.

Independent "cure cottages" where patients rested on porches year-round sprung up around Trudeau's laboratory. In winter, they purchased or rented fur coats to keep off the chill in the mountain town fifty miles south of Canada. Nurses brought hearty meals and fresh milk. Patients came to Saranac Lake from Latin America, Europe, and around the United States. Many of them stayed in cottages specialized for and by people from one ethnic or cultural group or occupation. Black, Greek, and Jewish patients found community in their own cottages. Among the most well-known of the cottages was run by Alfredo and Alice Gonzalez, from Puerto Rico and Cuba, respectively, who had both come seeking the "cure" and met and married in Saranac Lake. Their cottage gave rise to a Spanish-speaking culture and an interest in Latin music and dance in the town between the 1920s and 1950s. Saranac Lake was also a refuge from the outside world's prejudices against tuberculosis patients—although the disease was romanticized, recovered patients found it hard to find work or marry, as they were seen as frail and contagious.[2]

Once the US Immigration Service began screening newcomers in 1891, would-be immigrants with confirmed cases of tuberculosis were turned away at the border or hospitalized there for treatment. People with suspected cases were often turned away for "poor physique." Jewish people in particular were falsely reputed to have poor or "tubercular" skeletal and muscular development. In 1917, the US Public Health Service ruled that doctors could determine a patient had tuberculosis based on their observations of the patient's body alone, even if no tuberculosis bacteria were found in the patient's sputum when observed under a microscope. At the time, laboratory diagnosis based on bacteria was considered difficult, especially for early-stage cases. This change allowed doctors more power to exclude immigrants on health grounds, although in practice the exclusion was threatened more often than it was carried out.[3]

With patients from across the United States as well as international patients who were able to enter, Saranac Lake was one of the first sanatoriums. There were over 800 sanatoriums in the United States alone before their decline in the 1950s. Like hydropathy "water cures," an alternative medicine popular in the mid-nineteenth century, some patients felt their treatment was like staying at a health spa.[4] Sanatoriums also had a lot in common with other treatments (real or specious) that isolated patients in groups, for Hansen's disease (leprosy) or mental health. At these institutions, the governments or care providers had much more control over their patients than over the average citizen.

The "rest cure" gave some patients a respite from symptoms, but it was palliative care, not treatment. Some people did recover enough to get back on their feet, and many of them stayed local, where there was no stigma to tuberculosis. Some made a living off of crafts they had learned in occupational therapy, a new field at the time. Others became nurses, x-ray technicians, researchers, or landlords of cure cottages. For other patients, however, the rest cure was just a comfortable way to live out the remainder of their time.[5]

## PREVENTION AND A REAL CURE

German microbiologist Robert Koch isolated the tuberculosis bacterium in 1882, which proved that the disease is contagious but did not provide a cure. Doctors at the Saranac Lake Laboratory confirmed patients' diagnoses by looking at their sputum under the microscope. They also experimented with procedures to drain fluid off a patient's lungs.[6]

The confirmation that tuberculosis is contagious spurred public health work in the United States to catch up to the more developed sanitation movement in Britain. Anti-tuberculosis groups exhibited at fairs and in vacant storefronts, and created newspaper ads, pamphlets, and later, films. They encouraged people to spit their phlegm or chewing tobacco in cups called spittoons rather than in the street. Local, state, and federal governments tried a range of laws, from forbidding spitting to forcibly removing people suspected of recklessly spreading disease. Some of these laws gave legal weight to attempts to control the habits and movements of non-white people, immigrants, and the poor in the name of health.[7]

The antibiotic streptomycin made tuberculosis curable in the 1940s. The Saranac Lake Laboratory was reinvented in 1956 as the Trudeau Institute, studying infectious disease. Today, the historic laboratory building is a museum nestled in the village's downtown, which is dotted with porches where patients used to sit. However, tuberculosis is still a major global threat, and in the United States, it's largely a disease of the marginalized, present on Native reservations, in prisons, and among the homeless. The bacteria can evolve rapidly if the medication regimen is not strictly followed, and strains resistant to multiple drugs emerged in the 1980s among populations with poor access to healthcare. As extensively drug-resistant strains proliferate, it's possible antibiotics will be another "cure that wasn't."[8]

# Cocaine the Medicine and the Drug

In the time-honored tradition of self-experimentation, ophthalmologist Karl Koller applied a solution of cocaine to his own eye in 1884, after Sigmund Freud told him about the drug. His eye was numbed, and he realized this could be a middle option between putting a surgical patient unconscious and the patient feeling everything. Forty years after general anesthesia debuted, cocaine was the first local anesthetic, and it was a revolution. While it later proved to be dangerous and addictive, cocaine's modern identity and cultural meanings are wildly different from its medical use.[1]

## COCAINE, THE ANESTHETIC AND FEEL-GOOD DRUG

South Americans had used the coca plant for medical and recreational purposes for centuries, but new possibilities opened up in the 1860s when scientists isolated its potent active ingredient, cocaine. Doctors tried it as a stimulant, stamina enhancer, and treatment for morphine addiction, and one doctor used it as a local anesthetic on the throat.[2]

Once Koller publicized it, cocaine caught on in eye surgery, dental surgery, and more, especially in procedures that were difficult or impossible to do on an unconscious patient. Cocaine and other coca products were sold over the counter for labor pains, fatigue, anxiety, and asthma. Everyone from Pope Leo XIII to Thomas Edison endorsed Vin Mariani, a drink made from red wine and coca leaves and sold as a health tonic. An alternative cocaine tonic had caffeine but no alcohol—Coca-Cola, which now uses a de-cocainized coca flavor.[3]

Coca bottle, c. 1896.

LILLY STANDARDIZED COCA FLUID EXTRACT BOTTLE, ELI LILLY AND
COMPANY, COURTESY OF WOOD LIBRARY-MUSEUM OF ANESTHESI-
OLOGY, COPYRIGHT 2010. SCHAUMBURG, ILLINOIS.

Cocaine did not live up to its healthy reputation. It can lead to stomach
and lung problems, and cognitive effects like paranoia. Overdoses can induce
seizures, heart attack, or stroke. It was especially dangerous in dental surgery
where it went quickly from the gums into the bloodstream. It is also addictive.
In the late nineteenth century, the science of drug addiction was in its infancy;
the idea that addiction was something more than excessive use was only just
catching on. By the 1890s, scientists tried to synthesize a safer substitute for
cocaine. Eucaine and procaine (Novocain), both non-addictive and far less
toxic, were early successes, but cocaine is still used as an anesthetic, especially
when its properties as a vasoconstrictor (contracting the blood vessels) are
needed.[4]

## CHANGING MEANINGS

As cocaine addiction became common in the early twentieth century, the
drug developed social stigma and an underground market, even before it was
prohibited. Black people who used cocaine were painted as demonic, crazed
"fiends," and there was a myth perpetuated by white people that cocaine improved Black people's aim with a gun. These fears were used to justify police
violence against Black communities. Drug use was already painted differently

for people of different races and socioeconomic status; addiction came to be defined as a medical matter for the privileged in society and a matter of "degeneracy" for everyone else.[5]

The Pure Food and Drug Act, passed in 1906 amid changing attitudes about different drugs, required drug packages to specify if they included one of eleven substances, including cocaine. "U.S.P." on the label of this bottle also refers to federal standards, asserting that the drug follows the quality measures outlined in the United States Pharmacopeia guidelines. New laws in the 1910s and 1920s created the first federal restrictions on cocaine. Many of the leaders in the movement against alcohol turned their attention to cocaine and opiates during Prohibition, which lasted from 1920 to 1933.[6]

A pair of doctors wrote in 1988 of the "war on drugs": "Current fears and portrayals of cocaine's ravages bear an eerie resemblance to the sensationalized concern over 'drug madness' that characterized the last cocaine epidemic, in the late 1920s."[7]

Cocaine had long been available as a powder, but in the 1980s, the much cheaper solid form, crack cocaine, entered the market. News stories created a panic about "crack babies," based on the idea that babies born to cocaine-using mothers were predisposed to poor health, doing poorly in school and being violent and criminal. Later studies showed that poverty was the more significant cause of these outcomes, and that prenatal cocaine exposure had little effect on long-term health. Scholar of race and reproductive justice Dorothy Roberts has speculated, "This frightening portrait of damaged crack babies may have caused as much harm as the mothers' crack use itself," by inhibiting access to good care.[8]

Since the 1980s, US enforcement of cocaine bans has largely targeted crack, especially among Black and Latine people. Federal sentencing guidelines from 1986 had a 100:1 ratio—possessing one gram of crack was treated as equal to possessing 100 grams of powder cocaine. Doctors and civil liberties groups pushed to treat both forms of the drug the same. In 2010, the sentencing ratio was reduced to 18:1.[9]

Cocaine can seem like a dramatic example of what medicine got wrong in the past, but as a local anesthetic, it's unsensational. The drug improved an area of surgery when it was new, but over time its risks became plain. As safer alternatives were developed, it fell out of favor except in specific cases. That's the story of many medications. Cocaine would have a markedly different identity if not for its desirability as a recreational drug and its power to addict and kill people using it.

# Don Pedrito, a Legendary Healer

In the early to mid-twentieth century in the American Southwest, you could buy medicines marketed with the image of a bearded old man with a scar on his nose. Ironically, their namesake had preferred to prescribe treatments that cost little to nothing. Born Pedro Jaramillo and called "Don Pedrito" by his followers, he was probably the most famous *curandero*.[1]

## MIND, BODY, AND SPIRIT

*Curanderismo* is a set of traditions from Latin America and the Mexican-American border region, treating mind, body, and spirit and encompassing herbal medicine and faith healing. Practitioners are *curanderos* or *curanderas*. In 1881, Jaramillo moved from Guadalajara, Mexico, and began practicing as a *curandero* on a ranch near Falfurrias, Texas. This was a border culture, including people with Spanish, Native, and Anglo ancestry, and the healthcare practices and beliefs reflected that. *Curanderismo* has been called a form of folk psychiatry, and as in clinical psychiatry, treatment depends in part on trust and rapport between the patient and provider.[2] Jaramillo's practice did not focus on the mind, but he certainly had rapport and a shared culture with many of his patients.

Ruth Dodson, a white folklorist who interviewed Jaramillo's patients, wrote, "Mexicans would have preferred to consult a *curandero* even if doctors had been plentiful." As his fame grew, white Texans began to come to him as well. It is clear why people would choose him. Dodson relayed the report of a man who had a burr stuck in his throat. Several doctors had recommended surgery, but Jaramillo prescribed saltwater, which made the man vomit and brought up the burr. When Jaramillo traveled to heal in other cities, he left enough food behind to feed the people who would come to visit him in his absence.[3]

Much of Jaramillo's work used faith healing to treat physical and spiritual problems, such as *susto* (Spanish for fright or shock). Jaramillo taught that healing came from "the power of God released through your faith." He was said to know intuitively what traumas the patients had been through and who was a nonbeliever. Some of his cures seemed to his contemporaries like a test of faith, such as when he told a patient to put half a can of tomatoes in each shoe.[4] The results are lost to time.

Other prescriptions drew on herbalism. In a story told to Dodson, Jaramillo told a man who had traveled for miles to get to him that he had passed his remedy on the road. For the man's jaundice and sores, he recommended a bath with the wild plant *yerba soldado*. Jaundice is typically caused by diseases that harm the liver, and it's unlikely this prescription could have treated any of them. However, *yerba soldado* is reputed to have antimicrobial properties, so if the skin condition was bacterial, it's at least somewhat plausible the man did find his remedy on the road.[5]

## LARGER THAN LIFE

Jaramillo's followers reported that doctors tried to get him arrested because he drew such large crowds, but the police said that his work wasn't malpractice because, typical of *curanderos*, he didn't charge money. This story could be born of his folk hero status, or could be real evidence of doctors' concerns that he was stealing their patients or giving them false medical information. English-language newspapers dismissed his "ignorant" patients and treated him as an exotic novelty. They erroneously called him an "Aztec miracle worker" despite the fact that he was Catholic, and his family was Purépecha, a people never conquered by the Aztecs.[6]

After Jaramillo's death in 1907, Fernando M. Tijerina paid his son $500 to use the Don Pedrito name and his image. He sold thirty-five different herbal preparations under this brand, including this one-ounce box of *yerba soldado*. Known for his great generosity as well as healing, Jaramillo became as popular in death as in life. He is a folk saint, a venerated past leader in the spiritual community whom the Catholic Church does not recognize as a saint. People still seek his guidance and aid during spiritual ceremonies and at his shrine.[7]

Don Pedrito brand yerba del soldado, early twentieth century.
COURTESY OF MARGARET H. MCALLEN MEMORIAL ARCHIVES, MUSEUM OF SOUTH TEXAS HISTORY, EDIN-
BURG, TEXAS.

*Curanderismo* has much in common with other forms of faith healing. The practices are often restricted to believers and belief itself may have an important role in the treatment. Patients may find these practices more financially or culturally accessible than the "mainstream" alternative, or may feel that other treatments have failed them. However, *curanderismo* is unique to the communities that practice it, drawing on specific cultural roots. The tradition is not well represented in American museum collections. This could be because the stories of working-class Latine patients are not well represented generally, and because many common materials in treatments are too mundane or perishable for museums, like water, lemons, and eggs. This box of herbs is a rare artifact of this practice that has been meaningful to patients past and present.

# A Wooden Leg in a Mechanized World

Walking on and in between moving trains in railway yards, railway brakemen like Walter Sylvia knew there was risk to their job. The day in 1905 when he felt the impact of a train car on his body, he got away with his life, but he lost a leg. Many of his contemporaries wore prosthetic legs too, and often, demand is what inspires new solutions to engineering challenges in health. However, there hadn't been any serious advances in prosthetics in a generation. Sylvia lived at a time when most of the changes to prostheses on the market were about making them concealable, helping the wearer blend in with nondisabled society.

## PROSTHESES IN THE PROGRESSIVE ERA

Sylvia's wooden leg was made by the Hanger Company, which emerged out of a turning point in amputation history—the American Civil War. In this case, demand spurred change. Roughly sixty thousand soldiers lost at least one limb. Veterans often traded prostheses and modified or even made their own in search of a good fit. Between 1861 and 1873, eighty-eight new patents were filed for artificial leg designs, plus more for crutches, artificial arms, and other devices. James Hanger, who lost his leg in battle as an eighteen-year-old Confederate soldier, is said to have been the war's first amputee. He designed a prosthesis that was one of the first to use joints, rather than a solid block of wood, and launched a successful business with it.[1]

In the second half of the nineteenth century and the early twentieth century, increasing industrialization meant that a growing number of civilians were losing fingers, arms, and legs on the job in factories or on railroads. Reformers demanded laws to protect workers from needless risks, and injured brakemen were the plaintiffs in a series of court cases on the issue. Still, the changes lagged behind the need. The brakemen's union advocated for better conditions, but in the meantime, it provided death and disability insurance to its members and advertised prosthetic limbs in its journal.[2]

Although his own impressions of disability are not recorded, because Sylvia worked for a railroad, he almost certainly knew some amputees before he became one. Additionally, as the son of a Spanish immigrant, he may have followed the rapid changes in immigration law. Beginning in the 1880s, immigrants could be denied entry for being deemed "likely to become a public charge." Which conditions counted as likely to affect a person's ability to earn a living was open to interpretation. Some immigration officials were wary of anyone they thought might be concealing a prosthesis, while others took the person's career into consideration when deciding whether a missing limb would put them at risk of needing public assistance. It was never up to the immigrant. Public charge rules are part of immigration law to this day. In the same era, several cities banned people with "disfigurements," including missing limbs, from appearing in public without covering up.[3]

Meanwhile, advertisements for prostheses often portrayed users in before-and-after pictures. The customer without the limb was frequently shown half-naked, seated, looking vulnerable. The "after" pictures often showed the customer standing in a dignified full suit, although some showed a cutaway view of the prosthesis behind the pant leg. In 1905, the Hanger Company's ads touted that Hanger himself had made, sold, and worn prostheses for forty-four years. The ads described jointed prostheses as looking and feeling just like "natural" legs.[4]

### LIFE WITH A PROSTHESIS

Sylvia probably found that a wooden leg felt like a natural leg the way a voice on the telephone sounded like the person speaking. It was surprisingly good, but not an exact re-creation. After seeing a surgeon following his accident, it's likely that he got his new leg at a store specializing in prostheses. When he first tried it on, it could have made him feel like he was walking into a hole or up a hill, if the fit wasn't right.[5] He could adjust the fit somewhat by changing the lacing, and may have worn a heel-less sock on his stump to decrease chafing.

Wearing his prosthetic leg, Sylvia walked with a cane, and worked as an auto painter and later a city employee. He may or may not have viewed be-

Prosthetic Leg, 1905.
COURTESY OF THE WARING HISTORICAL LIBRARY, MEDICAL UNIVERSITY OF SOUTH CAROLINA, CHARLESTON, SOUTH CAROLINA.

ing an amputee as a medical condition. In the rhetoric of the time, peers may have seen him as a "successful cripple" because he could work. Nine years later when WWI began, prosthetics started advancing again, after changing very little since the Civil War. Improvements in adaptive technologies ranged from rubber-tipped crutches to lightweight aluminum limbs. However, after WWI, as government at all levels was paying more attention to the needs of disabled people, there was a renewal of rhetoric that distinguished the "successful cripple" from the "unsuccessful" or "dependent," defining people's success economically and ignoring the rampant job discrimination that amputees and other disabled people faced.[6]

Sylvia wore this leg until his death in 1937, but many people go through several prostheses in their lifetimes. Many WWII and Korean War veterans had wooden legs like his, which became an integral part of their lives and bodies. In the late twentieth century, some of them struggled to adapt when they needed new prostheses. The market had moved on, favoring new or newly affordable materials like plastics and carbon fiber that appealed to prosthesis wearers who wanted something strong and lightweight. In this case, it was new technologies that created change, rather than a period of particularly high demand. Many of the issues Sylvia and his contemporaries faced have been ameliorated but not solved, ranging from problems of comfort, fit, and useability to societal attitudes toward people wearing prostheses.[7]

# 20

# A Community Doctor's Legacy

As a child, Susan LaFlesche Picotte saw a neighbor die while waiting for a government-appointed doctor who never came. She observed pointedly, "It was only an Indian and it did not matter."[1] In her twenties, she was the doctor for the school on the Omaha reservation where she grew up, but adults came to her as well as students because she spoke their language. Near the end of her life, she founded a hospital, and the community is now working hard to preserve it as a historic site.

## THE HEALTH OF THE COMMUNITY

Susan LaFlesche was born in 1865, during a time of dramatic change for the Omaha people. Ten years before she was born, her people were relocated to a reservation. Her father was Joseph LaFlesche, also known as E-sta-ma-za or Iron Eye, their last recognized chief. Having seen what the US government did to tribes that resisted assimilation, he wanted the Omaha to know the language and skills to survive in white society. He sent his children to schools with the same goals, and Susan attended the Woman's Medical College of Pennsylvania.[2]

For generations, men had derided women with medical aspirations. While some trained in naturopathy or became self-taught doctors, women were excluded from mainstream medical schools. The first US woman to earn a medical degree was Elizabeth Blackwell in 1849. The Connecticut Indian Association paid for LaFlesche's education on the condition that she not get married for at least two years after she graduated, on the presumption that she'd stop working if she married. She graduated from the three-year program a year early and at the top of her class, in 1889. She came home to help treat Omaha people during a severe measles outbreak, then returned to Philadelphia for a year to complete a medical internship. LaFlesche was the first Native American to graduate from medical school; two others, Charles Ohíye S'a Eastman (Santee Dakota) and Carlos Wassaja Montezuma (Yavapai-Apache) earned their degrees later the same year.[3]

Traditional Omaha healers were experienced herbalists, but in the nineteenth century they were largely cut off from their cultural knowledge by depopulation and assimilation. Many diseases they faced, like smallpox, measles, and cholera, had been introduced by white settler-colonists. During the nineteenth century when Native peoples were forcibly relocated to reservations created by the US government, tuberculosis epidemics ravaged the reservation populations. By LaFlesche's lifetime, medicine in the European tradition had microscopy and other tools to understand the unseen causes of disease, advantages that her people's knowledge on its own was lacking.[4]

LaFlesche began working for the Omaha reservation school as a doctor in 1890. When the reservation's other doctor left shortly afterwards, she became the sole doctor for over one thousand people. She made house calls in all weather over an area of 450 square miles. She was employed by the Office of Indian Affairs, which routinely mishandled physician assignments by sending white doctors who spoke one Native language to the reservation of an entirely different Native nation, and rarely gave them adequate resources to do their jobs. She left her job in 1893 because of poor health, but returned to work a few years later. By then, she was Susan LaFlesche Picotte, married with two young sons who sometimes came along on house calls. Joining in the national effort to curb habits that spread tuberculosis, she spent many hours teaching the Omaha to give up communal drinking cups, which were common before modern water fountains.[5]

The Omaha had suffered a great deal from being forced to give up much of their culture, religion, and land. Some of them felt Picotte was embracing their oppressors. The school she attended as a child and the practice of assigning doctors to reservations were part of an aggressive assimilation trend in US policy often summed up with the phrase "Kill the Indian but save the man." In fact, reservation doctors were encouraged to try to eradicate any traces of traditional Native medicine. Picotte had a complicated role among her people, but some of them saw her assimilated education as an asset, and came to her for help navigating the legal and economic changes being thrust on the community. Like many reservation doctors, she was paid little, and in 1905, she took a second job as a Presbyterian missionary on her reservation. The work dovetailed with her passion for curtailing the double effects of alcohol and poverty on her patients' health.[6]

Alcohol abuse was one of the biggest threats to health on the Omaha Reservation in Picotte's lifetime. Her father had banned the sale of alcohol, but it was reintroduced after his death in 1888. It was not yet known that trauma is a risk factor for alcohol abuse, but whiskey peddlers knew that Indians were vulnerable targets. They conned their drunk customers in English-language legal issues and land sales. For over a century, various Native groups had tried diverse approaches to helping their community members who struggled with alcohol, including approaches influenced by Christianity and by Native religion. Picotte educated her community on the dangers of alcohol, and in 1906 she led a delegation to Washington, DC, to lobby for prohibiting alcohol on the reservation. Her hardline stance was controversial among her people, especially among people who already distrusted her preference for white medical doctrine.[7]

## A HOSPITAL OF THEIR OWN

After her husband's death in 1905, Picotte moved in with her sister in the town of Walthill. She set up an office in the garage, but she wanted to offer more and better care for her patients. She began fundraising to open a hospital, the Omaha community's first. She brought in donations from missionary groups, and her East coast connections made it possible to have a benefit concert at Carnegie Hall.[8]

In 1913, Picotte's dream was realized. With large windows, an airy floor plan, and a wide porch, the one-and-a-half-story hospital was reminiscent of a tuberculosis retreat. She did not get to enjoy the success of her hospital for long, as she died in 1915 of cancer. While she was ill, her family wrote to Marie Skłodowska Curie for help. Curie sent a pellet of radium, but it did not change Picotte's condition; in fact, effective uses of radioactivity in cancer treatment were decades away. Picotte died of cancer in 1915, and the hospital was renamed in her honor, operating until 1945. After that, the building was a nursing home for twenty years, and then had various commercial uses.[9]

Since the 1980s, a group of locals has worked to preserve the former hospital building, earning it National Historic Landmark status in 1993. In 2018, they received grants from the US Department of Agriculture and the Shakopee Mdewakanton Sioux Community, going toward restoration of the

Museum exhibits relocated during building restoration.
DR. SUSAN LAFLESCHE PICOTTE CENTER, WALTHILL, NEBRASKA, OMAHA RESERVATION.

building for a community center that includes a medical clinic and a museum. Michael Wolfe, former chairman of the Omaha Tribe, has noted that his people have felt forgotten, and the center's work celebrating Dr. Picotte has revived public awareness of the Omaha Tribe's history.[10]

# 21

# Carville, the "Louisiana Leper Home"

**"H**ave you decided on a new name?"

This was the first question many new residents heard in their medical exam on arriving at Carville. Especially in the early years at the beginning of the twentieth century, many residents took new names to protect their families from stigma. Carville was a quarantine hospital for people with Hansen's disease, better known as leprosy.

Residents' experiences varied widely, but most knew little about their illness until after they arrived. They knew the myths: "lepers" are sinful, shameful, and unclean, their limbs fall off, they spread the disease to anyone they touch. In fact, the main symptoms of Hansen's are nerve damage, often resulting in loss of feeling in extremities, and thickening of the skin in patches. Advanced cases can cause bone resorption after injuries, slowly deforming the hands or feet as the body metabolizes the minerals in the bones. It's not a mild disease, but it's nothing like its reputation. With or without quarantine, Hansen's never whipped through communities. It is slow to develop and transmitted with prolonged contact, and 95 percent of humans are naturally immune.[1]

## A NATIONAL QUARANTINE HOSPITAL

For years, Hansen's disease was said to be spread by association with immorality and sin. In 1873, Norwegian doctor Gerhard Armauer Hansen proposed that the disease known as leprosy was caused by a bacterium. It was soon clear that the disease is literally and not metaphorically contagious, but this did not yet temper the negative attitudes toward Hansen's disease patients. Dr.

R. D. Murray of the Marine Hospital Service wrote in favor of forced segregation, "Lepers shun people instinctively, but remain human for a long time." This cruel dehumanization is not uncommon in descriptions of people with deformities and disabilities, but it was particularly blatant in descriptions of people with Hansen's.[2]

It was in this context that Louisiana founded the "Leper Home" at Carville in 1894, following a state law calling for people with the disease to be quarantined. The law barred Hansen's disease patients from public transit, so the hospital's first residents arrived on a coal barge. The hospital was on the outskirts of the town of Carville, twenty miles south of Baton Rouge. In 1921, the federal government turned Carville into the National Leprosarium. It was one of the few leprosaria in North America, the largest of which was in Kalaupapa, Hawai'i. Some sought treatment at Carville voluntarily, and others were sent there for violating quarantine laws. In 1941, Carville researchers discovered the first antibiotics effective against Hansen's disease, and as the drugs advanced, it was demonstrated that people are no longer contagious once treatment starts. However, Carville remained an isolated inpatient site through the end of the century.[3]

José P. Ramirez Jr. remembers wondering when he arrived, "If I was in a hospital, why was I then in an infirmary? . . . Little did I know that the 'hospital' was composed of 350 acres and many buildings creating the infrastructure of a small community."[4] Over the decades, the site had movie theaters, chapels, sports teams, and an annual Mardi Gras celebration. There were two of almost everything: one for patients, and one for staff. Many buildings still stand and can be visited as a driving tour in addition to the museum. Mid-century, the dorm-style lodging was upgraded and included rooms for married couples. Before that, couples often built their own small cottages.

Children under sixteen were forbidden from Carville unless they were patients themselves; patient Julia Elwood said that after giving birth to her son, "I wasn't even allowed to touch him."[5] In the early years, residents were rarely allowed out to visit their families. Leonide Landry Manes, whose father was diagnosed when she was a child in 1924, recalled that he could only visit twice in eight years, when his mother was sick. "And he came under armed guard—and that's something I've never forgiven them for, and I never will."[6] Later, residents were regularly allowed a limited amount of "leave" from Carville. Some residents crawled through a well-worn passage under a fence for extra time away, leaving for a night on the town or to start new lives. The institution sometimes punished leaving "against medical advice" with a stay in the on-site jail.

Patient dormitories under construction, 1941.
FROM THE COLLECTIONS OF THE NATIONAL HANSEN'S DISEASE MUSEUM, CARVILLE, LOUISIANA.

## COMMUNITY AND CITIZENSHIP

Residents of the Carville hospital fought to be less cut off from the world, and in 1946, they were granted the right to vote. The Black residents were among the first Blacks in Louisiana to vote. The patients' newspaper, the *Star*, was nominally a community newspaper, a form of occupational therapy for its creators and a place to share news of Carville sports and entertainment. However, "the most important reason for its publication was . . . the placing of the disease, robbed of its traditional terror, among the list of chronic diseases, where it rightly belongs," according to Betty Martin, who wrote for the paper. It became the Carville residents' biggest advocacy tool, and its editor, Stanley Stein, one of the biggest advocates for destigmatizing the disease.[7]

After antibiotics created effective treatments, some people recovered and were discharged. Numerous former Carville residents challenged the stigma of their disease with their writing and speaking, describing their diverse experiences. Many of them began this work around the same time as the emerging disability rights movement in the 1960s and 1970s.

Their advocacy can teach us a great deal about Hansen's disease and about stigmatized conditions in our society. Religion, literature, and cultural norms influence our understanding of disease and disability. Disfigurement is seen as a reason to ostracize people. The way patients are managed and the rights they are given are not always in line with advances in medical understanding. Finally, many patients find self-advocacy an important part of the experience of having a stigmatized condition. After decades of advocacy, people with Hansen's no longer expect their families to disown them after diagnosis. The intentional shift toward calling it Hansen's disease has helped with the stigma. However, the word "leper" is still used to mean an exile or outcast. More broadly, literature, media, and popular culture still use deformity to note that a character is inhuman in some way.

Many early residents lived the rest of their lives at Carville. About 750 people are buried in the institution's cemetery under a grove of pecan trees. After the hospital closed, some former patients requested to return there to be buried alongside their friends. The markers note the deceased's patient number as well as their name—sometimes their given name, sometimes the one they took at Carville.[8]

# The Professional Nurse Only

Anna Merrill of Sioux Falls, South Dakota, mentally reviewed what she had learned in nursing school as she put on the Red Cross uniform for the first time. Married with children, she was more likely to be assigned a role in the United States than to be sent to Europe. It was the First World War, and decades of change in nursing were being put to use. These changes demonstrated increasing recognition that nursing is skilled work, and not the same as taking care of a family member or something women can do intuitively. Patients knew that they wanted nurses who were good at their work, but it fell to the nursing profession to demonstrate the importance of professionalization.

## CREATING PROFESSIONAL NURSING
In the early nineteenth-century United States, several Christian orders of nuns or deaconesses began offering nursing to their communities, following a centuries-old European tradition. Nurses often attribute the founding of their profession to Florence Nightingale, who led the English military's nursing service during the Crimean War (1854–1856). A keen statistician, after the war she reformed hospitals and developed nursing schools using data she had analyzed. The shift to professional nursing would take time, however. In the American Civil War, people of all races and genders served as nurses, nearly all without training. They worked with the army, religious organizations, or relief societies, or as independent volunteers.[1]

In the late nineteenth century, many places still saw nursing as an informal mantle women took on when needed. Nursing presentations at the 1893

Red Cross Nurse Uniform, c. 1914.
SIOUX EMPIRE MEDICAL MUSEUM, SANFORD
USD MEDICAL CENTER, SIOUX FALLS, SOUTH
DAKOTA.

World's Fair in Chicago helped spread the idea that trained nursing was valuable. Several people from Sioux Falls attended the fair, and returned home
determined to create the city's first hospital, which would boast a well-trained
corps of nurses.[2]

In 1898, the Sioux Falls hospital began its own nursing school. At the time,
it was common for hospitals to use student nurses as unpaid employees. They
laundered sheets and scrubbed floors as well as attending to patients. Hospital
administrators considered running a nursing school more cost-effective than
hiring nurses and separate cleaning staff. In many schools, the first several
classes of students had to transform their hospital from a dirty, unkempt place
to a modern healthcare facility. The students in Sioux Falls had an advantage,
as this hospital was quite new and had been formed in the era when an understanding of germs causing disease was finally mainstream in healthcare. Still,
a student nurse's day was scheduled from dawn to dusk with classes, work on

the wards, and designated rest periods. In the following decades, nursing leaders would stress that the students had to receive a good education in addition to their hours on the wards, or the system was exploiting them.[3]

## ADVANCING THE FIELD

By the first decade of the twentieth century, doctors and patients had begun to recognize the advantages of trained nurses. In Sioux Falls, nurses were in high demand as surgeons from surrounding rural areas began bringing their patients to the hospital for nursing care. Graduate nurses, who had completed nursing school, were hired to take care of patients in their homes. They treated pneumonia and typhoid and took care of new mothers and infants.[4]

This was an era of rapid development in the science of health. Good nursing schools taught anatomy, physiology, basic chemistry, and familiarity with surgery. Some doctors, both women and men, were wary of seeing nurses become more educated, worried that they would not submit to doctors' authority, but nurses argued that scientific understanding meant they could better serve their patients. Nursing associations advocated for fair labor standards, rigorous curricula in schools, and the establishment of nursing licenses. In 1903, the first four states passed licensure laws, creating the first Registered Nurses in the country. South Dakota followed suit in 1917 with the Nurse Practice Act that required minimum numbers of classroom and clinical practice hours in a nurse's training.[5]

These changes took place alongside a transformation within education for doctors. Building on the new emphasis on experimentation and research within the medical field in the mid-nineteenth century, by the end of the century leaders in medical education advocated for experiential learning. Medical students were required to do coursework in the laboratory and to provide care for patients under instructors' supervision. The focus shifted from memorizing facts to fostering critical thinking skills, a generation before leaders in childhood education made the same shift. This replaced the older model in which medical school consisted only of lecture-based classes offered in for-profit settings. Until this change, nurses of the late nineteenth century were more accustomed to learning by doing than doctors were.[6]

However, neither the professionalization of nursing nor the counterpart changes happening in medicine created a clear public understanding of what nursing entailed. From the start of World War I in 1914, American nurses and doctors went overseas with the Red Cross. A 1917 *Ladies' Home Journal* editorial noted, "Many women, untrained in nursing, have been disappointed to learn that their services were not wanted on the field of battle, nor even in a base hospital. It is the professional nurse only who has been called and accepted."[7] Nurses remarked that most people seemed to understand that nursing required training, but some thought that wartime nursing was somehow different. Nursing schools stepped up their recruiting, and managed to dramatically increase enrollment. During WWI, some schools began experimenting with moving nursing education into college settings followed by hospital training, and this trend continued as more students began getting bachelor's or higher degrees in nursing rather than training school certificates.[8]

Some of Merrill's peers spent their first years after nursing school inspecting wounds by a shaded lantern in hospitals in France, taking care not to let the light make their location an air raid target. Others did the equally important work of helping patients through tuberculosis or the pandemic flu, whether abroad or at home. In under a century, a new and essential field of healthcare had been created from a role that had been known in some form for thousands of years.

# The Pandemic of the Century: The 1918 Flu

"It hits suddenly and one's temperature nearly chases the mercury out thru the top of the MD's thermometer," wrote Sergeant John Acker after his bout of the flu in July 1918. "Face gets red, every bone in the body aches and the head splits wide open."[1] The 1918 pandemic killed between 50 and 100 million people, overtaking the world when science was unprepared. The lessons from that event about how individuals and governments can respond to worldwide health crises are still being learned.

### THE PANDEMIC OF THE TWENTIETH CENTURY

At first, doctors weren't sure what the new disease was. They called it bronchopneumonia, epidemic respiratory infection, cholera, or typhus. Once it was more widely recognized, the disease was often called three-day fever or Spanish flu, both misnomers. The disease could last for weeks, and there's no reason to believe the flu started in Spain. When many countries were censoring their newspapers because of WWI, Spain was neutral in the war and Spanish newspapers reported on the epidemic. The first wave from January to July was mild, with most people surviving. It isn't known how many civilians got the flu or died from it in the first wave; doctors weren't required to report this information to anyone. But the flu came back in the fall and had mutated into a much deadlier disease, often causing severe pneumonia. By September 1918, it was all over the world.[2]

People in 1918 were familiar with seasonal influenza outbreaks, but had little experience with what a truly bad flu could do. Many patients developed serious pneumonia, turning blue from lack of oxygen. For some, pneumonia only began to develop after several days of flu symptoms and high fevers, but others died gasping for breath days or even hours after their first symptoms. The 1918 flu killed the very young and elderly, but also disproportionately killed people aged twenty to forty. Crowded living conditions and other factors increased the danger of flu, but the impact did not vary by socioeconomic group as dramatically as with many other infectious diseases. In the United States, over a quarter of civilians and over a third of the military contracted the flu, and 2 percent of the population died. In some countries, up to 6 percent died. There were coffin shortages.[3]

## CARING FOR FLU PATIENTS

Sergeant Acker was given medications that made him sweat profusely, which he credited for his convalescence. In fact, the medications available at the time did little to nothing for the flu. Doctors advised codeine, whiskey, camphor oil, and a panoply of other drugs for the coughing. Some used laxatives for the fever or gave patients enough aspirin to kill them. One doctor wanted patients "drenched" with aspirin, recommending six times more than what's now known to be the maximum safe dose.[4]

Much of what could be done for patients was keeping them hydrated and comfortable. This work was mostly done by nurses. Instruments like this thermometer helped them monitor patients' symptoms. Decades later, IV nursing and other specialties would be very helpful for the flu, but not yet. One specialty that did exist by this point was public health nursing. These nurses checked on patients at home and ensured they had food and other basic supplies while waiting out the disease. Sometimes, nurses found children trying to fend for themselves after their parents had taken sick or died. The war had caused a shortage of nurses, as so many were aiding the military. However, many nursing schools refused to admit Black women, and had unofficial rules against other non-white women. The United States military did not allow qualified Black nurses to serve until December 1918.[5]

Some public health departments posted a warning on every building where a flu patient lived. Some closed schools, theaters, and other public places. People wore face masks, but they were often made of loosely woven gauze that was largely ineffective. That summer, cities across the United States threw parades to bolster morale in the war, with people packed tightly together in the crowds. It's not clear how much this contributed to the second wave. Meanwhile, although militaries consulted epidemiologists on troop move-

Thermometer, 1918.

NATIONAL WWI MUSEUM AND MEMO-
RIAL, KANSAS CITY, MISSOURI.

ments, they continued to move great numbers of people all over the world throughout the pandemic.[6]

There is still no cure for the flu. However, medicine is better prepared, because of advanced breathing support, antibiotics to treat secondary infections, and flu vaccines developed in the mid-twentieth century. Hospitals and governments also prepare better for pandemics than in the early 1900s, at least when the political will is there. Books and articles describing the 1918 flu pandemic at its centennial in 2018 read quite differently than those written after the beginning of the coronavirus pandemic. They marvel at old photos of people wearing face masks in public. They also warn that the next pandemic is likely to be borne out of antibiotic resistance, which may still be true of the following one. As both the flu and coronavirus have demonstrated, it takes both medical knowledge and public health initiatives to fight a pandemic.

# The Bubonic Plague Meets Bacteriology

In 1920, newly minted pathologist Anna Bowie was infected with *Yersinia pestis*, the bacteria that causes the bubonic plague. She lived during the third plague pandemic, and accidentally stuck her gloved finger with a needle while doing an autopsy on a victim.[1]

**THE THIRD PLAGUE**

The plague calls to mind medieval peasants with dark, egg-sized swellings in their groin, neck, and armpits, attended to by doctors who wore thick, waxed robes and birdlike masks in a misguided attempt to ward off what they thought were plague-causing evil spirits. All of this is accurate of the outbreak known as the Black Death, which killed many millions in Europe and the Middle East starting in the fourteenth century. The swellings are called "buboes," hence the name bubonic plague, but plague also has pneumonic and septicemic forms, causing lung or blood infections. It was not solely a medieval disease; the Black Death was the second of three plague pandemics. In the sixth century, the Justinian Plague swept the Byzantine Empire. From the 1890s to the 1950s, plague attacked port cities around the world, hitting China and India particularly hard.[2]

The third plague occurred at a time when science was able to intervene. In 1886, pathologist Alexandre Yersin was infected with the rabies virus after cutting his hand during an autopsy. The rabies vaccine, developed the year before by Louis Pasteur and Émile Roux, saved Yersin's life. He was inspired to go into vaccine research, and studied under Dr. Robert Koch in Germany.

In 1890, Koch published four criteria to establish that a particular microbe causes a disease. The microbe must be found in all examined cases of the disease, and be able to be grown in culture, like in a petri dish. The cultured microbe must be able to cause the disease in an animal, and then be retrieved from the sick animal and grown in culture again.

Using Koch's method, Yersin isolated plague bacteria in 1894. In 1897, scientists developed the first plague vaccine. These products of the new science of bacteriology saved countless lives. In the 1940s, plague was one of the many diseases considered banished by antibiotics. Today, some animals in the American southwest carry the disease, but humans who are exposed have good survival rates if they get treated quickly.[3]

## PLAGUE IN THE UNITED STATES

The first confirmed plague death in the United States was Wong Chut King in 1900, a Chinese immigrant in San Francisco. The white population already falsely stereotyped the Chinese as spreaders of disease, and as a doctor wrote in 1876, "A destructive earthquake would probably be charged to their account."[4] The San Francisco Board of Health declared Chinatown quarantined, but guards let white people out and Chinese people in. The press and state and local government believed the outbreak was bad for the economy, and even called it a hoax. In 1901, the quarantine officer who had confirmed the first plague cases was forced to resign.[5]

By 1920, when a cluster of outbreaks happened along the Gulf Coast, boards of health were more ready. The city of Galveston, Texas, hired forty rat-trappers. They dipped their quarry in kerosene to kill the fleas before bringing them to the lab to be tested for plague. New ordinances mandated that buildings be rat-proofed with concrete, and evidence of this change can still be seen around the city. Eighteen people in Galveston became sick with plague, including Bowie. Eleven got medical attention in time to receive anti-plague serum, and of those, five recovered. Dr. Bowie was one of them, and she was back to work a month later. In 1922, Bowie and a colleague published a paper on their autopsies in the *Journal of the American Medical Association*. She later became director of the pathology laboratory, and lived to age ninety.[6]

The field of pathology, which is about a generation older than the field of bacteriology, involves examining the causes of disease and its effects on the body. In the mid-nineteenth century, pathologists developed techniques to preserve dead cells on slides indefinitely. This slide from Bowie's study is not on display, but can be accessed for historical and scientific research.

Bubonic plague pathology slides, 1920.
UNIVERSITY OF TEXAS MEDICAL BRANCH HISTORICAL ANATOMICAL, PATHOLOGICAL AND SURGICAL SPECI-
MEN COLLECTIONS, GALVESTON, TEXAS.

If this story had a moral, it would be that we can learn from our past and our experiences, as scientists did in building on one another's work to understand what plague is and how it is transmitted, and as public health departments did in responding to the changing science. One hopes that studying the xenophobia and denial in the third plague can protect future generations.

# Safe, Simple, Sure?
# The Power of X-Rays

**"I** have seen my death," Anna Bertha Röntgen reportedly remarked after seeing the bones of her hand in the first ever x-ray of a person. No one had seen a skeleton in a living being. Later, a dentist marketed a "safety x-ray" with sensational news stories of dentists dying by electrocution in accidents with competitors' x-ray machines. The ads did not mention the hazards of radiation. In the first decades after their discovery, x-rays were regarded with both fear and wonder.

## AN IMAGING REVOLUTION

X-rays were an instant favorite subject for experimentation after Wilhelm Röntgen discovered them in 1895. In 1896, a Scottish doctor used x-rays to see a patient's kidney stones. At the 1904 St. Louis World's Fair, people flocked to an x-ray demonstration to see their bones revealed. For the first fifteen-odd years, x-ray machines were unreliable, sparking, zapping, burning monstrosities that required high voltage and had to be recalibrated before each use. By the 1910s, they were streamlined enough to be widely adopted for medical use. Portable x-ray machines in WWI allowed surgeons to locate shrapnel and bullets, and allowed doctors to see lung lesions in the 1918 flu pandemic. Hospitals and dentists' offices began to see x-ray machines as necessary equipment.[1]

Most dental x-ray machines had a head that could be positioned as needed, connected to a high-voltage power source by uninsulated wires on a long, articulated arm. An unlucky machine operator could be electrocuted. In 1920, dentist William Thwaites patented the design for a cylindrical wooden cabinet to house an x-ray machine. He sold his "Thwaites Safety X-Ray" with the tagline "Safe - Simple - Sure." The downside was that the patient had to position themselves in front of a small opening about chest-high, holding the x-ray plate at odd angles to get an image. In 1923, a rival company released the Victor CDS shockproof x-ray unit, which had no exposed wires but still had the

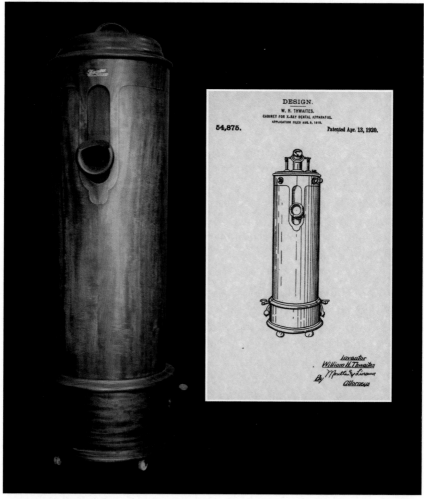

Thwaite X-Ray Machine, 1920.
FROM THE COLLECTIONS OF THE SINDECUSE MUSEUM OF DENTISTRY, SCHOOL OF DENTISTRY, UNIVERSITY OF MICHIGAN, ANN ARBOR, MICHIGAN.

positionable head. Thwaites's machine was obsolete, but he and his company continued to tout the supposed health benefits of x-rays.[2]

### THE POWER TO HEAL AND TO KILL

Doctors tried the power of x-rays on cancers, ringworm, syphilis, lupus, and tuberculosis. After discovering elements that emitted radiation similar to x-rays in the late 1890s, Marie Skłodowska Curie and others immediately applied these new radiation sources to health as well. Many of these uses would eventually be debunked. Thwaites believed he could cure many ills with x-ray exposures of over a minute. He was arrested twice in 1945 for practicing medicine without a license, after claiming he could heal skin lesions. A newspaper account of his arrest refers to a "ray machine" and says his claims were about the healing power of electricity.[3]

Early experiments also began to show radiation's real dangers. In 1902, a radiology technician in Germany developed skin cancer. By 1904, doctors, scientists, and technicians were dying from radiation. Many of them continued to work with x-rays even as they suffered. Thwaites died in 1945 of skin cancer that started on his nose, which may have been from x-ray exposure. As a competitive tennis player, he also may have had prolonged exposure to a different kind of radiation—UV rays from the sun, which would not be linked to cancer for another decade.[4]

By 1910, some x-ray operators wore lead vests, gloves, and masks, and some x-ray tubes were made with shields to prevent rays from scattering in all directions. However, it took decades for both the scientific community and the public to take the dangers of x-rays seriously. From the 1920s through the 1950s, shoe stores used x-ray machines to examine how a shoe fit on a customer's foot. As both medical and popular understanding of the dangers of radiation grew, shoe-fitting fluoroscopes were first advertised with increased safety features, then discontinued. The first standardized measure of how much radiation a tube emitted was created in 1937. Many people did not wake up to radiation's dangers until the United States dropped nuclear bombs on Japan in 1945.[5]

After WWII, the field of radiation dosimetry came into its own. This research determines acceptable doses of radiation exposure in healthcare and the workplace. Dosimetry makes it possible to weigh the risks and benefits of radiation's various imaging and therapeutic uses.[6] High-dose radiation is still used to treat many cancers, killing fast-growing cancer cells much quicker than more stable healthy cells. However, the dose a patient or practitioner is exposed to at the dentist's office is low—as is the risk of electrocution.

# "Are You Playing the Health Game?"

T is a Topic
which Trouble begins;
Both Tea and Coffee
for Children are Sins.

When Mabel Alice Taylor visited schools and homes, she sometimes carried a card game published by the Child Health Organization. The box read, "Are You Playing the Health Game?" Its didactic rhymes and illustrations taught children healthy habits. Taylor was a public health nurse, providing both patient care and education while visiting families at home. Education-based health initiatives were a new and growing concept at the beginning of Taylor's career in the 1920s, and they had their skeptics.

## PUBLIC HEALTH NURSING

The late nineteenth and early twentieth centuries saw a wave of social reform movements that aimed to protect the most vulnerable, as well as movements that aimed to apply science to daily life. The temperance movement was fueled in part by a desire to protect women and children from the effects of men's alcohol abuse; temperance organizations were early pioneers in introducing health education in schools. These trends also created a boom of new non-profits and government agencies devoted to public health and child health, as well as laws on related issues like child labor. Progressive Era changes in political culture enabled the creation and funding of these organizations, but also led to new questions on how to spend time and money most effectively to meet the great need.[1]

Some public health groups focused on health education, while others believed addressing poverty would do more for health than education ever could. These groups spoke of one another with barbed tongues. Health educators filled important gaps in public understanding as the science of health changed. Germ theory had created solid scientific backing for sanitation campaigns, which encouraged safely disposing of human, animal, and household waste and controlling disease-carrying pests. Kansas's Samuel Crumbine, a national leader in public health messaging, warned against the dangers of communal drinking cups. He also led a "swat the fly" campaign teaching that flies spread disease, and encouraged brick companies to stamp bricks with the phrase "don't spit on the sidewalk."[2]

The first public health nurses in the United States were from the nonprofit New York City Mission in 1877. They provided patient care and education based on the English model of district nursing, in which a city was divided into districts and each had a nurse who visited low-income patients at home. In the early twentieth century, many US cities began hiring public health nurses and school nurses. Mabel Taylor worked in public health nursing for sixty years, thirty of them for her home county, Harvey County, Kansas. She visited homes, schools, department stores, and factories.[3]

One school health inspector recalled that when children were asked to reveal the insides of their eyelids in examinations for the eye disease trachoma, they enjoyed the chance to make a funny face at an authority figure. However, many of these children had been through a painful and humiliating version of the same exam when they entered the country. Immigration officials quickly forced their eyelids inside out with a button hook dipped in Lysol. Once in the United States, immigrants often had an ambivalent relationship with public health efforts, including the introduction of nurses and health education in schools. While many efforts were benevolent, they were also tinged with the goal of "Americanizing" immigrants and the belief that middle-class American lifestyles were the healthiest. The worst treatment was aimed at Eastern Europeans and non-white immigrants. Mabel Taylor's young patients, who were mostly of English, Scandinavian, and German backgrounds, were more likely to have mostly positive experiences with public health authorities.[4]

## THE CHO AND CHO-CHO

In the early twentieth century, babies regularly died from diphtheria, poor nutrition, and diarrhea from bad food or milk. The first school nurse, Lina Rogers in New York City, was hired in 1902 on the recommendation of health inspectors. They had previously sent children home from school with no treatment when they showed symptoms of contagious diseases, but the children's families often did not have the means to get them care. The field of child health struggled to be taken seriously, as a field largely led by women (including women physicians) and one often considered charity work. In the First World War, many would-be soldiers were disqualified by preventable health issues that had followed them since childhood. Child health reformers used this as a new angle to explain the value of their work: they were working for the health of the soldiers, national defense, and civic good.[5]

The Child Health Organization, founded in 1918, produced a range of materials for health educators to use. In 1919, the federal Bureau of Education hired a circus performer to play "Cho-Cho," a clown who visited schools speaking to children about health. Soon, the Child Health Organization began publishing fables for children featuring Cho-Cho, although in these, he was an elf. Cho-Cho, along with the Health Fairy and other characters, taught children the importance of eating oatmeal, brown bread, and vegetables. Fables and other didactic tales were a well-established part of children's literature, but they had previously largely focused on religion, morality, and conduct, rather than health. This card game features Cho-Cho and advice to get enough sleep, eat healthy food, and to make sure food is cooked in a clean pan.[6]

The cards pictured warn, "Both tea and coffee for children are sins." In earlier generations, before it was known that heat kills disease-causing microbes, many people believed that coffee and tea (which were always served hot) were safer beverages than water or milk. In this era, it was not altogether unusual for children to drink tea or coffee with the adults. Caffeine was sometimes painted as a refreshing health tonic ingredient and other times a dangerous poison that should be banned. Child health educators taught that caffeine was bad for growing children. Before meals were available to purchase in schools, concerned school and health officials found some young children from poor households spent their breakfast or lunch money on coffee. They liked coffee because it kept them warm.[7]

Health card game, 1921.
IMAGE COURTESY OF THE CLENDENING HISTORY OF MEDICINE LIBRARY & MUSEUM, UNIVERSITY OF KANSAS
MEDICAL CENTER.

Today we take for granted that certain knowledge such as coffee being bad for children is commonplace. We assume that some level of public health infrastructure exists, and that schools and other entities encourage children to understand nutrition and other elements of health. In the early twentieth century, nurses like Taylor charted new territory to make these things standard.

# The Problem
# with "Good" Genes

In the 1920s and 1930s, you could take your prized brood to the state fair to be evaluated. The highest scorers won medals and were encouraged to breed more, while the lowest were not supposed to reproduce at all. Each individual was given blood, urine, and intelligence tests, a physical exam, and a psychological evaluation.[1] Chickens and cattle were judged in other pavilions at the same fairs, but these contests were for humans.

## FITTER FAMILIES

The contests were in the "Fitter Families" pavilion, sponsored by the American Eugenics Society, usually with the support of local boards of health. In this era, states were more involved in public health education than ever, and the fairs also included educational posters and films about tuberculosis, venereal disease, sanitation, nutrition, and childcare. However, Fitter Families pavilions' displays had headings such as, "Some people are born to be a burden on the rest." Flashing lights indicated how often "defective" children were born. The society instructed fairgoers on the "mathematics" of marriage, declaring that a marriage of "pure + pure" meant the children would be "normal," and anything else was "abnormal" or "tainted."[2]

Normalcy reigned supreme, and while the people with the most power in society decided what was normal, fairs made eugenics, the promotion of "good" genes, a household word. Fitter Families contests considered white and nondisabled people to be the best "stock," and denigrated deviations from the ideal by describing various traits as "fit" or "unfit" for society. In the eugenic

Fitter Families medal from the Kansas Free Fair,
c 1920s-30s
IMAGE COURTESY OF THE MUSEUM OF DISABILITY HISTORY,
BUFFALO, NY.

interpretation of science, hereditary traits included intelligence, leadership, patriotism, conforming or not to gender roles, intersexuality, homosexuality, poverty, and criminality. These contests were part of a mindset combining value judgments and medical ones. Newspapers covered the contests uncritically, like they would a high school football game.[3]

Many of the traits deemed negative were associated with one another. For example, Black girls and women were believed to be oversexualized, and being overly interested in sex was often treated as a mental illness, so people with one "undesirable" quality were labeled with three. With categories like "criminality," it got even muddier. Some people labeled criminals were causing harm, and others were convicted of crimes like being homeless or queer. In the late nineteenth and early twentieth centuries, science began to dismantle the theory that criminality was inherited, but it stayed part of the eugenicist lexicon.[4]

### THE EUGENIC MINDSET

In 1803, the English economist Thomas Malthus described a "natural law" that human population growth would always outpace food supply. He claimed the hungry were inherently unfit to improve their situation. This law has been disproven many times, but Malthus's thinking remained influential. Later that century, his followers mixed his claims with scientific racism and enthusiasm for the young field of genetics. Francis Galton of England coined the word "eugenics," for "good genes," in 1883. By the 1890s, Americans adopted the idea, using it to prop up a narrow definition of "true" Americans and justify restrictive immigration policies. Movements that had once advocated for better conditions to help people out of poverty were weakened and altered to accommodate this new, "scientific" understanding of why some people thrive and others struggle.[5]

Eugenics flourished in elite American medical schools and spread from there. It inspired profound human rights abuses in medical practice, including doctors and parents letting disabled and interracial babies die of neglect. It tainted research too. The federally funded Pellagra Commission studied a debilitating condition that mostly affected the poor. Their 1917 report claimed pellagra was hereditary, despite several years of evidence that it's a vitamin B-3 deficiency caused by malnutrition.[6]

In 1912, psychologist Henry Goddard published *The Kallikak Family: A Study in the Heredity of Feeblemindedness*, and soon it was cited in a quarter of American high school biology textbooks. The book purported to trace a family's genetic "taint" that supposedly caused syphilis, tuberculosis, immorality, and various disabilities over many generations, although as a study it was deeply flawed. That year, Goddard was invited to consult on Ellis Island's methods for evaluating immigrants' intelligence. Francis Galton had been among the first to try to create a standardized intelligence test, but Goddard used a more updated test, a predecessor of the Stanford–Binet test that is still used to measure IQ today.[7]

Eugenics had already played a major role in shaping United States immigration policy for decades. The 1882 Immigration Act banned people with certain diseases and real or perceived disabilities. Nativists encouraged extremely stringent requirements excluding people with "defects" ranging from blindness to epilepsy, arguing that they were a burden on national resources. Eugenicists added that these "defects" would spread in successive generations. These reasons for exclusion were codified into law in the 1900s and 1910s. Leaders in the US Public Health Service felt eugenic considerations were not within the purview of the law, but Immigration Service decisions were frequently guided by the belief that some nationalities had "inferior" genetic stock.[8]

What began with Fitter Families medals progressed beyond immigration restrictions to forced sterilization. The Eugenics Record Office, a research institute in New York State, published a model sterilization law after several states had implemented their own. The German Third Reich based their sterilization law on this model, and leading American eugenicists openly praised the German "racial hygiene" movement. In the 1927 case *Buck v. Bell*, the Supreme Court ruled that state institutions could sterilize people deemed "unfit." The plaintiff, Carrie Buck, had been deemed "feebleminded," but like many targets of eugenics, she probably did not have the supposed "defect" she was labeled with. As an impoverished single mother in poor health who had grown up in foster care, other characteristics made her a target. Her mother had also been designated "feebleminded," a catch-all term for intellectual disabilities, and Chief Justice Oliver Wendell Holmes proclaimed, "Three generations of imbeciles is enough." *Buck v. Bell* was never overturned, and although later cases made forced sterilization legally murky, some states practiced it into the 1980s if not longer.[9]

After the Holocaust, some institutions began to distance themselves from the name "eugenics." The scientific backing for many eugenicist claims had been dismantled decades before, even before the Fitter Families contests began. In 1948, the United Nations defined "measures intended to prevent births within the group" as a form of genocide. However, eugenics didn't disappear. Many leaders in the birth control movement wanted poor Black and Latina women to have fewer children. In the mid-twentieth century, some surgeons sterilized patients, especially poor Black women, without their knowledge. It happened enough in the South that it was nicknamed the "Mississippi appendectomy." In the 1970s and 1980s, several leading eugenics societies changed their names in an attempt to distance themselves from the recent past.[10]

The fairgoers who competed for Fitter Families medals were not necessarily hostile to everyone different from them. However, they enjoyed the societal benefits of having their relative power recognized, and on some level they accepted a hostile system. Fair medals are a reminder of the early years of eugenics, but the legacy of eugenics is not in museum artifacts. Eugenics equates health with worth. It relies on the idea that some heritable traits are more valuable to society, and that people with "inferior" traits are less deserving of human rights. These ideas reappear within medical ethics, reproductive health, and reactions to people with disabilities to this day.

# Machinery and Machinations

"At best, it is all an illusion. At worst, it is a colossal fraud," said a *Scientific American* writer on Dr. Albert Abrams's theories and devices.[1] In 1916, Abrams announced his theory "Electronic Reactions of Abrams" (ERA), claiming that good and bad electrons determine our health. *Scientific American* magazine printed a twelve-part article series on Abrams, continuing even after he died in January 1924. Why continue disproving him? He had many ardent followers, both practitioners and patients, so his ideas had the potential to outlive him.

Abrams stood out to *Scientific American* not because he was unique, but because he was a particularly influential example of a very common phenomenon: charismatic health entrepreneurs who capitalized on ideas that sounded scientific. He created a wide variety of devices and accessories, including this "oscilloclast." The theory was that the oscilloclast created waves of electrons that would counteract the destructive waves of electrons in a patient's body, curing any ailments. The problem is that the Electronic Reactions of Abrams have not been observed in any scientific setting, and the devices are useless.[2]

## MIRACLES OF SCIENCE

An explosion of new medical devices came from technological advances of the nineteenth and early twentieth centuries. For example, scores of gadgets purporting to harness the power of electricity for health came onto the market. Among the most popular was the I-ON-A-CO, an electric belt that was supposed to allow the body to cure itself of disease. In the same era, physicians

Dr. Abrams's Oscilloclast, 1923.
THE BAKKEN MUSEUM, MINNEAPOLIS, MINNESOTA.

used electricity in physical therapy and for neurological disorders with some legitimate success. To the first generation who had electricity in their homes, it seemed there was nothing this natural force couldn't do. Abrams's ideas rode a related wave of enthusiasm. The idea that matter is made up of subatomic particles with positive, negative, or no electric charges had recently percolated into public consciousness from physics. A doctor who claimed that something to do with electrons could transform healthcare may not have sounded far-fetched to a non-expert.[3]

Some people who developed and sold fringe devices believed their own theories. They arrived at their ideas by unorthodox means, but they felt their ideas worked about as often as those of the medical establishment. Others were in it for the money. Abrams leased his oscilloclast to practitioners, who were self-proclaimed doctors, or trained doctors who had broken with scientific medicine. They paid $200 down (around $3,000 today adjusted for inflation) plus $5 per month. They also signed a contract stating they would not open the device. Had they opened it to find it a mostly empty box, they might have become suspicious.[4]

## PUTTING ELECTRONIC REACTIONS OF ABRAMS TO THE TEST

While Abrams did not allow his work to be tested in a scientific setting, some people who practiced Abrams's methods were willing to try to prove themselves. In one test, investigators mailed a blood sample to an ERA practitioner, who diagnosed the person with a Streptococcus infection in the fallopian tube. It was a trick. The investigators had sent blood from a healthy male guinea pig with no fallopian tubes. The results of the tests on the oscilloclast were simpler: the investigators couldn't get it to do anything, other than its characteristic tick. Major medical journals decried Abrams's work. Robert Andrews Millikan, who had won the 1923 Nobel Prize for Physics for his work involving electrons, examined this oscilloclast as part of a court case, and declared it not scientifically valid. Abrams's more charitable detractors offered that the devices might work by the power of suggestion.[5]

After Abrams's death, other fringe doctors preserved some of his ideas in their own work, but overall, his theories lost traction as new science and pseudoscience came along to capture the public's imagination.[6] With hindsight, it's easy to call Abrams and his contemporaries quacks, but their influence highlights the allure of new technologies inside and outside the scientific community, an allure not limited to his time.

# Diabetes: A Fatal Disease Becomes Chronic

It looked scarily like an eating disorder, but it was doctor's orders. Twelve-year-old Elizabeth ate one thousand calories most days of the week, about half of what a healthy child her age would need. She usually satisfied this with an egg, some chicken, and boiled vegetables. After five days of that menu, she'd eat nothing for a day, then three hundred calories the next day. It was 1919, and this was the best treatment for diabetes that science had to offer.[1]

Elizabeth had type 1 diabetes, an autoimmune disease that attacks the pancreas. Her body did not produce enough of the hormone insulin, used in processing food. She was at risk for organ failure or falling into a coma; life expectancy was a year after diagnosis. The extremely difficult diet would prolong her life, but many children died of starvation on this plan. In one case, a boy in a hospital snuck toothpaste and birdseed to eat. Noting his spike in blood sugar and not knowing he had eaten, the staff reduced his food even more. He weighed forty pounds at his death.[2]

## NO LONGER A DEATH SENTENCE

Science began to understand diabetes in the nineteenth century, as early endocrinologists started doing experimental physiology—performing tests to alter and understand the various secretions and hormones in the body. Researchers proved that diabetes is a problem with the pancreas by removing dogs' pancreases and observing to see if the dogs developed diabetes, which they did. In 1907, US doctor Stanley Rossiter Benedict developed a test for glucose in the urine that a doctor or the patient themselves could do. This allowed patients to monitor how well their dietary restrictions were working to control their diabetes. However, by the late 1910s, the outlook for diabetes research was bleak. Endocrinology had promised great things in its early years, after the 1890s discovery that thyroid replacement therapy could cure several serious diseases. Now, with no exciting new results in years, that promise seemed empty.[3]

Possibly four hundred researchers had tried to use an extract from the pancreas to treat diabetes. The Ontario-based team that succeeded included physician Frederick Banting, his assistant Charles Best, physiologist John Macleod, and biochemist James Collip. After tests on hundreds of dogs, they began treating patients in 1922. People spoke of miracles and resurrection. A single injection of insulin could bring a patient out of a coma.[4]

### MANAGING A CHRONIC DISEASE

When Elizabeth Hughes was fifteen and weighed forty-five pounds, she was brought to Toronto for insulin treatment. With insulin, she could manage most of her daily medical care herself. A child of privilege and the daughter of US Secretary of State Charles Evans Hughes, she always had access to insulin, and she lived to age seventy-three.

In the decades after insulin was first purified, the biggest advances for diabetics were longer-acting types of insulin that continued working between meals. Patients gave themselves insulin with reusable needles and glass syringes that had to be boiled for twenty minutes between uses and resharpened with a pumice stone. Single-use syringes with smaller, less painful

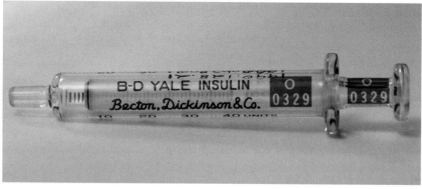

Insulin syringe, c. 1961.
STATE HISTORICAL MUSEUM OF IOWA, DES MOINES, IOWA.

needles came out in 1961, and soon, new urine strips and glucometers to test blood sugar made it easier for people with diabetes to manage their condition at home.[5] The syringe in the figure on the previous page was used at Camp Sunnyside, a camp founded by the nonprofit Easter Seals in 1961.

Much of diabetes research today is on preventing and treating complications such as damage to the eyes, feet, kidneys, and heart. However, disparities in access to healthcare create dramatic differences in rates of complications. Today, insulin is much more expensive in the United States than elsewhere. One US study found that a quarter of patients surveyed have rationed insulin because of the cost.[6] Even a short-term gap in insurance coverage or the ability to pay a copay can and does rapidly kill people. Diabetes was inescapably deadly until the miracle of insulin, but it is serious even today as a chronic condition.

# The Tools of a Contested Trade: A Midwife's Kit

A decade after she retired, Janie Clara Breckenridge could still remember the first child she delivered after getting her midwife's license in 1925, and the last child she delivered in 1972. She delivered over fifteen hundred babies in between them.[1] She learned to be a midwife in a program designed to reduce healthcare disparities, giving more families access to childbirth assistance rooted in modern scientific principles. These programs also sharpened the ideological and skill-based divide between midwives and doctors.

## A MIDWIFE'S TOOLS

Breckenridge, or "Mama Janie" as friends called her, became a fixture in the Black community of Claiborne County, Mississippi. We can imagine a day in her life by looking at what was and what wasn't inside the leather kit she was issued by her local health department. Arriving at a family's home, she scrubbed from her nails to her elbows with her scrub brush. She donned a hand-sewn surgical mask and a bleached white cotton gown over her clothes. Manuals for expectant mothers encouraged women who were planning a home birth to make their room hospital-clean, but few of her patients were able to do that.[2] She created a clean surface on the bed with pads she had made of cotton and folded newspaper.

Breckenridge coached the birthing parent through the delivery and welcomed the child into the world. She tied off the umbilical cord with umbilical tape (a soft rope), and placed drops of silver nitrate in the baby's eyes to prevent conjunctivitis. Then, she weighed the baby on a small scale she brought

Midwife kit, c. 1925.

COLLECTION OF THE MUSEUM DIVISION, MISSISSIPPI DEPARTMENT OF ARCHIVES AND HISTORY, JACKSON, MISSISSIPPI.

with her. Her clients were largely poor, and she would help a family whether they paid her the fee set by the board of health, paid her in livestock or produce, or did not pay at all.[3]

In Mississippi starting in 1921, midwives were trained by a public health nurse, and required to attend the local "midwife club" monthly. Breckenridge was in one of the first cohorts in her community trained in this way; generations of midwives before her had trained by observing their own mothers or other midwives deliver babies. At the midwife club, women were taught songs like "Why does the midwife wear a clean gown? To protect the mother and baby," to the tune of "Mary Had a Little Lamb." The curriculum assumed that the midwives were illiterate and already practicing midwifery according to old, dangerous ideas. Breckenridge was neither; she had graduated from her local school, which went until seventh grade, and had been a farm worker rather than a midwife before taking this training. The midwife club was also where midwives returned completed birth certificates and received silver nitrate, the one medication they were permitted to use.[4]

## THE BATTLE OVER MIDWIVES

A midwife would lose her license for giving medications to ease pain or speed the delivery. She would also lose it for using tools such as forceps, an instrument shaped like tongs used to grasp and pull the baby. If anything went wrong during a birth, she was supposed to call for a doctor. Until about 1900, most children were delivered by midwives. The midwife often assisted with postnatal care as well. However, doctors had pushed to bring childbirth under their own control since the late eighteenth century, even when their skill at using medications and tools varied widely. Several schools of midwifery were founded in the US in the 1880s and 1890s, but by the early twentieth century, urban middle- and upper-class white American-born people preferred to give birth with a doctor. Everyone else used midwives. They often charged less than half of what doctors charged, and usually knew and honored their patients' cultural practices and their preferences for who was present at the birth.[5]

Most American medical journals in the 1910s and 1920s discussed "the midwife question." The question, depending on who you asked, was how midwives could be educated and governed so they could safely supplement the work of obstetricians, or whether midwives should be permitted to practice at all. Obstetrics had emerged as a growing field in the latter half of the nineteenth century, as specialization within medicine became more common. Obstetricians saw midwives as rivals, because it was difficult to argue the necessity of a specialized practice of medicine when people without advanced degrees were also delivering babies successfully. They had a similar rivalry with general practice doctors who delivered babies, but less intense and less tinged with attitudes about gender, race, and class.[6]

Doctors who opposed midwives believed they were dirty, ignorant, and superstitious. While many midwives did use folk remedies including some based in superstition, the stereotype had less to do with actual practice and more to do with prejudice toward Black people and immigrants, who made up a large portion of midwives. Many children in the Antebellum South were birthed with the assistance of an enslaved midwife, and for years afterwards, southern Black women known as "granny midwives" served Black and white patients. Also in the late nineteenth and early twentieth centuries, immigrant communities were largely served by midwives who had attended formal midwifery schools in their home countries in Europe. Some doctors suspected both immigrant and "granny" midwives of providing abortions, which were illegal in most states at the time.[7]

While prominent doctors called for midwifery to be eliminated, public health leaders saw that not enough doctors delivered babies to meet the need. The federal Sheppard-Towner Act of 1921 required states to regulate and license midwives. Some of the new training programs only offered the basics, like what Breckenridge received. Others trained women as both nurses and midwives in order to fill gaps in care. The Frontier Nursing Service, founded in 1925 by Mary Breckinridge (no relation), brought nurse-midwives to rural white Appalachians, funded by wealthy white northeasterners interested in supporting what they saw as "old stock" Anglo-Saxon Americans. Other nurse-midwife programs served poor Black and Puerto Rican people in New York City.[8]

During the forty-seven years that Breckenridge practiced, the skills of midwifery changed little, but the patient base sometimes changed. Beginning in the 1960s, federal programs like Medicaid relied on nurse-midwives. Discussions of childbirth are often enmeshed with concepts of womanhood, although a person's body and not their gender determines whether they can give birth, and the feminist and new age movements of the 1960s and 1970s popularized midwife-attended home births. They saw home birth as a way to allow the mother greater agency in the process than in the heavily medicated, doctor-controlled environment of the midcentury hospital.[9]

Today, midwives attend only about 10 percent of births in the United States, but this has not necessarily made births safer as doctors predicted in the era Breckenridge was trained. The United States has the highest infant mortality rate among industrialized countries, with large disparities in infant and maternal mortality by race, ethnicity, income, and geography.[10] Both in historical context and over the course of her career, Janie Breckenridge's profession meant different things to different people. She could be a holdout in a stopgap system that outlived its usefulness, a devoted community servant, or simply the first hands to hold many hundreds of children.

# Sipping on the Sunshine Vitamin

The word "vitamin" wasn't expected to stick around. In 1912, biochemist Casimir Funk coined "vitamin" from the Latin *vita* for "life" and the amines, a group of organic compounds. Eight years later, another biochemist dropped the "e" after it became clear that not all vitamins are in the amine group. Several contemporaries thought the whole word should be scrapped once the chemical properties of the different vitamins were uncovered, but "vitamin"—the word and the concept—caught on among scientists, marketers, and the public. The previous generation had started thinking about nutrients separately from the foods that provide them, but they were thinking in terms of fuel—protein, fat, and carbohydrates. Once, only naturopaths and eclectic doctors (part of the irregular or alternative medicine trends) recommended fruits and vegetables. Now, eating fruits and vegetables for their vitamins featured prominently in mainstream medical advice.[1]

## SUNNY VITAMIN D

Vitamins are organic compounds that we need for certain chemical reactions. Our bodies can't produce most vitamins, so we get them from food. We can produce vitamin D if we get enough sunlight, but in cities during the Industrial Revolution, vitamin D deficiency was widespread in children who worked in factories dawn to dusk. An extreme vitamin D deficiency causes rickets, a debilitating disease affecting calcium absorption and bone formation. The children had a bowlegged, unsteady, "rickety" walk. The concept that disease could be caused by a deficiency was initially tricky for science to grasp. Germ theory predisposed researchers to look for the *presence* of a disease-causing substance. Once the idea that the lack of a substance could cause disease, it opened up a new avenue of investigation.

By the 1920s, it was clear that sunlight, cod liver oil, a mercury vapor lamp, or certain foods exposed to this lamp could all cure rickets.[2] These things didn't seem related to one another, but there was vitamin D in the oil, and UV rays in the sunlight and the lamp. Harry Steenbock made the connection when he determined that UV rays convert certain fats to vitamin D. In 1924, Steenbock and the University of Wisconsin patented a method to use UV on foods. Wisconsin dairies were among the first to buy the rights to fortify their food this way. Another local industry was beer, particularly lagers. At the time, Schlitz, Miller, Pabst, and other major beer brands were based in Milwaukee. In 1936, three years after Prohibition ended, Schlitz debuted "Sunshine Vitamin D beer," touting it as providing the health benefits of the summer sun.[3]

Schlitz 'Sunshine' Vitamin D Beer Can, 1936.
OBJECT WHI-148349, WISCONSIN HISTORICAL SOCIETY, MADISON, WISCONSIN.

wooden box lined with a pillow, with ventilation holes and a glass window in the top. A dial on the side adjusts the heat provided by a lightbulb. The whole thing is about one and a half times the size of a shoebox. When electric power was unavailable, the incubator could be heated with a hot water bottle. Indeed, some doctors at the time advocated using hot water bottles instead of incubators.

While the Trans-Mississippi Expo made Nebraska the first place in the country infant incubators were used, the 1938 plan to distribute them was in line with when they caught on in the rest of the country. The first textbook on the care of premature infants and those with birth defects came out in 1922. In 1935, Chicago created a plan for premature infant care which became the model for other cities. In 1943, New York's first premature infant unit opened and Martin Couney closed his last exhibit, a seasonal one on Coney Island.[7]

The newspaper ended its story, "Wanda's poundage, or ounceage, puts the University hospital one up on the Denver hospital, which Monday announced that it expected to save a 42-ounce baby." Forty-one and a half ounces at birth, Wanda pulled through and lived to age sixty-three.[8]

# The Penicillin Revolution

The story goes that absentminded biology professor Alexander Fleming forgot an experiment when he went on vacation, and when he came back, he had serendipitously discovered the first-ever antibiotic. The famous tale isn't too far from the truth, but it glosses over the difficulty of making penicillin into a usable drug.

It is true that Fleming found penicillin by accident. He returned from a vacation in 1928 to find that a felt-like mold seemed to be chasing out the bacteria in a petri dish. However, Fleming was stymied in finding help making his discovery useful. Few bacteriologists and chemists worked together, and few worked on applied medicine.[1] Dr. Gladys Hobby, a microbiologist on the team that later began penicillin's mass production, wrote, "The scientific community was not ready for penicillin in 1928–1929. It was not ready to perform or even permit the experimental procedures necessary to establish its therapeutic efficacy."[2]

## FROM DISCOVERY TO DRUG

In the next decade, university scientists began collaborating more closely with industry, and interdisciplinary teams worked on drug development. Antibiotics began to seem like a real possibility worth investigating. The compound salvarsan had been available to treat syphilis since 1907, but it could be toxic to humans. The antimicrobial sulfanilamide debuted in 1935. It was the first of the sulfa drugs, which stop bacterial growth but do not kill bacteria. In 1938, Dr. Howard Florey, a pathologist at Oxford, read Fleming's paper on the penicillium mold. Recognizing that it could kill bacteria, he and colleagues tackled the problem of creating a medication.[3]

Producing a meaningful amount of penicillin in order to test and use it presented a real challenge. The mold that makes penicillin only grows in the top few millimeters of a nutrient broth. Florey's colleague Norman Heatley found that a discontinued style of bedpan about the size of a casserole dish worked well to maximize the broth's surface area. He ordered them custom from a ceramics manufacturer.[4]

Container for producing penicillin, c. 1940s.
COURTESY OF HISTORICAL COLLECTIONS & SERVICES, CLAUDE MOORE HEALTH SCIENCES LIBRARY, UNIVERSITY OF VIRGINIA, CHARLOTTESVILLE, VIRGINIA.

In 1940, Florey and his team began experiments on mice, and the following year, they began testing on humans. The first was Albert Alexander, dying of an infected wound from a rose thorn. After ten days of treatment, it looked like he would recover. Penicillin production was still very slow, so they used what little they had left on another patient. That patient survived, but Alexander's condition worsened and he died. Three other patients lived and one more died in the initial tests.[5]

At the start of WWII, Florey's team prepared to destroy their laboratory if the Germans invaded. They smeared penicillium mold in their clothes, hoping they could restart their work from spores. One of their colleagues, Dr. Ernst Chain, was a Jewish biochemist who had left his home in Germany. As the war increased the pressure to quickly mass-produce the drug, Florey and Heatley came to the United States in 1941 in the hope of interesting pharmaceutical companies. Working with a US Department of Agriculture laboratory, they soon realized that penicillin grew better and faster in the United States—because of the high nitrogen content in the corn-based nutrient broth used for mold cultures. They also improved on the vessels used to grow the mold and tested related penicillium molds to cultivate the most potent form of the drug.[6]

## THE ANTIBIOTIC ERA

The first great victory for penicillin was with Anne Miller, who battled septicemia for a month following a miscarriage in 1942. All other treatments had failed. It was pure coincidence that her doctor heard about penicillin. Another of his patients was friends with Florey and had mentioned it to him. Miller was the first patient cured by penicillin who would certainly have died without it. The first mass-produced penicillin was designated for war hospitals. The drug was made available to the public in 1945. Penicillin, and the other antibiotics that followed, transformed healthcare. Surgery, childbirth, organ transplantation, and managing severe burns all became dramatically less dangerous. Once-deadly bacterial infections could be cured with something more reliable than rest and sheer luck.[7]

However, accepting the 1945 Nobel Prize along with Florey and Chain, Fleming warned that penicillin would not be a miracle drug forever: bacteria can become resistant to antibiotics. Today, experts frame antibiotic effectiveness as a natural resource to be managed with careful use and continued research. Cautious use can slow the development of resistance while researchers race to develop new antibiotics. Problems that seem to have been hit by magic bullets are not always permanently solved, and so medicine has to keep evolving.[8]

# 34

# Blood Transfusion Comes of Age

As a small-town doctor in Fryeburg, Maine, Kenneth Dore tried to be prepared for anything. Among the tools tucked in his bag was this nine-inch-long blood transfusion kit. He might need to use it if a patient lost too much blood giving birth, or if a patient was injured at work in the lumber mill or was in a car accident. The most dangerous cases might be driven to a hospital in a neighboring community ten or fifteen miles away, but many patients were cared for at home. When Dore began his practice in 1938, blood transfusion had recently matured from an inconsistently used procedure to one that was well understood and widespread.

## COMPATIBILITY

Experiments with blood transfusion began in the early seventeenth century, after British doctor William Harvey proved that blood circulates rather than flowing unidirectionally from the heart. Most experiments transfused blood into humans from cows or sheep. They failed because blood is not compatible across species. In the early nineteenth century, English obstetrician James Blundell did work to advance human-to-human blood transfusion. When blood transfusion began to grow in popularity in the early twentieth century, the donor was often a member of the recipient's family, partly for convenience, and partly on the assumption that relatives were likely to have similar blood.[1]

In 1900, Austrian doctor Karl Landsteiner noticed that mixing blood samples from different people sometimes formed clumps of red blood cells. His experiments led him to discover the blood types A, B, AB, and O, which

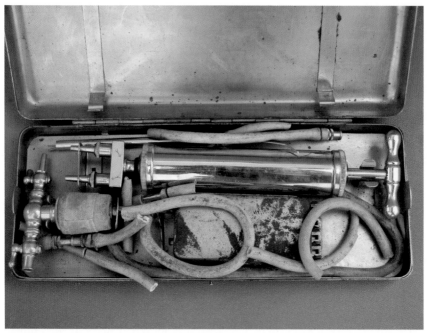

Blood transfusion kit for house calls, c. 1938.
COLLECTIONS OF FRYEBURG HISTORICAL SOCIETY, FRYEBURG, MAINE, COURTESY OF MAINEMEMORY.NET,
ITEM #20386.

react differently to one another because of the antigens they carry. Nearly forty years later, Landsteiner would be part of the team that discovered Rh factors, which are labeled positive and negative. Three groups of doctors independently discovered blood types in the early twentieth century, each giving the types a different set of names. Until the mid-1940s, many hospitals used all three classifications.[2]

Clumps formed by incompatible blood could kill the recipient, but early on, doctors frequently skipped typing the blood because it could take three hours to do. They just transfused a small amount of blood and waited to see if there was a reaction before giving more. During WWI, a new process reduced the time dramatically, and by the time Dr. Dore was practicing, he could test samples of blood against one another in about five minutes. If more than one potential donor was available, the doctor would do each of the tests at the same time.[3]

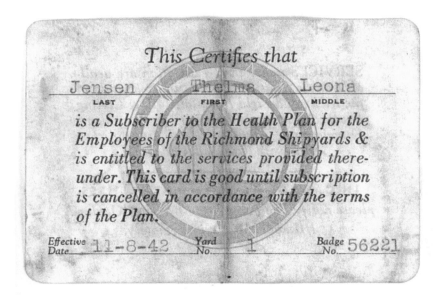

This Certifies that

Jensen          Thelma          Leona
LAST            FIRST           MIDDLE

is a Subscriber to the Health Plan for the
Employees of the Richmond Shipyards &
is entitled to the services provided there-
under. This card is good until subscription
is cancelled in accordance with the terms
of the Plan.

Effective Date 11-8-42     Yard No. 1     Badge No. 56221

Insurance card, 1942.

IMAGE COURTESY OF THE NATIONAL PARK SERVICE, ROSIE THE RIVETER/WWII HOME FRONT NATIONAL HIS-
TORIC PARK, RICHMOND, CALIFORNIA, RORI 75 _C-1

existing patchwork of insurance coverage to cover more people and conditions. In response, the insurance industry began working more closely with
physicians, and insurance became the primary means to afford most medical
procedures.[5]

Economic historian Christy Ford Chapin summarizes, "Insurance companies did not gain their dominant role because of their ability to minimize
transaction costs, offer efficient organization, or compete with other forms
of financing. The way federal politics interacted with the private sector positioned insurance companies . . . as the principal managers and coordinators
of the US healthcare system." The health plan Thelma Jensen enrolled in arose
because of a business need as well as a human need. Jensen probably thought
much more of her shipfitting crew's accomplishments than of this paper card,
but it ultimately signified a big change in the landscape of healthcare.[6]

# Nursing at War

Nurse Mattie Donnell Hicks saw things in her career that neither nursing school nor Army training had prepared her for. She recalled, "We had to run a tube down in their throat and clean—and get all the fluid and stuff off of their stomach. And you know, through that tube live worms would come through. Live! Have you ever heard of such? Live worms!"[1]

These parasites were in Korea, and in her twenty-one-year career as an Army nurse, Hicks saw the human cost of war as well as unfamiliar pathologies. She recalled, "A young fellow coming in for basic training and get that sick and then die, you know, it kind of gets you. It kind of gets next to you. But we had to play nurse, we had to play mama, because some of the soldiers were just right out of high school and they didn't know too much about army life, and we had to play preacher, we had to play friend."[2]

## THE ARMY NURSE CORPS

Founded in 1901, the Army Nurse Corps initially worked closely with the Red Cross Nursing Service. Nurses were not granted military rank until 1944, after many veteran nurses organized for it. Rank was not just a matter of respect, but of authorizing senior nurses to make decisions relevant to their expertise during crises. Hicks earned the rank of Major, allowing her to make management-level decisions as well as choices about individual patients' care.

Hicks's two uniforms from WWII, a white dress and this checked one never saw much wear. She only served about a month at the end of the war. Both dresses were cut just below the knee, a style adopted for wartime fabric

Army Nurse Corps seersucker dress, 1945

WOMEN VETERANS HISTORICAL PROJECT, UNIVERSITY OF NORTH CAROLINA GREENSBORO UNIVERSITY LIBRARIES, GREENSBORO, NORTH CAROLINA.

rationing, and each had a matching cap. Starting in the Korean War, Hicks wore a uniform of brown fatigues, including pants. The Korean War was also the first in which the Army Nurse Corps allowed men. Scrubs would come into fashion for civilian nurses in the 1970s.

In 1950 when the Korean War began, nearly a third of women in the US Armed Forces were healthcare professionals—the Army Nurse Corps and the dietitians, occupational therapists, and physical therapists of the Women's Medical Specialist Corps. Hicks was stationed at the 11th Evacuation Hospital, the stage between the front lines and longer-term recovery care. After the war, she stayed with the Army. She served in Germany and on relief missions, such as one to Chile after a series of earthquakes in 1960. In addition to general duty, Hicks was an OB/GYN nurse, assisting physicians who attended deliveries.[3]

## ADAPTING TO CHANGE

Hicks was one of 479 Black nurses in the 50,000-woman Army Nurse Corps at the end of WWII. The Army had limits on the number of Black nurses admitted until 1944, when the limits were dropped due to public pressure. Nonwhite people's experiences in the Army in WWII and Korea were mixed. Some encountered systemic and interpersonal racism, but others remembered only collaboration. Hicks described her integrated unit as feeling like a family. Still, she mentioned that her unit was sent to a POW hospital and "then somebody must have reported it, because they shipped us out of there and [we] went to where it was integrated." When asked about her heroes, Hicks recalled looking up to nursing leaders who were Black, including Brigadier General Hazel Johnson, Chief of the Army Nurse Corps. [4]

Major Mattie Hicks's career spanned the first years of penicillin, improvements in blood transfusions, and patients arriving from the battlefield by helicopter for the first time. She also rode a helicopter to administer recently developed vaccines to remote areas. She worked in both racially segregated and integrated units, and served in over ten different hospitals around the world. If one theme could be applied to the experiences of WWII and Korean War nurses, it's probably adaptation in the face of change, and Hicks's career exemplified this.

# The Science and Politics of Inhaling Dust

"The dust would be so thick in the sheds you could not see the man next to you," recalled Iside Brusetti, who began working in a Barre, Vermont, granite-cutting shed in 1906.[1] Vermonters had mined granite for buildings, statues, and gravestones since the 1820s, and workers cut and sanded it in buildings referred to as sheds. The pneumatic drills introduced later in the century created significantly more dust than older methods. A disease called "stonecutters' TB" or "granite cutters' consumption" emerged, causing shortness of breath until workers could barely breathe after simple tasks. The problem would have legal as well as medical ramifications.

## DEFINING A DISEASE

As with many occupational health concerns, the questions to be answered were both about what the risks were, and about who should be responsible for those risks. Most lung problems at the turn of the twentieth century were assumed to be tuberculosis (also called TB, consumption, or phthisis). Chimney sweeps were said to get TB from soot, and coal miners from coal dust. Public health officials at the time knew the granite cutters' disease was an occupational problem, but they believed the workers themselves caused it by spreading bacteria with unsanitary habits. They focused their efforts on educating the workers on good hygiene. Barre was home to the Washington County Sanatorium, ostensibly treating tuberculosis, from 1921 through 1968. "Silicosis" was coined in 1870 to describe their actual disease, but it would be decades before it was well understood.[2]

Barre granite cutters found an ally in local physician DeForest Clinton Jarvis, who was among those who argued that the granite cutters' disease was silicosis caused by working conditions the workers had no control over, not by their lack of sanitary habits. In the early twentieth century, the granite industry began funding medical research. Sometimes, this furthered both workers' and employers' needs, but other times, employers relied on biased research while claiming they had done their due diligence for workers' health.[3]

Until the 1920s, research into occupational diseases was mainly done in field studies. At that point, scientists began testing the effects of various pollutants in laboratories, which helped separate silicosis from tuberculosis. They found that silica particles irritated and cut the lungs. This caused fibroids in which the tissue around the air sacs in the lungs was thick, stiff, and scarred. Silicosis does put people at higher risk for developing tuberculosis, if they are exposed to the bacteria. Meanwhile, a similar disease caused by inhaling coal dust, black lung or coal miner's pneumoconiosis, had ravaged Appalachia and other coal-mining regions around the world since at least the late eighteenth century. When research on Barre granite cutters demonstrated that silicosis is caused by mining dust and not pneumonia, many people assumed that this was the coal miners' ailment as well, until a group of doctors in Great Britain identified coal miner's pneumoconiosis as a separate disease in 1942.[4]

### PREVENTION AND RESPONSIBILITY

From the 1890s through the 1930s, the Barre community struggled as sons followed fathers into the granite industry, where all the local jobs were. The local cemeteries are filled with stones cut by the workers who then died in their forties or fifties. In the early years, the granite industry didn't provide any insurance or compensation to silicosis victims. In 1910, Vermont was one of the first states to require businesses to carry workers' compensation insurance. This made it easier for workers to get compensated for workplace accidents, but prevented them from being able to sue. However, work-related illness was not included. Pressure from granite workers' unions inspired Vermont to form a commission to study the problem in 1947. Over the next two decades, workers' compensation was made available to more sick and injured workers. Compensation cases centered around medical questions including diagnosis, how disabling a particular condition was, and the time needed to recuperate. In legal cases about workers' compensation, testimony from a doctor became the norm.[5]

Compensation for silicosis, of course, is not as helpful to the workers or to their employers as prevention. Generally, the United States was slower to enact legislation protecting workers' health than other industrialized nations. In 1932, a group of doctors and industry experts formed a discussion group to coordinate research efforts around silicosis, which they called the "Konicide Club" (an approximation of Greek for "killer dust"). However, in this and other groups, there was no effort made to include workers or their representatives, which made the problem an abstract and economic one. Meanwhile, workers had been saying since at least 1900 that something had to be done. In the 1920s and 1930s, their unions agitated for change.[6]

Finally, in 1937, the Vermont Department of Health created the Silicosis Control Program based on an agreement between workers' unions and granite shed owners. The previous year, silicosis had received national attention because of a workers' compensation case in West Virginia in which hundreds of workers died of silicosis working in Hawks Nest Tunnel. The state used portable x-ray machines to evaluate workers' lung health annually, at first during workers' free time, and then on company time once it was clear that more workers could be examined that way. Suction devices were installed in granite sheds, filtering excess dust from the air. Silicosis cases dropped dramatically, but did not disappear.[7]

Even with dust removal, workers need breathing protection, like this style of mask used starting in the 1930s. The reusable, lightweight metal frame could be bent to fit the wearer's face, and the fabric filter could be replaced. This style was phased out by the 1970s in favor of more fitted styles that filtered more dust. In the 1990s when N95 masks were developed for filtering airborne disease particles, workers in a number of dust-generating industries began using them as well.

Despite the victories, national legal standards to protect against workplace hazards were decades off. In 1968, a deadly explosion in a coal mine in Farmington, West Virginia drew national attention towards mine safety. The United Mine Workers of America and the newly formed West Virginia Black Lung Association campaigned for change. Congress passed safety laws for coal mine workers the next year, which included a mandate to eradicate black lung by creating maximum acceptable levels of coal dust in the air in mine shafts. Coal mine owners were also required to provide chest x-rays, as was done for granite workers. This progress helped catalyze the passing of the federal Occupational Safety and Health Act in 1970.[8]

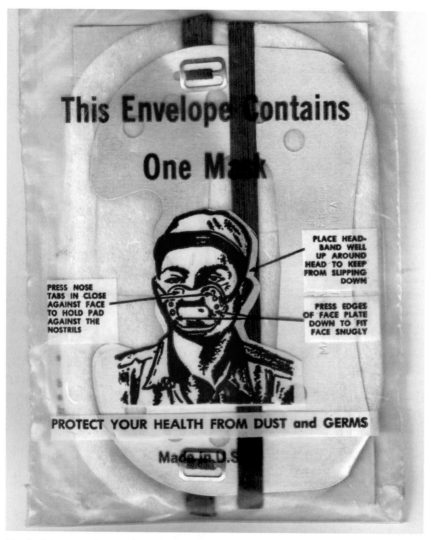

Martindale protective mask, c. 1930s-1950s.
VERMONT GRANITE MUSEUM OF BARRE, BARRE, VERMONT.

Silica is only dangerous when inhaled, but it continues to be a hazard in mining, pottery, manufacturing, and construction. There is no known cure for silicosis, so prevention is vital. This is true of black lung, asbestosis (caused by inhalation of asbestos fibers), and other industrial lung diseases as well. The history of "granite cutters' TB" and its relatives is an example of medicine intersecting with policy around individual and industry responsibilities.

# Health Uplifted,
# Health Upended

A young Black couple might have looked at this poster hanging in their church parlor or community center and seen a family like theirs. A Black middle-class family in a moment of domestic sweetness was not a portrayal they saw often in an age of racial caricatures. The poster announced that year's National Negro Health Week, an event put on by government and nonprofit agencies from 1915 to 1951.*

There are no happy posters and public health booklets from the Tuskegee Syphilis Study. The documents and artifacts that remain from this forty-year study are autopsy records, patient examination cards that note how many years a patient had been infected with syphilis, and photographs of doctors taking blood samples from men they were lying to. Taken together, these two programs exemplify some of the progress and some of the worst abuses in health in the twentieth century, showing how both systemic factors like poverty and education and the direct effects of racist decisions have had significant impacts on people's health.

### NATIONAL NEGRO HEALTH WEEK

When National Negro Health Week began, the death rate for Black people was one and a half times higher than for white people. Black people were dramatically underrepresented in the health professions. The 1910 Flexner Report, a

---

* The word "Negro" was used by many Black people in the United States until the 1970s.

# NATIONAL NEGRO HEALTH WEEK

## APRIL 2-8, 1922

THE HEALTH OF
THE CHILDREN
IS
THE WEALTH OF
THE NATION

## Better Health

## for

# HOME - SCHOOL - COMMUNITY

*This Poster Designed and Contributed by the*
### NATIONAL CHILD WELFARE ASSOCIATION, Inc.
70 Fifth Avenue, New York City
*Publishers of*
Educational Picture Panels
For Churches, Schools, Y. M. C. A's., Y. W. C. A's., etc.
Suitable for Health Week and Every Other Week in the Year.
(See Other Side)

Please Hang This Poster in Conspicuous Place Before and During Health Week.

National Negro Health Week poster, 1922.

landmark in improving standards in medical schools, also recommended clo-sure of schools that weren't up to standards. Only two Black medical schools had the resources to pass muster. At the same time, women in Black commu-nity organizations laid the groundwork for a Black public health movement. The founder of the Tuskegee Institute (now Tuskegee University), Booker T. Washington, built on their work to start National Health Improvement Week in 1915. He died that year, but his project continued as the annual National Negro Health Week, managed by a Tuskegee Institute committee. In 1921, the US Public Health Service became involved, producing a newsletter, a poster, a sermon, a leaflet for school children, and a radio broadcast each year.[1]

Schools and community groups observed the week with medical screen-ings, vaccine clinics, and short-term projects tackling health issues. It was also a platform for public health departments to provide practical education. Some of the biggest health challenges of the time were infectious diseases, including tuberculosis and syphilis. Relatively recent discoveries about how diseases spread weren't always common knowledge. National Negro Health Week included hundreds of health clinics and thousands of public lectures each year, plus more tangible improvements like the thousands of outhouses built nationwide.[2]

The week aimed for "racial uplift," on the theory that individual and community self-help could defeat poverty, poor education, and poor health. Booker T. Washington had adhered to this theory, in conflict with some other Black leaders who argued that a focus on self-help would not succeed without addressing systemic factors affecting Blacks. The fact that medical schools were segregated was one such factor. National Negro Health Week did enable individuals and communities to create at least incremental change. However, some advice dispensed by official National Negro Health Week materials showed the writers' naïveté about the larger issues at play, like the booklet that advised, "Overcrowding makes bad air, bad morals, discomfort, disease. If your house is crowded, enlarge it."[3]

## THE SYPHILIS STUDY
Seventeen years after National Negro Health Week began at the Tuskegee Institute, another program was launched there. It is often called the Tuskegee Syphilis Study, but it was largely run by the US Public Health Service, not the school. It was planned as a short-term examination of Black men who had already had syphilis for at least five years, but the researchers decided to continue the study indefinitely, following the men until their death while withholding treatment. The typical recommendation for syphilis at the time

was harsh but moderately effective mercury-based drugs. Untreated syphilis was known to damage the heart and brain.[4]

Study officials repeatedly lied to the impoverished study subjects and said it was a medical treatment program. The men never consented to being in a study and were never told they had syphilis. Some were told they had "bad blood," an imprecise slang term for syphilis and other diseases that not all of them had heard. The men received rides to and from the Tuskegee Institute for examinations, some treatment for minor ailments, and free hot meals on examination days. Later on, the researchers offered the men burial insurance, which ensured they would have access to the subjects' bodies for autopsy. The Public Health Service enlisted the cooperation of local doctors, and even the draft board to ensure they did not get outside treatment. Penicillin became available in the 1940s, a safe and effective treatment for syphilis. Nothing changed for the 399 men with syphilis in the study.[5]

Papers in top medical journals laid the study out in full detail, but only a few of the thousands of readers raised concerns. The 1962 Pure Food and Drug Act Amendments included regulations on human experimentation, but the United States was far behind the international standards created in the aftermath of Nazi atrocities. In 1966, Public Health Service physician Peter Buxtun learned of the study and proposed the agency halt it on moral grounds. They continued the study. In 1969, a group of physicians convened at the CDC to discuss whether the study was a public relations liability in the era of civil rights. By then, over one hundred of the men had died because of syphilis or its complications. A minority of doctors present wanted to offer the remaining subjects treatment. Others claimed the subjects wouldn't want treatment. They noted there would never be a chance to study so many subjects with untreated syphilis again. They continued the study. In 1970, a leading Public Health Service official declared that the study's outcomes would never "find, prevent, or cure a single case of syphilis," but said it provided laboratories with useful blood samples. They continued the study.[6]

Finally, in 1972 Buxtun spoke with a reporter from the Associated Press. Soon, the whole country knew the true purpose of the study, including the men who were its subjects. The Department of Health, Education and Welfare ordered an end to the study on November 16, four months after the scandal broke and forty years after the study began. The study took center stage at the Kennedy hearings on human experimentation in February and March 1973. In their wake, Congress passed the 1974 National Research Act. It required that institutional review boards evaluate studies receiving federal funding.

These committees had to include people who represented ethical perspectives as well as research agendas. The act also created a federal commission which released the Belmont Report in 1979. The report articulated principles of medical research ethics: studies must respect personal autonomy, must benefit someone (unlike the syphilis study), and must distribute costs and benefits justly. Two years later came the first version of the Common Rule, a standard of medical ethics that guides most regulations today.[7]

National Negro Health Week ended in 1951 during a move to racially integrate the roles of government agencies. Meanwhile, the Tuskegee Syphilis Study would continue for twenty-one more years. The experiment seemed to be a touchstone for why Black Americans did not trust doctors or the government for decades, although surveys show that the study is no longer as important to most Black Americans' minds as more recent personal or national experiences. Racial disparities in health persisted, perpetuated in part by racism, whether overt, covert, or unconscious. Too many medical professionals and institutions continued to treat Black people and other marginalized groups as expendable, excusing their actions with the myth that these groups were uninterested in taking care of their own health.[8] Some contemporary efforts to improve health in Black communities and among other marginalized groups work along similar principles as National Negro Health Week did and focus on empowerment, while others attempt to address the broader context that contributes to poor health. It is likely that both approaches are needed.

# DDT: The Double-Edged Sword

In 1939, a Swedish chemist looking for a way to moth-proof wool discovered the pesticide properties of dichloro-diphenyl-trichloroethane. This chemical, abbreviated DDT, did not just deter insects—it killed them, days and even months after application. DDT initially appeared to be surprisingly safe for humans, but when its effects were better understood, it became the cornerstone of a movement.

## THE ATOM BOMB OF THE INSECT WORLD

While humans have fought with insects for hundreds of thousands of years, pest control as we know it is a recent invention. In the nineteenth century, insect control was mostly studied by hobbyist entomologists. The practical applications they found elevated the science of insects from a gentleman's pastime to a field considered socially and economically important, as natural and chemical pest control gained a reputation for increasing crop yields and preventing disease. In the 1890s, scientists began to confirm that insects could be disease vectors, carrying specific diseases from person to person. People had long known that certain illnesses are common around swamps, but they believed this had to do with poisonous air. The word "malaria" literally means "bad air." In 1897, scientists discovered that the *Anopheles* mosquito, which often breeds in swamps, carries malaria. At the time, there was no effective treatment for malaria, a disease with flu-like symptoms which can be fatal.[1]

DDT's long-lasting ability to kill insects made it powerful in preventing insect-borne disease. During WWII, the United States was the first country to use DDT on a wide scale. Soldiers coated their clothing and scalps with the chemical. DDT prevented hundreds of thousands of deaths from disease: typhus carried by lice, and malaria and yellow fever carried by mosquitoes. It hit the US consumer market in August 1945, after years of free advertising in newspaper and magazine articles about its power in the war. Many early pesticides had been acutely toxic to humans; they harmed people right away. The idea of a safer pesticide was exhilarating. DDT was a part of a post-WWII narrative of humanity's conquest over nature and America's conquest over enemies, and indeed, it was dubbed "the atom bomb of the insect world."[2]

## QUESTIONING AND CHALLENGING

Like the atom bomb, though, DDT has extended fallout. People raised concerns immediately. High doses cause vomiting, tremors, and seizures in humans. Dorothy Coulson, a farmer in Georgia, campaigned against DDT from the late 1940s. The press noted scientists' concerns about its power to kill beneficial insects alongside harmful ones, especially when used on farms.[3] This can of DDT, sold for farming and gardening, demonstrates that at least

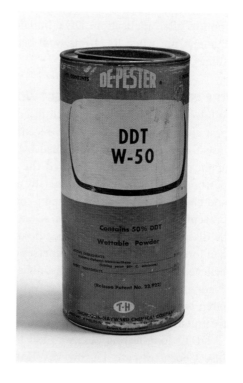

DDT canister, mid-twentieth century.
DDT W-50, COURTESY OF SCIENCE HISTORY
INSTITUTE, PHIL ALLEGRETTI PESTICIDE
COLLECTION, PHILADELPHIA, PENNSYLVANIA.

some of the risks were common knowledge. The back of the can has instructions for using it on livestock; in barns, mills, and grain storage areas; and on crops. The label warns to stop use on crops at least thirty days before harvest, and not to let it come in contact with food.

"Like the constant dripping of water that in turn wears away the hardest stone, this birth-to-death contact with dangerous chemicals may in the end prove disastrous," wrote marine biologist Rachel Carson in her 1962 blockbuster book *Silent Spring*.[4] Her book was a flashpoint in a growing environmental consciousness that was new in Western culture, one that saw the well-being of humans and the environment as interdependent, rather than seeing nature as a place to retreat to. Carson used DDT to explain and dramatize key ecological concepts: persistence, biomagnification, and long-term toxicity. Persistent pesticides like DDT stay in the water and soil for years. As animals higher on the food chain eat animals with DDT in their bodies, it accumulates in ever higher concentrations. This is biomagnification. These two problems aggravate the other big problem with DDT—it's toxic when it builds up over time. While some of Carson's claims in the book were overblown, these problems are real. The Environmental Protection Agency, which formed in 1970, banned DDT in 1972, and many countries followed suit in the next few decades.[5]

Malaria is still a serious health threat in many places, mainly tropical areas. Some advocates of using DDT for modern malaria control see hypocrisy or selfishness in people from developed Western nations calling for DDT bans when their countries used it to regionally eradicate malaria before DDT safety concerns went mainstream. In 2001, an international treaty limited the use of DDT to disease control only, and not agricultural pest control. The World Health Organization approves of DDT only for treating the insides of buildings.[6] Both these decisions have been controversial, and the WHO has gone back and forth on the topic. When a medication has the potential to save human lives and to end them, doctors and regulators make difficult judgments based on individual risks and benefits. When a preventative measure applied on a community scale has the same potential, as with DDT, that judgment is even more difficult.

# The Iron Lung
# and the Polio Epidemics

"A painful trip down a hallway ended with another fiery sea of agony crashing against me . . . On the peak of a high wave I descended with my nose flattened against someone's hand. Later I learned that the hand belonged to a physical therapist who was protecting my nose as my head slid through the collar of an iron lung." Martha Mason had never seen an iron lung until she contracted polio in 1948 at age eleven.[1]

From the 1910s through the 1950s, epidemics of poliomyelitis struck North America, Europe, Australia, and New Zealand. Immigrants, the poor, and crowded, dirty cities were all quickly made scapegoats. Polio appeared to whip unstoppably through communities, but it was not as ubiquitous as it seemed, and it's not unusually contagious. Most polio patients recover after no symptoms or a few weeks of flu-like symptoms and muscle pain. However, in some cases polio destroys motor neurons, temporarily or permanently paralyzing one or more parts of the body. Some patients lose the ability to breathe on their own. In the 1910s, polio patients were taken to hospitals to be quarantined, and some parents feared they were sending their children off to die. A few decades later, in large part due to the lifesaving iron lung, parents were eager to get their polio-stricken children into a hospital's care.[2]

### ENTER THE IRON LUNG

Prior to the iron lung, there were no good options for treating a patient whose respiratory muscles had failed. Various people had attempted making external respirators since the 1830s, including Alexander Graham Bell, with some successful prototypes, but nothing was on the market for use. In some cases, doctors or nurses would try to manually resuscitate a patient, but this was exhausting for patient and provider alike and couldn't be sustained.[3]

The "lung" was a respirator, a metal cylinder three feet in diameter and over seven feet long. Philip Drinker devised the first iron lung in 1928, but three years later it was eclipsed by a less expensive model invented by John Haven Emerson. The patient lay on their back on a bed inside the tank, seeing the world through a mirror above their head. A pump changed the pressure in the tank at intervals, forcing the patient to inhale and exhale. Polio survivor Larry Alexander wrote, "The weight, the unbearable weight on my chest continued for a few breaths; then, as the dials [on the side of the iron lung] were regulated, it lifted as if death itself were lifting from my body and my soul." Breathing and speaking with the machine's rhythm took getting used to, but it kept people alive.[4]

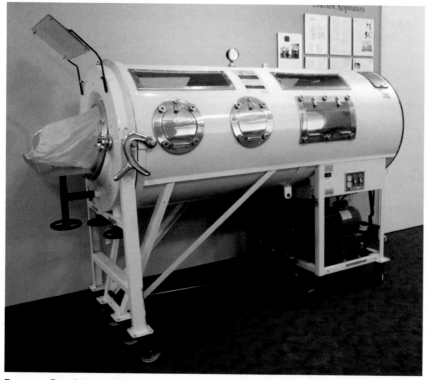

Emerson Respirator, 1952.
MELNICK MEDICAL MUSEUM, YOUNGSTOWN STATE UNIVERSITY, YOUNGSTOWN, OHIO.

Hospital halls were filled with the iron lung's squeaks, whines, and unmistakable whooshing. Iron lung wards were typically segregated by patient age, gender, and sometimes race. The long drive to a hospital was even longer for many Black families who had to find a hospital willing to admit them. Life on the wards was often dull because patients could not move, but they could talk with other patients, or read while a nurse or relative turned the pages. Some patients found the hospital a scary place, where you quickly learned that a drawn curtain meant a wardmate had died. However, some missed the camaraderie of their ward when they returned to the outside world, meeting both overt discrimination and barriers to their new access needs at schools, homes, and workplaces.[5]

After the acute stage of polio passed in about a week, the patient was out of immediate danger, but it might be days or months before they could be weaned off the iron lung. Some stayed on breathing support for life, with iron lungs in their homes, or with newer technology. Portable chest respirators were developed as early as the 1940s, but they provided less powerful breathing assistance than iron lungs did. In the 1950s, physicians in Europe responded to a series of polio outbreaks with the new Engström respirators. While iron lungs are negative-pressure ventilators, changing the pressure around the body to move the diaphragm, Engström respirators are positive-pressure ventilators, blowing air through a tube inserted in the trachea (windpipe). The majority of ventilators used today work by positive pressure.[6]

## POLIO PREVENTION

While respirator technology was advancing, the polio vaccine was what ended the era of iron lung wards. Researcher Jonas Salk and his team had been working on the hotly anticipated vaccine for years. They quietly conducted the initial trials of their vaccine at institutions for disabled children. In 1955, it was ready for a clinical trial with hundreds of thousands of volunteers, called Polio Pioneers. A vaccine must be able to provoke the body's immune system to recognize a pathogen without replicating and causing the disease. Salk and his team honed new techniques that killed the polio virus used in the vaccine.[7]

The 1955 press release cut to the chase: "The vaccine works. It is safe, effective and potent." Later that year, forty thousand children contracted polio from a defective version of the vaccine in which the virus wasn't properly killed, inspiring stronger federal oversight in vaccines. In 1960, Salk's main competitor, Albert Sabin, debuted a faster-acting vaccine. This one used a live virus strain that had been attenuated, or weakened, by repeatedly growing the virus in either a tissue culture or a non-human animal such as a mouse. It was essentially a slow form of genetically modifying the virus, akin to the way selective breeding of plants or animals is a slow form of genetically modifying vegetables or livestock.[8]

Youngstown, Ohio, was one of the first cities in the United States to use the new vaccine, which was more effective against the spread of polio than Salk's. The local medical society sponsored a mass immunization program, a bright spot in a difficult decade for the city. Volunteers mixed the tasteless vaccine with water in small paper cups by the thousands and distributed them at sites in the community, mostly schools. Because of vaccines, polio cases in the United States dropped 96 percent by 1962, inspiring researchers who would find vaccines for other fatal childhood illnesses.[9]

There is still no cure for polio, but the World Health Organization has been working to eradicate it through vaccination. In the twenty-first century, polio cases have dropped from hundreds of thousands of cases a year to a few hundred a year globally. The hulking, now-silent iron lung is an oddity to people who don't remember that era. Its mustard yellow or sickly green shell has been turned black and white in the public imagination by old photographs and television footage. However, polio and the iron lung are still within living memory. It evokes both the fear and the hope felt by patients who relied on it to breathe.

# Two Eras of Change in Pharmacy

Walking into the building marked Upjohn Pharmacy on the corner of Main and Center streets, visitors saw scales, mortar and pestle sets, and ceramic and glass jars of bulk medications. However, the pharmacists didn't fill prescriptions, but handed out souvenir postcards and sample bottles of vitamins, one of Upjohn's most successful products. In the next room, visitors could browse displays about the company's products and manufacturing in the present day. This idyllic late nineteenth-century drugstore was created with the real Upjohn company's sponsorship as part of the "Main Street USA" attraction at Disneyland from 1955 to 1970. It was one of Disneyland's original features when the park opened. "Main Street, with its calm charm, will associate reliability with the brand names displayed there," noted an article in Upjohn's employee magazine. While the attraction was aiming for a sense of nostalgic timelessness, both the era that the fictional display was trying to capture and the era in which the attraction existed were times of notable change.[1]

## FROM ASSEMBLY TO SELLING A STANDARDIZED PRODUCT

The attraction's contents were antiques scavenged from across the country, including nineteenth-century syringes, microscopes, cosmetics, and jars of pills and powders. In the pharmacy of the actual late nineteenth century, a great deal of the medications were assembled or "compounded" on site. They were prepared for the individual patient by a pharmacist who may have learned by apprenticeship, or in one of the schools of pharmacy that began proliferating in the mid-nineteenth century. However, some medications were premade

Upjohn Disney Collection, nineteenth century, assembled 1955–1970.
UNIVERSITY OF ARIZONA COLLEGE OF PHARMACY MUSEUM, TUCSON, ARIZONA.

tinctures, ointments, and plasters, which had been made in bulk in Europe since the Renaissance. The nineteenth century had seen a gradual increase in the types of medicines that came to the pharmacy in ready-to-use forms. A big step forward was premade tablets, arriving around the Civil War. Some pharmacists, seeing the shift in their field, moved from operating local drugstores to manufacturing drugs.[2]

The Upjohn Pill and Granule Company was founded in 1886, in the midst of a growth period for the field of pharmacy. Germ theory ushered in a wave of optimism that science could bring new cures, and the era saw a rise in American drug manufacturing. Upjohn initially found its niche in pills that the body could effectively break down. In the nineteenth century, pills were coated with a range of substances, from sugar and gelatin to silver and gold, not all of which broke down enough for the body to use what was inside. Upjohn's signature was a pill that could easily be crushed to a powder.[3]

As more and more medications were arriving ready-made, pharmacists added a new specialty that they could prepare on site: sodas. Carbonated water was thought to be healthy, and both it and sugar made various medicines (real and pseudoscientific) more palatable. Drugstore soda counters thrived as a temperance-era alternative to bars, with brands like Coca-Cola and Dr. Pepper promising to give customers vitality and health. By the mid-twentieth century, federal regulations limited which products could be sold with health claims and restricted the sale of certain popular soda ingredients like cocaine. This sapped the energy of the health soda fad, but soda remained a popular treat. While it would have been appropriate, Disney's Upjohn Pharmacy storefront did not include a soda fountain, perhaps because in the 1950s it was not yet nostalgic.[4]

### THE DRUG DISCOVERY BOOM

Between the era of the real Upjohn's early years and the era when the Disney storefront welcomed tourists, pharmacies changed at a fast pace. In its "Main Street" attraction, Upjohn painted itself as a modern company that had a long history of withstanding rapid changes in the field. It opened around the height of a surge of new drugs, but this era was also marked by incidents that revealed a need for advances in drug safety.

The precursors of the boom had begun decades before. In Europe, industrial chemistry began to flourish in the late nineteenth century as companies that made dyes began investing in research. They tinkered with existing compounds to create synthetic ones, including compounds of medicinal value. One of the successes of that period that's still around today is aspirin, developed by the dye company Bayer in 1899. During WWI, a shortage of supplies from Europe, the difficulty of getting drugs from enemy countries, and the desire to get any advantage possible for the soldiers inspired American drug companies to invest in research as well.[5]

In 1937, over one hundred people died from taking elixir sulfanilamide, a drug prepared with a toxic solvent. Drug safety was in the headlines, and people worried about the poisons that lurked in their medicine cabinets. In the wake of this incident, Congress passed the 1938 Food, Drug, and Cosmetic Act, requiring that new drugs be tested for safety. A few years later, the field of pharmacy was buoyed by the discovery of antibiotics, which restored excitement over medications. By the mid-twentieth century, companies competed to be the best at developing new drugs, not just manufacturing them. The Upjohn company developed a process for the large-scale production of cortisone in 1952. This steroid, used for autoimmune diseases, acute respiratory problems, and other needs, went from impractically expensive to highly profitable. By 1955 when Disneyland opened, faith in pharmacy from both scientists and the public had reached what may have been an all-time high.[6]

While it may have seemed in 1955 that science would continuously propel Upjohn and other drug companies forward, during the fifteen years that the Disney Upjohn "store" was open, the drug discovery boom tapered off. Revolutionary new chemical finds were becoming less frequent. Drug safety received renewed attention in the 1950s when thalidomide, often prescribed for morning sickness, caused miscarriages and severe, life-altering birth defects. Dr. Frances Oldham Kelsey and her colleagues at the FDA blocked it from approval in the United States. This era was also the beginning of the shift towards medications that target risk factors for disease, such as blood pressure medications. Targeting risk factors meant that companies had to change advertising techniques in order to attract customers who felt healthy. The Upjohn company's marketing department shifted priorities as well, and ended its sponsored display at Disneyland in 1970.[7]

The collection of drugstore antiques assembled for the Upjohn Disney attraction is now housed at the University of Arizona College of Pharmacy Museum. The Upjohn company was absorbed by Pfizer in the 1990s, but the Upjohn Disney collection is more than a defunct company's corporate history. It captures two eras: the late nineteenth century when the items were made, and the mid-twentieth, when pharmaceutical companies vied to become trusted household names while the science of pharmacy experienced a complicated golden age.

# More Than a Metaphor: The Straitjacket

A straitjacket brings to mind movie depictions of mental illness—dangerous people, and people treated like they're dangerous. *One Flew over the Cuckoo's Nest* was filmed at Oregon State Hospital, which has both a modern mental healthcare facility and a museum of asylum history. Caring for patients with mental illness in asylums or inpatient hospitals started out as a humanitarian project, but it has a history fraught with abuses. Countless people have invoked straitjackets as a metaphor for restricting or robbing someone of their freedom. In fact, a major theme in the history of mental health treatment is finding the appropriate amount to restrict patients' freedom, if any amount is appropriate. This can be on the small scale of a garment and on the large scale of their control of their life.

## RESTRAINT AND RESTRAINTS

Actual straitjackets, primarily intended to prevent a person from hurting themselves or others, evolved from other cloth restraints and have existed since at least the 1730s. In that era, many mentally ill people were imprisoned. Many others lived with their families, some of whom abused or neglected them out of malice, poor understanding of their needs, or inadequate resources to take care of them. Better treatment of the mentally ill was one of a number of nineteenth-century reform movements that worked for a more humane society. Inspired in part by similar changes in Europe, American Dorothea Dix campaigned to create state hospitals for the insane starting in the 1840s.

Some nineteenth-century doctors believed mental illness was a disregard for self-control. They thought they could train people to exercise more personal restraint by physically restraining them. Others saw mental illness as an innate, incurable flaw. Women could be committed to asylums (often by a family member) for arguing, masturbating, remaining single, and a host of other reasons, and people who would today be described as transgender or nonbinary were also deemed mentally ill. In 1851, a doctor proposed that enslaved people who tried to escape suffered from a mental illness called "drapetomania." In short, mental illness was construed as any failure to conform to the restraints of social and moral expectations. Treatment for white and wealthy people tended to be kinder and more solution-focused, and for non-white people and the poor it tended to be more punitive.[1]

In a parallel with mental illness, people began seeing alcohol misuse as a treatable disease starting early in the nineteenth century. Still, the older interpretation of drinking as a failure of restraint and a moral problem remained popular. Many people struggling with alcoholism were sent to state hospitals in the nineteenth and early twentieth centuries, even if they had no underlying mental health condition.[2]

Especially when they were involuntarily committed, insane asylum patients were deprived of both liberty and dignity. During the same period, psychiatrists and reformers argued that a well-run mental health institution used no physical restraints whatsoever. "Moral treatment" hospitals aimed to create a positive social environment and care for patients' mental well-being. However, even "moral treatment" hospitals used straitjackets when staff were overworked and short-handed. In that regard, not much had changed a century later. In his 1961 book *Asylums*, sociologist Erving Goffman showed that asylums typically used systems of rewards and punishments, rather than the treatment methods recommended by doctors. This canvas straitjacket was used at the Oregon State Hospital in the 1960s. The sleeves, which go past the patient's hands, are strapped down at the sides and buckled around the back. Straitjackets were often used to punish insubordination and "bad" behavior, violent or not. Patients were sometimes left in restraints for days or even years.[3]

The turn of the twentieth century saw a number of changes in mental health treatment. The eugenics movement pushed to strip people with a mental health diagnosis of their rights. Meanwhile, new schools of thought like Sigmund Freud's psychoanalysis persuaded many people that mental illness is treatable. This expensive new therapy also sharpened the class divide

is necessary to keep her
hands in a strait jacket to
prevent her from picking on
her hands and head.

Patient History for Elizabeth
November 9, 1896

Straitjacket, c. 1960.

OREGON STATE HOSPITAL MUSEUM OF MENTAL HEALTH, SALEM, OREGON.

in how people with mental illness were treated. At the same time, reformers continued to fight against mental health "treatments" that robbed the patient of any agency. In 1913, reformer and patient Clifford Beers founded the first outpatient mental health clinic in the United States.[4]

Also in 1913, it was proven that the psychiatric disorder called general paralysis of the insane was caused by third-stage syphilis. This discovery inspired researchers to look for biological origins and cures for other mental illnesses. Doctors studying shell-shocked soldiers returning from WWI also began to understand the role of trauma in mental health.[5]

## MID-CENTURY MENTAL HEALTH

Mid-twentieth-century treatments aimed to soothe excitability or snap the person out of the grips of their illness. The restraint itself was not intended as therapy, but restraints including straitjackets and bed straps were used to keep the patient in place during treatment. One treatment was "hydrotherapy," in which patients sat in extremely cold water, sometimes for hours at a time, or were sandwiched between cold, wet bed sheets. The "tub room" featured in *One Flew over the Cuckoo's Nest* was for hydrotherapy. Another treatment was insulin shock "therapy," introduced in the 1930s, causing seizures and comas with high doses of the hormone insulin. After emerging from the coma, the patient was typically docile and helpless for a short period of time. This practice fell out of favor when antipsychotic drugs became available. The most famous treatment was electroconvulsive therapy, inducing seizures by passing an electrical current through the brain. It is still used for certain disorders, but with informed consent, and while the patient is under general anesthesia.[6]

Some mental health treatment in this period aimed specifically to prepare people for life outside the asylum. Psychiatrist Joshua Bierer, an Austrian who began working in London in 1942, taught the "social approach," which centered on both patient independence and creating close, supportive communities. He began working at Oregon State Hospital in 1960 and taught this approach to clinics in the United States.[7]

In 1951, hospitals began using a daily injection of the new drug chlorpromazine to prevent manic and psychotic states. A number of copycat drugs were soon released, broadly called "antipsychotics." Patients often resisted these medications because of their side effects. Like straitjackets, the drugs were often used as a means of control and sometimes punishment. The first drugs for people outside of institutional care who had moderate anxiety also debuted in the 1950s. More people began seeing mental health as a spectrum, rather than believing insanity was something that happened to a certain kind of person. The 1960s saw the start of the deinstitutionalization movement, in which mental health patients are given the support they need to live independently. These changes ushered out the era of the straitjacket as a mainstay in mental health facilities.[8]

Today, many people lead independent lives while living with serious mental illness, assisted by counseling, medications, and for some people, short- or long-term inpatient treatment at psychiatric hospitals or clinics. There are many serious issues facing the mental health community, including stigma, barriers to access to high-quality care, and one of the same problems that reformers tried to solve in the early nineteenth century: a large number of people with severe mental illnesses are imprisoned rather than cared for. Prisons use restraints, sometimes including straitjackets, in much the same way that they had long been used in mental hospitals.[9] While restraint in the abstract sense remains relevant to discussions of mental health, straitjackets, their use, and their misuse are still more than a metaphor.

# 43

# Changing Ways of Looking at the Gut

In the nineteenth century, doctors used reflected light from a candle to try to see ulcers, polyps, and cancer in the stomach. When that wasn't bright enough, they used light from a burning mixture of alcohol and turpentine.[1] Edison's 1879 incandescent lamp allowed great strides forward, but it wasn't until the 1950s that researchers solved the problem of seeing around curves in the digestive tract.

## EARLY CHALLENGES

In 1902, the laryngologist Chevalier Jackson designed an endoscope to see the esophagus that became the standard for almost a century. An endoscope is the general name for a tool inserted in a surgical incision or a natural orifice like the mouth in order to see deep inside the body. Developing a gastroscope, a tool specifically to see the stomach, stayed an unsolved challenge. Before fiber optics, the most widely used endoscope for the rest of the GI tract was Rudolf Schindler's 1932 hinged semiflexible gastroscope. The doctor had to be excellent and the patient had to tip their head back to align the mouth, throat, and esophagus like a sword-swallower. Endoscopes for other purposes, such as gynecology, were limited by the risk of burns from the hot lightbulb.[2]

## THE MODEL T OF ENDOSCOPES

In 1954, Basil Hirschowitz, a physician studying ulcers, was struck by two papers he read about using fiber optics to transmit images. They suggested practical possibilities for the known concept that a strand of glass could carry light. Hirschowitz met with the authors, but was disappointed by the amount of light loss and the green tint to the images in the existing technology. He began working with two physicists, Dr. C. Wilbur Peters and Larry Curtiss. They wrestled with engineering problems such as detangling glass fibers that snarled in the mail, and polishing the fibers' ends to get good surfaces for the light to enter and exit. The worst problem was "cross talk," when light jumps between fibers, losing the image. Curtiss, who was an undergraduate at the time, solved this by insulating the optical glass strands with a different glass.[3]

"I looked at this rather thick, forbidding but flexible rod," Hirschowitz wrote later, "took the instrument and my courage in both hands, and swallowed it over the protest of my unanesthetized pharynx and my vomiting center." A few days later, he used his prototype to view an ulcer in a patient's small intestine. The team had some trouble getting a company to commercially produce the gastroscope, and a few companies claimed to be developing a rival product, which never materialized. However, in 1960, American Cystoscope Makers, Inc. produced the first model based on the team's design, soon releasing the ACMI Model 4990, which Hirschowitz called "the model T of fiber-optic endoscopy."[4]

Model 4990 fiber optic gastroscope, 1960.
ALABAMA MUSEUM OF THE HEALTH SCIENCES, THE UNIVERSITY OF ALABAMA AT BIRMINGHAM, BIRMING-
HAM, ALABAMA.

Other industries borrowed the idea of using fiber optics to see around curves and corners, and in 1962, Rolls Royce began using a variation on the AMCI 4990 gastroscope to inspect aircraft engines without dismantling them. Meanwhile, gastroendoscopy literally brought light to diagnosis and treatment of many GI issues, greatly improving diagnosis for many kinds of cancer.[5] The next innovation in endoscopy was to incorporate surgical tools in the same instrument as imaging tools. Today, fiber optics have been replaced with tiny video cameras, as the back-and-forth exchange between medical and non-medical innovations continues.

# The Pill's New Era of Choice (For Some)

"You are murdering us for your profit and convenience," charged one woman, part of a group who interrupted a 1970 Senate hearing about the side effects of hormonal birth control. Controversy has always surrounded hormonal birth control pills, colloquially called "the Pill." Some of the Pill's first advocates hoped that the poor, disabled people, and people of color would reproduce less. The Pill was initially tested on marginalized communities, with sloppy to nonexistent consent practices. When the Pill first came out, the doses and side effects were much stronger than today, and many people were angered by doctors who seemed to prescribe it carelessly. Yet millions of people take it, and many considered it life-changing when it debuted.[1] Prospective patients launched a national discussion on patients' involvement in their own health. The Pill is myriad things in a small package, and its history includes many questions of choice, not just reproductive choices.

## PRODUCTION AND TESTING

The Pill was the product of years of research on human hormones. Progesterone, the hormone in the initial pill formula, was synthesized in Mexico by Mexican and American scientists from a local yam called barbasco. This tuber was also used to make cortisone and other medical products. Both harvesting it and testing its chemical purity in the lab became important Mexican industries in the 1940s. However, once the Pill went on the market, it was unaffordable to most people in Mexico, including people who were involved in its making.[2]

Once the hormone was ready for clinical trials, the scientists working on the Pill only found sixty people willing to be study subjects, and half didn't comply with the study's stringent requirements. They turned to forcing people to participate, including women in long-term psychiatric care who had nothing to gain from contraception.[3]

The first large-scale clinical trials took place in a housing project in Puerto Rico in 1956. In Puerto Rico, over a third of women were sterilized—some involuntarily, and some because it was the most accessible form of contraception. Many women were eager for effective but reversible alternatives. The study directors erroneously assumed they could do a trial there quietly, believing the locals to be ignorant and docile. There was an outcry from some of the two hundred test subjects and others in their community who were concerned that the tests were being done there for racist reasons. Indeed, some notable birth control advocates believed it could protect society from the "lower classes" out-reproducing the "upper classes." Just as in Mexico, the commercial Pill was unaffordable to most Puerto Ricans involved in its making. Neither this nor the problem of poor consent practices in testing are unique to the Pill, but they are particularly resonant given that many of the conversations around the Pill focus on enabling patients to make their own choices.[4]

### SIDE EFFECTS: WHOSE CHOICE?

The Pill was part of a shift around sexual and reproductive health that had been in progress for the better part of a century. In 1873, the Comstock Act banned sending contraception or information about contraception through the mail. This federal law, which also banned mailing sex toys and pornography, limited the sale of condoms, diaphragms, and spermicides. However, a growing movement advocating family planning pushed back against this law and its state and local counterparts. In 1936, the U Circuit Court of Appeals ruled that physicians could receive contraceptive devices in the mail, and the American Medical Association also began recognizing birth control as within doctors' purview.[5]

When the first birth control pill appeared under the brand name Enovid in 1960, some women had already begun taking their reproductive choices out of doctors' total control. They questioned their lack of agency during childbirth, especially the practice of strapping laboring patients to beds. Now, the Pill meant that contraception was wholly in the hands of the person who could get pregnant, unlike older methods. Happy patient-customers said the Pill freed

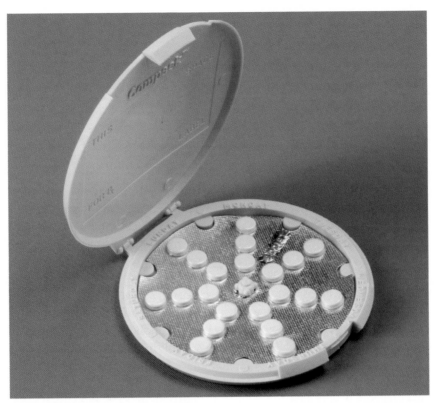

Enovid birth control pill pack, c. 1960.
DITTRICK MEDICAL HISTORY CENTER, CASE WESTERN RESERVE UNIVERSITY, CLEVELAND, OHIO.

them from having another child every year. Within five years, over six million people were taking the Pill.*

Enovid's side effects ranged from headaches and vomiting to increased risk of blood clots, heart attack, cancer, and stroke. The book *The Doctor's Case against the Pill* by medical journalist Barbara Seaman caught the attention of Senator Gaylord Nelson, who was investigating abuses in the pharmaceutical industry. In 1970, the US Senate held the Nelson Hearings on the Pill's safety and side effects. Women were not called to testify about their own experiences

---

* Such statistics often describe all pill users as women. Transgender men, nonbinary people, and others who get pregnant are presumably included in counts of Pill users, although they are frequently underrepresented or left out of studies entirely. Tone, *Devices and Desires*, 233–34; Richard W. Wertz and Dorothy C. Wertz, *Lying-In: A History of Childbirth in America* (New York: Free Press, 1977), 170; May, *America and the Pill*, 128.

on the Pill, but a group of women stood up and spoke from the audience. That year, hundreds of women wrote to the FDA, demanding that the Pill come with a list of side effects and risks. While some considered the increased health risks to be tantamount to murder, for many women, the discussion was as much about informed consent and the doctor-patient relationship as about the medication's risks.[6]

Doctors had been claiming since the trials in Puerto Rico that the symptoms women reported were psychosomatic. Some claimed that giving patients more information would increase side effects by the power of suggestion, and members of the nascent women's health movement condemned the doctors for being patronizing. Consumer organizations and women's health groups argued that giving patients more information and the ability to make their own choices is always better. Critics argued that the FDA should not mandate providing a list of side effects when doing so had not been studied. However, within six months, advocates succeeded in getting a seven-sentence insert in Pill packages. A more thorough insert was several years off. The Pill was one of the first medications with a mandated patient package insert.[7]

Also starting mid-century, women advocated for more attention to sex-specific health needs beyond prenatal care and childbirth. In 1970, the newly formed Boston Women's Health Collective published the first edition of the book *Our Bodies, Ourselves*, addressing topics from sexually transmitted infections to sexual assault. In 1973, the United States Supreme Court affirmed that pregnant people have the right to an abortion. By 1974, more than 1,200 women's groups in the United States offered health resources.[8]

The changes created by patient-activists allowed patients more choices about their healthcare, but access to the changes was often limited to women who were white, nondisabled, and middle- or upper-class. Exacerbated by the rise of the "welfare queen" myth in the 1970s, numerous government and nonprofit initiatives have favored longer-term contraceptives for women who receive public assistance, regardless of the individual's desires or health needs. Furthermore, some patients have been compelled to submit to sterilization as a condition of receiving an abortion.[9]

The doses of hormones in the Pill are much lower today than they were when it came out, but none of these related debates are resolved. There is ongoing discourse about whether doctors take women's concerns seriously. The United States has giant economic and racial disparities in access to reproductive care, and both contraception and abortion are still debated as social and moral divisions as well as health needs.[10] The Pill opened the door to new choices for patients, but also to public conversations about whose choices they should be.

# Smoking under Scrutiny

When Alton Ochsner was a medical student in the 1910s, a doctor invited his class to watch a lung cancer autopsy, thinking they might not see another case in their lifetimes. In 1933, Ochsner saw nine cases in six months. The patients had all smoked since WWI, and it set him on a path to investigating a possible link between cigarettes and lung cancer. He wasn't the only one, but other theories abounded, blaming influenza, chemical weapons, or asphalt for the rise in lung cancer. It took hundreds of scientists until the 1960s to prove conclusively that smoking causes cancer, in part because they couldn't rely on the gold standard in science, laboratory experiments.[1]

## TOBACCO MEETS THE LABORATORY

Native North and South American cultures had used tobacco for thousands of years, often in ceremonies, but in the sixteenth century, Europeans began smoking pipes and cigars recreationally. By the mid-nineteenth century, some people worried that tobacco was a stimulant and an unsanitary habit, but many believed smoking was fine in moderation.[2] In the 1880s, two changes meant people smoked more and inhaled more while smoking: cigarette-making machines enabled mass production, and new ways to cure tobacco produced a less acidic smoke. During WWI, several countries gave soldiers cigarettes in their rations to keep them calm. By the 1930s, veterans had been smoking for over a decade. In 1936, the rate of death by lung cancer had more than tripled over what it had been in 1920.

In the 1920s and 1930s, several researchers began devising machines to study which components of a cigarette made it into the smoke. Smoking machines use a mechanical vacuum pump or other machine method to puff on a cigarette at intervals to mimic human smoking. They trap the gasses and collect particles from the smoke on filter pads to be analyzed.[3]

By the early 1950s, the public was beginning to understand that cigarette smoke was dangerous. Cigarette companies responded by trying to position their products as safer than their competitors' cigarettes. The race between companies to demonstrate that their cigarettes had lower tar outputs than their competitors was dubbed the "tar derby." Tobacco companies used smoking machine tests to try to stay one step ahead of one another. Each claimed their products had the lowest nicotine as well as the lowest tar. Filtered cigarettes had become popular as the dangers of tobacco became known, and companies claimed that their cigarettes' filters removed any danger. Their results were questionable, because the machines they used were far from standardized, using different puff volumes and other variables, but smoking machines also played a role in legitimate research.[4]

## CAUSES AND EFFECTS

Thousands of studies on the health effects of tobacco were done from the 1930s through the 1960s, but smoking was everywhere. Both the 1962 Royal College of Physicians' report in England and the 1964 Surgeon General's Report in the United States re-evaluated the first three decades of research in order to make official recommendations regarding tobacco use. The main concern was lung cancer, but they studied other cancers, heart disease, and

Machine smoking filter pads, undated.
DAVID J. SENCER CDC MUSEUM, U.S. CENTERS FOR DISEASE CONTROL AND PREVENTION, ATLANTA, GEORGIA.

other issues as well. For the Surgeon General's Report, a team of ten doctors and biostatisticians (plus two dozen staff) reviewed nearly seven thousand studies that had been done to that point. However, given the state of science at the time, they did not just need to answer whether the evidence showed that smoking causes cancer. They also needed to answer whether it was possible to draw a conclusion from the type of studies that had been done.

Some respected scientists wanted to rule out the possibility that some other factor predisposed people to both smoking and lung cancer. They felt that the causal link between cigarettes and lung cancer could not be proven otherwise. Moreover, a number of experienced biostatisticians and epidemiologists had very serious concerns about judging hypotheses based on a diverse body of evidence. Some of them were in the pockets of the tobacco industry, but many of them were simply being cautious. Scientific consensus had recently begun to converge around the necessity of well-designed experiments, specifically randomized controlled trials, as a standard for much-needed scientific rigor within medical testing. However, there were no studies in which people were assigned to smoke, for practical and ethical reasons. Researchers cannot ask test subjects to expose themselves to something being evaluated for its likelihood of causing cancer.[5]

The studies the Surgeon General's committee reviewed included animal experiments about the carcinogenic properties of tobacco. The report includes a chapter on the composition of cigarette smoke, which relied on smoking machines. However, the most significant studies they reviewed used one of two methods, both of which were fairly new and considered unproven. Case-control studies looked at people with cancer and compared how many of them had been smokers or nonsmokers. Cohort studies followed smokers and non-smokers over time and tracked which ones developed cancer.[6]

In the battle over what types of evidence could make a scientific case, those who favored a rigorous but broad approach including case-control and cohort studies won. The 1964 Surgeon General's Report is considered a landmark statement of methods for assessing evidence. In 1965, British tobacco researcher Sir A. Bradford Hill laid out nine principles for evaluating the suspected cause of a disease. For example, the stronger the correlation, the stronger the likelihood that it's the real cause. He noted that heavy smokers were twenty to thirty times more likely to die of lung cancer than non-smokers, an extremely strong correlation. The Bradford Hill criteria are still a touchstone in epidemiology.[7]

Many of the researchers and policymakers were themselves smokers. There was little support for the process of quitting, and most doctors considered smoking a habit, not an addiction. The surgeon Evarts Graham initially dismissed Alton Ochsner's suspicion that the rise of cigarette smoking caused the rise of lung cancer. He pointed out that there had also been a rise in the sale of nylon stockings, but no one thought nylons caused cancer. A few years later, he reduced his smoking to six cigarettes a day after a student, Ernst Wynder, showed him compelling data. In 1953, Graham and Wynder published an animal study demonstrating a link between cigarette tar and skin cancer, and he quit smoking altogether. Two weeks before his death from lung cancer in 1957, he wrote to Ochsner, "After having smoked as much as I did for so many years, too much damage had been done."[8]

The history of tobacco research is littered with the stories of people who quit too late, and of tobacco companies wielding their money as power. However, over 40 percent of adults in the US smoked in the 1960s. Thirty years later, per capita cigarette consumption had been cut nearly in half because of a combination of regulations, education, and support for quitting. The CDC estimates that this reduction prevented about 1.6 million deaths from smoking-related causes, including lung cancer, other cancers, and heart disease.[9] While smoking is still a major global public health concern, recent history boasts many successes. The development of scientific consensus around the dangers of tobacco was a victory for science, both in terms of the knowledge gained about smoking and about study methods, opening the doors for future research.

# Ed Roberts and the Independent Living Movement

L ater in life, Ed Roberts periodically referenced a horrible comment his doctor made in front of him when he had polio at fourteen in 1953. The doctor said to his mother, "You should probably hope he dies, because if he lives he will be nothing more than a vegetable." Roberts decided that if he was a "vegetable," he would be an artichoke, "a little prickly on the outside with a big heart."[1] He went on to cofound a movement for greater autonomy for disabled people, both in their role as patients and in other areas of their lives.

## FIGHTING FOR FREEDOM

A few years after surviving polio, Roberts attended the University of California at Berkeley, but administrators almost rescinded his acceptance when they found out he was a quadriplegic. The campus hospital was the one building that could accommodate the iron lung he slept in at night, so he lived there despite not being a patient. He wanted a motorized wheelchair, but his doctors said he wouldn't be able to operate the controls because he only had use of two fingers. He had a controller installed on a chair backwards, positioned so he could use his two fingers to the best advantage. This freed him to go to class and go on dates without an attendant pushing his chair.

Soon, more disabled students joined Roberts in using the hospital as a dorm. They worked together to get the university to remove obstacles to their education. They needed curb cuts in the sidewalks, ramps into the buildings, and other basic features that were quite rare in the 1960s. Roberts cofounded UC Berkeley's Physically Disabled Students Program, which provided support

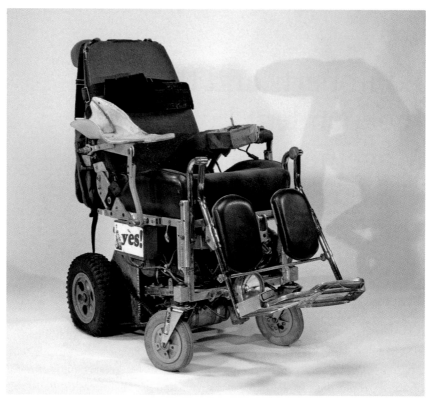

Wheelchair, c. 1960s.

DIVISION OF MEDICINE AND SCIENCE, NATIONAL MUSEUM OF AMERICAN HISTORY, SMITHSONIAN INSTITU-
TION, WASHINGTON, DC.

in navigating bureaucracy and ableism. The program also helped students re-
pair their wheelchairs and other assistive devices, many of which weren't built
for active college life. In 1972, Roberts became the first executive director of
a nonprofit based on the same model—the Center for Independent Living,
which inspired hundreds of similar centers across the country.[2]

As more disabled people were becoming activists, they made change on a
national level. Disabled organizers helped pass Section 504 of the Rehabilita-
tion Act of 1973. This civil rights provision banned discrimination against
disabled people in programs that received federal funds. It took years of activism, and Roberts took part in a twenty-five-day sit-in organized by Judith
Heumann and Kitty Cone. It was the longest sit-in at a federal government
building in United States history. Section 504 was a victory, but its reach was

limited. In one case, a court ruled that if a bus driver opened the doors for a wheelchair user, the bus system was accessible, even if there were stairs to get onto the bus. Disabled activists kept fighting for a stronger law. The Americans with Disabilities Act (ADA) was passed in 1990. It covers much of the private sector as well as the public sector, and clarifies terms and closes loopholes from Section 504. Even now, many disabled people need to advocate for their right to access public places on a regular basis.[3]

## BEYOND THE MEDICAL MODEL

The history of healthcare is incomplete without disability, but viewing disability through the lens of healthcare is extremely limiting. What's often termed the medical model of disability assumes disabled people need a cure. Many disabled people want their healthcare to help them live their best lives, whether or not that means making their bodies work the same as others. Public health professionals are more used to looking at problems as systemic rather than individual, but many still rely on the medical model and see disability as an outcome to prevent, to the exclusion of seeing a population to serve. Many disabled activists prefer the social model of disability. This view looks at the cultural, political, architectural, and economic factors in a disabled person's life. Disability is what an impairment (such as Roberts's paralysis) means for the person living in society.[4]

Ed Roberts is remembered as the father of the independent living movement, which works to get disabled people the freedom to make their own decisions. Much of what Roberts fought for is not medical, like accessible public transit and an end to employment discrimination. Other issues for the disabled community are at the intersection of medical and social issues, like health insurance. The independent living movement is based on the idea that disabled people deserve independence, not defined as doing everything without assistance, but as making their own decisions. Some disability activists critique or qualify this model, saying it caters disproportionately to the people who have the ability, education, and societal power to stand up for themselves. Others argue that these critiques oversimplify the movement's goals. As Judy Heumann said, "The main point in the movement, to us, is that disabled people gain political power and self-respect."[5]

It is all too common for non-disabled people to see an assistive device and overlook the person using it. This wheelchair was special; Roberts customized it with an adjustable seat and space for a respirator, and decorated it with a bumper sticker. But it was Roberts, and not the wheelchair, making history.

It is perhaps even more common to describe people as "bound" or "confined" to their assistive devices. Like many people who use assistive devices, Roberts didn't see his wheelchair as confining—he was confined by almost being turned away from school, by sidewalks with a five-inch drop to cross the street, and by inaccessible buildings, including places he had meetings or was an invited speaker. His wheelchair was freeing, and allowed him to work for further freedom. After he died of a heart attack in 1995, Roberts's family donated the wheelchair to the Smithsonian according to his wishes.[6] Its presence in the museum's collection is a testament to the traction disability rights gained in his lifetime, although the work is far from done.

# 47

# Bypassing the Heart

In 1896, surgeon Stephen Paget wrote, "Surgery of the heart has probably reached the limit set by nature to all surgery," asserting that it would be impossible to do surgery inside a heart. That same year, German Ludwig Rehn proved Paget wrong, performing the first suture within the heart.[1] Half a century later, surgeons could correct several valve defects, but it was clear that certain surgeries could not be done on a beating heart. The heart pumps blood into the lungs to receive oxygen, then pumps oxygen-rich blood to the body. Stopping the heart safely requires a way to bypass these organs and temporarily take over their roles. This was achieved in the 1950s, and heart surgery has seen a series of improvements small and large, building on one another with no "limit set by nature" yet found.

### INNOVATIONS COMING TOGETHER

Dramatic near-successes and near-failures mark the history of heart surgery. John Gibbon of Philadelphia completed the first heart-lung machine to perform pulmonary bypass in 1952. Gibbon's first patient on the machine died because of an incorrect diagnosis. The following year, Gibbon successfully repaired an atrial septal defect on a teenager who had been hospitalized for heart problems three times in six months. His machine was a new use for a peristaltic or roller pump, which uses rollers to stroke a flexible tube of blood, propelling the blood forward. The pump was invented by Lebanese-American Michael DeBakey, a preeminent cardiac surgeon who also co-authored one of the first papers on cigarettes and lung cancer.[2]

Gibbon's machine passed blood over a series of wire mesh screens to create a film of blood that was then exposed to oxygen. By contrast, in the machine pictured here, bubbles of oxygen gas were pumped into the blood. Doctors had been attempting to use bubbles for perfusion since the 1880s, well before open-heart surgery. However, bubbles of gas can be deadly if introduced into the body, so there can't be any bubbles left when the blood is pumped back into the patient. Early experiments with heart-lung machines included a number of failed bubble oxygenator designs. In 1955, surgeons at the University of Minnesota introduced a bubble oxygenator that let all the bubbles rise to the top of a tube and burst, creating safe, oxygenated blood. This became the dominant type of oxygenator until the 1980s, when devices for gas exchange over a thin membrane rose to prominence.[3]

### A TIME OF CHANGE
This heart-lung machine was used by the University of South Alabama Medical Center (now University Hospital) in Mobile, Alabama, starting in 1969.

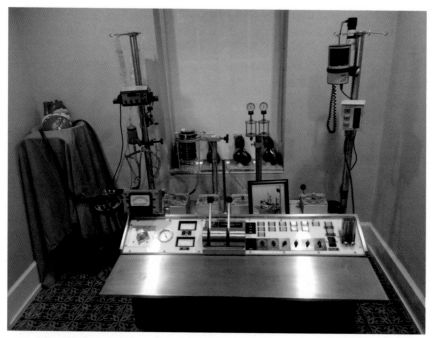

Heart-Lung Machine, 1970s.
MOBILE MEDICAL MUSEUM, MOBILE, ALABAMA.

The dozen-plus years this machine was in use were a time of change in more than one way. Hospitals across the country had recently racially integrated or closed following the passage of Medicare, which mandated that hospitals receiving funding comply with the Civil Rights Act.

Also in that time, heart-lung machines enabled more innovations. In 1969, a patient lived with an artificial heart for three days, before receiving a transplant of a donated human heart. This was just two years after the first successful heart transplant. The first ventricular assist device, a partial artificial heart that can sustain patients for months before a transplant, debuted in the 1980s.[4]

Heart-lung machines and other complex machinery often get taken apart and remade, especially in the first years of the technology. Because of this, early examples are held by relatively few museums, compared with how important a development the heart-lung machine is. This particular example was not ground-breaking in and of itself, but it is a compilation of advances that occurred not long before it was made. To the patients in Mobile who would not have survived without this machine, it is assuredly priceless.

# False Hopelessness or False Hope: The Early Years of AIDS

In the early 1980s, people from certain groups started dying terrible deaths. Gay men, Haitians, and people who used intravenous drugs were dying from diseases their bodies should have fought off easily. In 1982, their condition was named Acquired Immunodeficiency Syndrome, or AIDS. When it was mysterious and new, it seemed that AIDS was somehow connected to these marginalized groups. In fact, the virus can spread to anyone through sexual contact or exchange of fluids such as blood. Especially in the 1980s and early 1990s, patients faced massive amounts of stigma, and many doctors refused to treat them. Meanwhile, many of the first medications seemed to have miraculous effects but fell short in later testing. It's little wonder that groups of patients and doctors came to different conclusions about risky new treatments, as was the case with Compound Q. This drug was one of the most famous medications people took to try to treat their AIDS, but it was never approved by the Food and Drug Administration.

## TRUST AND DISTRUST

Today, people with HIV (Human Immunodeficiency Virus, which causes AIDS) can live long and healthy lives with the right care, but there is still no cure. Around 690,000 people died from HIV-related causes in 2020. The vast majority died from poor access to prevention and care, but another factor is HIV/AIDS denialism. Denialism can include refusing to believe that HIV causes AIDS, or that proven drugs work. Its adherents go against a large and conclusive body of evidence, justifying their beliefs with cult-like theories and often encouraging people to seek alternative therapies.[1]

Early in the epidemic, many doctors turned AIDS patients away, some out of fear of contagion, and others out of a belief that patients brought the disease on themselves. Prejudice compounded poverty and other barriers to staying healthy. Many gay and bi men, trans women, and gender nonconforming people were stranded by their families, employers, landlords, and doctors when AIDS outed them. Some doctors suggested "overexposure" to semen caused AIDS in men. Meanwhile, straight, bi, and gay cisgender women with AIDS were often ignored or misdiagnosed.

Globally, HIV was an increasing problem in Africa and Haiti, and racism fueled more stigma in the United States. Until 1985, the CDC considered all Haitian immigrants at high risk for HIV, causing Haitians to face housing and employment discrimination regardless of their actual HIV status. From 1987 to 2010, the United States restricted immigration by people with HIV. Meanwhile, people who used intravenous drugs were often already without support systems, and the disease marginalized them further. Some politicians attacked harm-reduction strategies like needle exchanges that reduced transmission. In response to all of this, people who were HIV-positive formed activist and community groups to fight for their survival. In work that echoed the women's health movement's goals to include patient voices in care, HIV-positive activists helped make AIDS research part of the national health agenda, influenced improved research practices, and mitigated drug companies' price racketeering.[2]

## HOPES

Not only did early AIDS patients often die horrible deaths, but many watched loved ones die of the same disease first. Stuck in a dire situation, many people with AIDS tried alternative therapies. "Any glimmer of hope was better than none," recalled AIDS activist Martin Delaney. "We used to have a saying in those days that there was no such thing as false hope, that there was only false hopelessness. But I think in retrospect, certainly some of the things we dabbled with were false hopes."[3]

Alternative therapies included treatments being scientifically studied but not yet approved by the FDA (or another country's regulating body), and some that were untested or had performed poorly in trials. One example was Kemron, a low-dose version of the drug interferon which was not tested in the

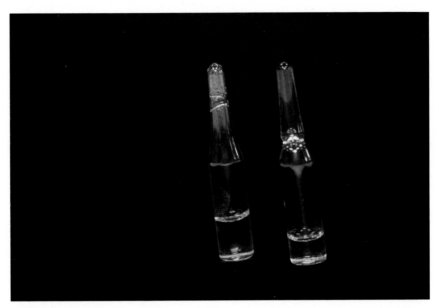

Vials of Compound Q, c. 1990.

United States. Many patients believed it was being overlooked because it was developed in Kenya. People with HIV formed "buyers' clubs" which imported and distributed alternative and unapproved HIV medications. Some doctors even referred their patients to these groups.[4]

The nonprofit Project Inform worked to help people with AIDS make educated choices about unapproved medicines. After trichosanthin or "Compound Q" showed some promise in laboratory tests in 1991, Project Inform worked with several doctors to create an illicit clinical trial with no ethics and process oversight from an institutional review board. Their goal was to convince the FDA and researchers that standard trial procedures were slower than necessary. However, formal trials found that Compound Q was too toxic to be used safely, and the FDA did not approve it. The Dallas Buyers' Club in Texas was the lone holdout that continued distributing Compound Q after the FDA asked buyers' clubs to stop.[5]

The AIDS epidemic inspired many people to become more active advocates in their own care and in the healthcare system. However, some patients were wary of a system that included people who hated them and who had made choices they didn't understand. They focused on the potential harm in drugs that had been approved, and the potential good in drugs that were not. Compound Q is one of those unapproved drugs that had more cultural significance than medical significance.

# September 11 and Emergency Response

S corched and crushed, this ambulance bears the scars of the terrorist attacks on September 11, 2001. By that evening, about six hundred emergency medical personnel had come to the scene where hijacked airplanes crashed into the World Trade Center in Manhattan.[1] That day's events were a landmark in how far emergency response has come.

## SLOW BEGINNINGS

Ambulances have a long history, starting with Byzantines on horseback who carried wounded soldiers, and thirteenth-century stretcher-bearers who carried the sick in Florence. Napoleon's chief physician created the first modern ambulance corps in the early nineteenth century. Partway through the American Civil War, Congress overhauled the Union ambulance service with more horse-drawn vehicles, transforming a system that was the butt of soldiers' jokes into a real asset. However, throughout the Civil War, ambulance services brought patients to the surgeons, with no medical staff riding along.[2]

A former Union Army surgeon created an ambulance team during a New York City cholera epidemic in 1869. At first, the team disinfected victims' and patients' homes and carted patients off to quarantine hospitals. Soon, it was working in coordination with Bellevue Hospital to provide first aid and transport for all kinds of illnesses and injuries. The need for ambulances grew with increasing vehicle traffic and accidents, and by 1880, cities across the country had them. They had some hallmarks of modern ambulances, like central dispatch systems (by telegraph, at first), but they did not have specialized staff. Ambulance services run by hospitals, police, or fire departments sometimes had a surgeon or medical intern providing care. Private ambulance services were often staffed by people with no medical training. However, there was a growing movement of training laypeople in first aid, spearheaded by American Red Cross founder Clara Barton. During WWI and again during WWII, first aid training was part of heightened national interest in emergency preparedness.[3]

## PARAMEDICS AND EMTS

By the mid-twentieth century, the hodgepodge of available emergency care was increasingly inadequate. Many companies sent out dirty, poorly equipped ambulances and extorted patients for money. Medical organizations began to call for change, and emergency services rapidly modernized in the 1960s and 1970s. In 1967, the first professional paramedics aided their own underserved Black neighborhoods in Philadelphia. That same year, a young girl's accidental death in Haywood County, North Carolina inspired what may have been the first all-volunteer paramedic operation in the country. The word "paramedic"

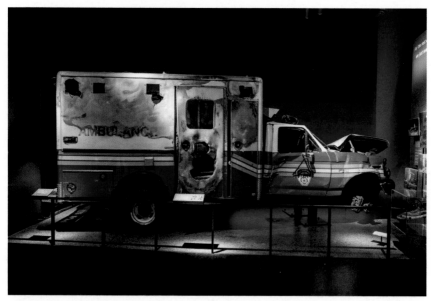

Ambulance recovered from the World Trade Center site after September 11, 2001.
COLLECTION 9/11 MEMORIAL MUSEUM, NEW YORK, NEW YORK, COURTESY OF THE PORT AUTHORITY OF NEW YORK AND NEW JERSEY; PRESENTED WITH PERMISSION OF THE NEW YORK CITY FIRE DEPARTMENT, PHOTOGRAPH BY JIN S. LEE.

meant they were trained to provide care but were not doctors or nurses. Two years later, Los Angeles County formed a paramedic team which inspired the TV show *Emergency!* (1972–1977). The show inspired new emergency services departments across the country. As local departments proliferated, the 1973 Emergency Services Systems Act encouraged them to create regional networks that shared resources.[4]

On September 11, 2001, emergency medical technicians (EMTs) from several public and private groups showed up at Ground Zero to help. When Benjamin Badillo and Edward Martinez arrived in this ambulance, an officer sent Martinez to the triage area and directed Badillo to stay with the vehicle. Emergency medical services (EMS) workers are not typically trained in rescues under hazardous conditions, or given protective clothing or breathing devices. They work from a triage center in a safe area, treating patients brought to them by firefighters.[5]

That day, the safe area wasn't safe. Different agencies' radio equipment did not work with one another, complicating evacuation. Martinez was in the triage center when he heard an explosion. He tried to grab the nearest patient and run to safety, but the patient slipped from his hands and he couldn't find them again in the smoke. Falling debris slammed Martinez to the ground, and he was hospitalized for four days with his injuries. Badillo rushed from the ambulance into a nearby building for cover when the first tower fell, but he inhaled a significant amount of smoke and debris. He spent much of the day evacuating people by boat, with no word on whether Martinez was alive and getting only static when he tried to radio him.[6]

Since 2001, there have been repeated calls for increased workplace safety for EMS personnel, resulting in improvements but not large systemic change. After 9/11, the Federal Communications Commission (FCC) created an "interoperability" agency to create a nationwide system for EMS communications. While there is still progress to be made, the inspiring work of the paramedics and EMTs on 9/11 shows that emergency medical response has become an irreplaceable part of healthcare.

# Saving Lives amid the Opioid Crisis

A twenty-year-old woman was near asphyxiation, but not gasping for breath. Her brain wasn't telling her body to breathe. Her mother found her unconscious and blue and called 911, and police arrived instead of EMTs. However, a few months before in mid-2016, police officers near her home in Montevideo, Minnesota, had started carrying naloxone to reverse opioid overdoses. Thirty seconds after receiving the medication, the woman was awake and talking.[1]

## ORIGINS OF THE OPIOID CRISIS

Opium was used as a pain reliever and sleep aid for at least five thousand years. In the nineteenth century, chemists began creating more powerful narcotics from opium, called opiates, including morphine in the 1820s and heroin in the 1890s. They were used unsuccessfully to treat opium addiction and alcoholism. Opiates were widely prescribed for pain and coughs, and used in over-the-counter tinctures and syrups, including those given to children. New synthetic opioids were developed in the early twentieth century, including hydrocodone (Vicodin), oxycodone (Percocet or Oxycontin), and methadone. Today they are used to ease severe pain during cancer or following injuries or surgery.[2]

Opioids are addictive, and part of dependence on them is needing larger and larger doses to feel the same effects. While many opioids create a high or euphoria, as the dose escalates, patients need the drug just to feel normal. Dose escalation puts patients at risk of overdose. The young woman in Minnesota who almost died of a fentanyl overdose would not have been alone. In 2019, 130 Americans a day died of opioid overdoses. The opioid epidemic in Minnesota has hit its Native American and Black residents disproportionately hard. Most deaths occur where emergency responders are spread thin over rural areas.[3]

## HARM REDUCTION FOR OPIOID USE

Naloxone hydrochloride, best known by the brand name Narcan, was developed in the 1960s to block the effects of opioids in the body. It can stop an overdose in progress and save the patient's life. In 2015, the FDA approved intranasal administration—spraying naloxone in the patient's nose. Naloxone is available without a prescription in many places, and in 2018 the US Surgeon General urged the public to carry it. Making naloxone available is a harm-reduction strategy, meaning it minimizes the negative effects of a behavior such as drug use. Harm reduction was first described and given a name in the 1980s, when needle exchange programs helped intravenous drug users avoid transmitting HIV. Harm reduction is a more effective and humane alternative to using the criminal justice system to address a medical problem. Criminalizing drug use increases risk factors for addiction, like unstable income and housing.[4]

One of the major ideological alternatives to harm reduction is the model that prioritizes abstinence from drug use above all else. When doctors began looking at addiction as a medical issue in the late nineteenth century, some were influenced by the Protestant revivalist ideas of the temperance movement. When Alcoholics Anonymous was founded in 1935, it taught that giving oneself up to a higher power is the only way to avoid temptation and inevitable ruin. It is not a medical program, but it became the dominant model of addiction treatment in the United States and influential in many other parts of the world. Narcotics Anonymous, founded in 1953 to help people struggling with opioid and other drug addiction, used the approach nearly exactly. While today a great number of addiction treatment programs are secular, religious concepts such as purity continue to influence the abstinence-based approach, for example in the idea of staying "clean" of a drug. Studies show that abstinence is often ineffective for opioid addiction.[5]

Instead of total abstinence, some researchers and clinicians advocate for a medication-based approach. Beginning in the 1920s, some doctors offered a controlled supply of heroin to people struggling with addiction, preventing them from using higher doses as their body habituated to the drug. This is

# Notes

## CHAPTER 1. UNWASHED GROINS AND CHILD LABOR: CANCER IN THE EARLY INDUSTRIAL AGE

1. George Lewis Phillips, *American Chimney Sweeps: An Historical Account of a Once Important Trade* (Trenton: Past Times Press, 1957), 52.

2. H. A. Waldron, "A Brief History of Scrotal Cancer," *British Journal of Industrial Medicine* 40, no. 4 (1983): 391–92; Phillips, *American Chimney Sweeps*, 53–55.

3. Herbert K. Abrams, "A Short History of Occupational Health," *Journal of Public Health Policy* 22, no. 1 (2001): 34–80, http://doi.org/10.2307/3343553, 38.

4. Paul A. Gilje and Howard B. Rock, "'Sweep O! Sweep O!': African-American Chimney Sweeps and Citizenship in the New Nation," *The William and Mary Quarterly* 51, no. 3 (1994): 524, http://doi.org/10.2307/2947440.

5. Waldron, "A Brief History of Scrotal Cancer," 396.

6. Ritva Vyas et al., "Squamous Cell Carcinoma of the Scrotum: A Look beyond the Chimneystacks," *World Journal of Clinical Cases: WJCC* 2, no. 11 (November 16, 2014): 654–60, http://doi.org10.12998/wjcc.v2.i11.654.

## CHAPTER 2. GEORGE WASHINGTON'S TOOTHBRUSH

1. Kathryn Gehred, "Did George Washington's False Teeth Come from His Slaves?: A Look at the Evidence, the Responses to That Evidence, and the Limitations of

History," *Washington's Quill, The Washington Papers, University of Virginia*, October 19, 2016, http://gwpapers.virginia.edu/george-washingtons-false-teeth-come-slaves-look-evidence-responses-evidence-limitations-history/.

2. "W-615A-D Mount Vernon Fact Sheet," Mount Vernon Ladies' Association, May 20, 2019; Stuart L. Fischman, "The History of Oral Hygiene Products: How Far Have We Come in 6000 Years?," *Periodontology 2000* 15, no. 1 (November 1997): 7–14, http://doi.org/10.1111/j.1600-0757.1997.tb00099.x.

3. Bernhard Wolf Weinberger, *An Introduction to the History of Dentistry*, vol. 2, 2 vols. (St. Louis: C. V. Mosby Co., 1948), 91, https://catalog.hathitrust.org/Record/001571139.

4. American Dental Association, "History of Dentistry Timeline," accessed July 21, 2019, https://www.ada.org/en/about-the-ada/ada-history-and-presidents-of-the-ada/ada-history-of-dentistry-timeline.

5. American Dental Association, "History of Dentistry Timeline"; George Washington to Richard Varick, September 26, 1785, *The Writings of George Washington from the Original Manuscript Sources, 1745–1799* (Washington, DC: United States George Washington Bicentennial Commission, 1931), 281–82, http://archive.org/details/writingsofgeorge28wash.

## CHAPTER 3. THE AGE OF THE VACCINE

1. Thomas Jefferson to Benjamin Waterhouse, December 1, 1801, Benjamin Waterhouse papers, Box: 01, Folder: 24 Identifier: H MS c16, Countway Library of Medicine, https://hollisarchives.lib.harvard.edu/repositories/14/archival_objects/1910488.

2. S. L. Kotar and J. E. Gessler, *Smallpox: A History* (Jefferson, NC: McFarland, 2013), 6–9.

3. Kotar and Gessler, *Smallpox*, 9, 27; David S. Jones, *Rationalizing Epidemics: Meanings and Uses of American Indian Mortality since 1600* (Cambridge, MA: Harvard University Press, 2004), 32.

4. Elizabeth A. Fenn, *Pox Americana: The Great Smallpox Epidemic of 1775–82* (New York: Hill and Wang, 2002), 17.

5. Barbara Alice Mann, *The Tainted Gift: The Disease Method of Frontier Expansion*, ill. ed. (Santa Barbara, CA: Praeger, 2009), xiv, 12; Jones, *Rationalizing Epidemics*, 95.

6. Fenn, *Pox Americana*, 17, 31.

7. Fenn, *Pox Americana*, 18.

8. Jack Eckert, "To Slay the Devouring Monster," Online exhibit, *Center for the History of Medicine* (2013), http://collections.countway.harvard.edu/onview/exhibits/show/to-slay-the-devouring-monster/edward-jenner.

9. Eckert, "To Slay the Devouring Monster"; Walter L. Burrage, *A History of the Massachusetts Medical Society* (Norwood, MA: Plimpton Press, 1923), 58, http://archive.org/details/historyofmassach00burr; Jones, *Rationalizing Epidemics,* 91; Benjamin Waterhouse to John Coakley Lettsom, November 5, 1801, Harvard University Libraries, https://hollisarchives.lib.harvard.edu/repositories/14/archival_objects/1910494.

10. Eckert, "To Slay the Devouring Monster"; Jones, *Rationalizing Epidemics,* 89.

11. Mann, *The Tainted Gift*, 50; Jones, *Rationalizing Epidemics,* 115.

12. World Health Organization, "Smallpox," accessed December 8, 2019, https://www.who.int/health-topics/smallpox#tab=tab_1.

## CHAPTER 4. NO WRONG WAY TO EAT

1. Mark McCamish, Gustavo Bounous, and Maureen Geraghty, "History of Enteral Feeding: Past and Present Perspectives," in *Clinical Nutrition: Enteral and Tube Feeding* by John L. Rombeau and Rolando Rolandelli (Philadelphia: W. B. Saunders Company, 1997), 1.

2. Valerie A. Fildes, *Breasts, Bottles and Babies: A History of Infant Feeding* (Edinburgh: Edinburgh University Press, 1986), 215, 308, 315.

3. Alexis C. Madrigal, "Disposable America," *The Atlantic*, June 21, 2018, https://www.theatlantic.com/technology/archive/2018/06/disposable-america/563204/.

4. Stanley J. Dudrick and J. Alexander Palesty, "Historical Highlights of the Development of Enteral Nutrition," *The Surgical Clinics of North America* 91, no. 4 (August 2011): 946, http://doi.org10.1016/j.suc.2011.05.002; Gail Cresci and John Mellinger, "The History of Nonsurgical Enteral Tube Feeding Access," *Nutrition in Clinical Practice* 21, no. 5 (October 2006): 522, http://doi.org/10.1177/0115426506021005522.

5. Laura Harkness, "The History of Enteral Nutrition Therapy: From Raw Eggs and Nasal Tubes to Purified Amino Acids and Early Postoperative Jejunal Delivery,"

*Journal of the American Dietetic Association* 102, no. 3 (March 1, 2002): 401, 403, http://doi.org/10.1016/S0002-8223(02)90092-1; Cresci and Mellinger, "The History of Nonsurgical Enteral Tube Feeding Access," 522.

## CHAPTER 5. A PIONEERING OPERATION

1. August Schachner, *Ephraim McDowell, "Father of Ovariotomy": His Life and His Work* (reprinted from *The Johns Hopkins Hospital Bulletin* 24, no. 267 [May 1913]), 12, http://archive.org/details/b30619658.

2. Schachner, *Ephraim McDowell, "Father of Ovariotomy,"* 4–6, 363; James S. Olson, *Bathsheba's Breast: Women, Cancer, and History*, revised ed. (Baltimore: Johns Hopkins University Press, 2005), 13.

3. Schachner, *Ephraim McDowell, "Father of Ovariotomy,"* 4–6, 363; Olson, *Bathsheba's Breast*, 13.

4. Schachner, *Ephraim McDowell, "Father of Ovariotomy,"* 4–6.

5. "Virtual Tour," *McDowell House Museum Website*, accessed March 8, 2020, http://www.mcdowellhouse.com/virtual-tour/; McDowell report reprinted in Schachner, *Ephraim McDowell, "Father of Ovariotomy,"* 8.

6. M. A. Fallouji, "History of Surgery of the Abdominal Cavity. Arabic Contributions," *International Surgery* 78, no. 3 (September 1993): 236–38.

7. Kat Eschner, "This American Doctor Pioneered Abdominal Surgery by Operating on Enslaved Women," *Smithsonian Magazine*, accessed February 27, 2020, https://www.smithsonianmag.com/history/father-abdominal-surgery-practiced-enslaved-women-180967589/.

8. August Schachner, *Ephraim McDowell, "Father of Ovariotomy" and Founder of Abdominal Surgery, with an Appendix on Jane Todd Crawford* (Philadelphia, London: J. B. Lippincott Company, 1921), 284, http://archive.org/details/ephraimmcdowellf00schaiala.

9. Eschner, "This American Doctor Pioneered Abdominal Surgery by Operating on Enslaved Women."

10. Vincent T. DeVita and Steven A. Rosenberg, "Two Hundred Years of Cancer Research," *New England Journal of Medicine* 366, no. 23 (June 7, 2012): 2207–14, http://doi.org/10.1056/NEJMra1204479; Archibald Barkley, *Kentucky's Pioneer*

*Lithotomists* (Cincinnati: C. J. Krehbiel & Company, 1913), http://archive.org/details/kentuckyspioneer00bark.

## CHAPTER 6. HEALING BY A HIGHER POWER

1.  Amy Carpenter, "Church History: The Handkerchief Healing and Raising the Dead," *Third Hour*, November 14, 2018, https://thirdhour.org/blog/faith/lds-history/church-history-handkerchief-healing/.

2.  Claudia L. Bushman, *Contemporary Mormonism: Latter-Day Saints in Modern America* (Westport, CT: Praeger, 2006), 16.

3.  Paul Offit, *Bad Faith: When Religious Belief Undermines Modern Medicine* (New York: Basic Books, 2015), 155; Lester E. Bush, *Health and Medicine among the Latter-Day Saints: Science, Sense & Scripture* (New York: Crossroad, 1992), 74; Bushman, *Contemporary Mormonism*, 20.

4.  Bush, *Health and Medicine among the Latter-Day Saints,* 62–63, 69–70.

5.  Offit, *Bad Faith*, 184–87.

6.  Marek Jantos and Hosen Kiat, "Prayer as Medicine: How Much Have We Learned?," *The Medical Journal of Australia* 186, no. 10 (May 21, 2007), http://doi.org/10.5694/j.1326-5377.2007.tb01041.x; Wendy Cadge, "Saying Your Prayers, Constructing Your Religions: Medical Studies of Intercessory Prayer," *The Journal of Religion* 89, no. 3 (2009): 299–327, http://doi.org/10.1086/597818.

## CHAPTER 7. MORTON'S ETHER INHALER AND THE ADVENT OF ANESTHESIA

1.  J. M. Fenster, *Ether Day: The Strange Tale of America's Greatest Medical Discovery and the Haunted Men Who Made It* (New York: Harper Perennial, 2002), 44; Henry Jacob Bigelow, "Insensibility during Surgical Operations Produced by Inhalation," *The Boston Medical and Surgical Journal* 35, no. 16 (November 18, 1846): 310.

2.  Fenster, *Ether Day*, 7; Bigelow, "Insensibility during Surgical Operations Produced by Inhalation," 310.

3.  Rajesh P. Haridas, "Horace Wells' Demonstration of Nitrous Oxide in Boston," *Anesthesiology: The Journal of the American Society of Anesthesiologists* 119, no. 5 (November 1, 2013): 1019, http://doi.org/10.1097/ALN.0b013e3182a771ea; Masaru Izuo, "Medical History: Seishu Hanaoka and His Success in Breast Cancer Surgery

under General Anesthesia Two Hundred Years Ago," *Breast Cancer* 11, no. 4 (November 1, 2004): 319–24, http://doi.org/10.1007/BF02968037.

4. William Bynum and Helen Bynum, eds., *Great Discoveries in Medicine* (New York: Thames & Hudson, 2011), 221; Fenster, *Ether Day*, 164.

5. Bigelow, "Insensibility during Surgical Operations Produced by Inhalation," 309; John Collins Warren, "Inhalation of an Etheral Vapor for the Prevention of Pain in Surgical Operations," *Boston Medical and Surgical Journal* (December 3, 1846): 376.

6. Fenster, *Ether Day*, 121; W. Clay Wallace, "Remarks on the Inhalation of Ether Previous to Surgical Operations," *Boston Medical and Surgical Journal* (n.d.): 435; Bigelow, "Insensibility during Surgical Operations Produced by Inhalation," 313; Bynum and Bynum, *Great Discoveries in Medicine*, 221.

7. Fenster, *Ether Day*, 92, 195; A. B. Gould, "Charles T. Jackson's Claim to the Discovery of Etherization," in *Anaesthesia*, ed. Joseph Rupreht, Marius Jan van Lieburg, John Alfred Lee, and Wilhelm Erdmann (Berlin, Heidelberg: Springer, 1985), 384–87, http://doi.org/10.1007/978-3-642-69636-7_81.

8. J. F. Flagg, "The Inhalation of an Ethereal Vapor to Prevent Sensibility to Pain during Surgical Operations," *Boston Medical and Surgical Journal* (November 23, 1846); Fenster, *Ether Day*, 75, 178.

9. Frederic Washburn, "Remarks on the History of the Old Surgical Amphitheatre," *The Boston Medical and Surgical Journal* 195, no. 26 (December 23, 1926): 1194, https://doi.org/10.1056/N EJM192612231952602.

## CHAPTER 8. BITTERS AND IRREGULARS: ALTERNATIVE HEALING IN THE NINETEENTH CENTURY

1. Hostetter's United States Almanac 1867, quoted in James Harvey Young, *The Toadstool Millionaires: A Social History of Patent Medicines in America before Federal Regulation* (Princeton, NJ: Princeton University Press, 1961), 128, http://archive.org/details/toadstoolmillion00youn.

2. Young, *The Toadstool Millionaires*, 128–29.

3. Young, *The Toadstool Millionaires*, 94–95, 133.

4. *Hostetter's Illustrated United States Almanac, for the Year 1868* (Pittsburgh, PA: Hostetter and Smith, 1868), 11, http://archive.org/details/hostettersillust1868amer.

5. Young, *The Toadstool Millionaires*, 134.

6. Erika Janik, *Marketplace of the Marvelous: The Strange Origins of Modern Medicine*, reprint ed. (Boston: Beacon Press, 2015), 117–19.

7. Marshall Scott Legan, "Hydropathy in America: A Nineteenth Century Panacea," *Bulletin of the History of Medicine* 45, no. 3 (1971): 267; Kenneth M. Ludmerer, *Time to Heal: American Medical Education from the Turn of the Century to the Era of Managed Care*, rev. ed. (New York, Oxford: Oxford University Press, 2005), 4.

8. Legan, "Hydropathy in America," 267.

9. Janik, *Marketplace of the Marvelous*, 29, 149.

10. Janik, *Marketplace of the Marvelous*, 260.

11. Ludmerer, *Time to Heal*, 5; Young, *The Toadstool Millionaires*, 248.

## CHAPTER 9. BLOOD SHED AFTER THE BATTLE: BLEEDING CUPS

1. U.S. National Park Service, "The Ray House—Wilson's Creek National Battlefield," accessed October 6, 2019, https://www.nps.gov/wicr/learn/historyculture/the-ray-house.htm.

2. Margaret Humphreys, *Marrow of Tragedy: The Health Crisis of the American Civil War* (Baltimore: Johns Hopkins University Press, 2013), 29.

3. Faith Lagay, "The Legacy of Humoral Medicine," *AMA Journal of Ethics* 4, no. 7 (July 1, 2002), http://doi.org/10.1001/virtualmentor.2002.4.7.mhst1-0207.

4. Glenna R. Schroeder-Lein, *The Encyclopedia of Civil War Medicine* (New York: Routledge, 2008), 9; Humphreys, *Marrow of Tragedy*, 26.

5. Shauna Devine, *Learning from the Wounded: The Civil War and the Rise of American Medical Science* (Chapel Hill, NC: University of North Carolina Press, 2017), 4, 8–9, 17, 55.

6. Devine, *Learning from the Wounded*, 100, 112.

## CHAPTER 10. UNDER THE SURGEON'S TENT: THE PHYSICIAN IN THE CIVIL WAR

1. William Stryker, *Record of Officers and Men of New Jersey in the Civil War, 1861–1865*, vol. 1 (Trenton, NJ: John L. Murphy, Steam Book and Job Printer, 1876), 267, http://slic.njstatelib.org/slic_files/searchable_publications/civilwar/NJCWn267.html.

2. Glenna R. Schroeder-Lein, *The Encyclopedia of Civil War Medicine* (New York: Routledge, 2008), 11.

3. Margaret Humphreys, *Marrow of Tragedy: The Health Crisis of the American Civil War* (Baltimore: Johns Hopkins University Press, 2013), 43.

4. Schroeder-Lein, *The Encyclopedia of Civil War Medicine*, 16.

5. Schroeder-Lein, *The Encyclopedia of Civil War Medicine*, 261; Shauna Devine, *Learning from the Wounded: The Civil War and the Rise of American Medical Science* (Chapel Hill, NC: University of North Carolina Press, 2017), 94.

6. Schroeder-Lein, *The Encyclopedia of Civil War Medicine*, 261; Devine, *Learning from the Wounded*, 122.

7. Devine, *Learning from the Wounded*, 32, 50, 176.

8. Devine, *Learning from the Wounded*, 9, 209.

## CHAPTER 11. "INFLAMMATORY MISCHIEF" MEETS ANTISEPTIC TECHNIQUES

1. Lindsey Fitzharris, *The Butchering Art: Joseph Lister's Quest to Transform the Grisly World of Victorian Medicine* (New York: Farrar, Straus and Giroux, 2017), 85, 201.

2. Joseph Lister, "On the Antiseptic Principle in the Practice of Surgery," *The British Medical Journal* 2, no. 351 (1867): 246; Fitzharris, *The Butchering Art*, 215.

3. Charles Brooks Brigham, *Surgical Cases with Illustrations* (Cambridge: Houghton and Co., 1876), 56, 108, https://books.google.com/books/about/Surgical_Cases_with_Illustrations.html?id=kbW-uPRcy7UC.

4. Fitzharris, *The Butchering Art*, 210.

## CHAPTER 12. ANSWERING THE MILK QUESTION

1. John Mullaly, *The Milk Trade in New York and Vicinity: Giving an Account of the Sale of Pure and Adulterated Milk* (New York: Fowlers and Wells, 1853), 24, https://books.google.com/books/about/The_Milk_Trade_of_New_York_and_Vicinity.html?id=KXIZAAAAYAAJ.

2. Mark Kurlansky, *Milk!: A 10,000-Year Food Fracas* (New York: Bloomsbury Publishing, 2018), 179.

3. Kurlansky, *Milk!*, 184, 182; *The Industrial Advance of Rochester: A Historical, Statistical & Descriptive Review* (Philadelphia: National Publishing Company, 1884), 66, https://books.google.com/books/about/The_Industrial_Advance_of_Rochester.html?id=VSEaAAAAYAAJ.

4. Kurlansky, *Milk!*, 186.

## CHAPTER 13. SKULL SHAPE AND SCIENTIFIC RACISM

1. Allan Chase, *The Legacy of Malthus: The Social Costs of the New Scientific Racism* (New York: Knopf, distributed by Random House, 1977), 94–96.

2. Harriet A. Washington, *Medical Apartheid: The Dark History of Medical Experimentation on Black Americans from Colonial Times to the Present*, reprint (New York: Anchor, 2008), 83; Samuel J. Redman, *Bone Rooms: From Scientific Racism to Human Prehistory in Museums* (Cambridge, MA: Harvard University Press, 2016), 8, 26, 28; Barbara Alice Mann, *The Tainted Gift: The Disease Method of Frontier Expansion*, ill. ed. (Santa Barbara: Praeger, 2009), 45.

3. Chase, *The Legacy of Malthus*, 98.

4. Washington, *Medical Apartheid*, 65.

5. Chase, *The Legacy of Malthus*, 183; Amy L. Fairchild, *Science at the Borders: Immigrant Inspection and the Shaping of the Modern Industrial Labor Force* (Baltimore: Johns Hopkins University Press, 2003), 59, 182.

6. Kim TallBear, *Native American DNA: Tribal Belonging and the False Promise of Genetic Science* (Minneapolis: University of Minnesota Press, 2013), 12; Institute of Medicine (US) Committee on Understanding and Eliminating Racial and Ethnic Disparities in Health Care, "Executive Summary," in *Unequal Treatment: Confronting Racial and Ethnic Disparities in Health Care*, ed. Brian D. Smedley, Adrienne Y. Stith, and Alan R. Nelson (Washington, DC: National Academies Press, 2003), https://www.ncbi.nlm.nih.gov/books/NBK220355/; Kelly M. Hoffman et al., "Racial Bias in Pain Assessment and Treatment Recommendations, and False Beliefs about Biological Differences between Blacks and Whites," *Proceedings of the National Academy of Sciences of the United States of America* 113, no. 16 (2016): 4296–4301.

## CHAPTER 14. "HEALTH AND COMFORT OF BODY, WITH GRACE AND BEAUTY OF FORM"

1. John S. Haller, *The Physician and Sexuality in Victorian America* (New York: W. W. Norton, 1974), 168, http://archive.org/details/physiciansexuali0000unse.

2. Barbara Ehrenreich and Deirdre English, *For Her Own Good: Two Centuries of the Experts' Advice to Women*, 2nd ed. (New York: Anchor, 2005), 98; Valerie Steele, *The Corset: A Cultural History* (New Haven, CT: Yale University Press, 2003), 49.

3. Johanna Goldberg, "Did Corsets Harm Women's Health?," *Books, Health, and History: The New York Academy of Medicine Blog*, May 29, 2015, https://nyamcenterforhistory.org/2015/05/29/did-corsets-harm-womens-health/; Steele, *The Corset*, 49.

4. Patricia A. Vertinsky, *The Eternally Wounded Woman: Women, Doctors, and Exercise in the Late Nineteenth Century*, Illini Books (Urbana, IL: University of Illinois Press, 1994), 15.

5. Marylynne Diggs, "Romantic Friends or a 'Different Race of Creatures'? The Representation of Lesbian Pathology in Nineteenth-Century America," *Feminist Studies* 21, no. 2 (1995): 317–40, http://doi.org/10.2307/3178264, 335; Susan Stryker, *Transgender History: The Roots of Today's Revolution* (Berkeley: Seal Press, 2017), 56.

6. Quoted in Carroll Smith-Rosenberg and Charles E. Rosenberg, "The Female Animal: Medical and Biological Views of Woman and Her Role in Nineteenth-Century America," in *Women and Health in America*, ed. Judith Walzer Leavitt, 2nd ed. (Madison, WI: The University of Wisconsin Press, 1984), 112–13.

7. Smith-Rosenberg and Rosenberg, "The Female Animal," 112, 115; Diane Price Herndl, "The Invisible (Invalid) Woman: African-American Women, Illness, and Nineteenth-Century Narrative," in *Women and Health in America*, ed. Judith Walzer Leavitt, 2nd ed. (Madison, WI: The University of Wisconsin Press, 1984), 132.

8. Smith-Rosenberg and Rosenberg, "The Female Animal," 117; Vertinsky, *The Eternally Wounded Woman*, 5; Quoted in Gerhart Schwarz, "Society, Physicians, and the Corset," *Bulletin of the New York Academy of Medicine* 55, no. 6 (June 1979): 551–90, 583.

9. Goldberg, "Did Corsets Harm Women's Health?"

10. Tracy L. Bale and C. Neill Epperson, "Sex as a Biological Variable: Who, What, When, Why, and How," *Neuropsychopharmacology* 42, no. 2 (January 2017): 386–96, http://doi.org/10.1038/npp.2016.215; Claire Ainsworth, "Sex Redefined," *Nature News* 518, no. 7539 (February 19, 2015): 288, http://doi.org/10.1038/518288a; Vertinsky, *The Eternally Wounded Woman*, 5.

## CHAPTER 15. EAST MEETS WEST IN THE MEDICINE CABINET: A CHINESE DOCTOR IN AMERICA

1. Tamara Venit Shelton, *Herbs and Roots: A History of Chinese Doctors in the American Medical Marketplace* (New Haven, CT: Yale University Press, 2019), 15; Paul Unschuld, *Traditional Chinese Medicine: Heritage and Adaptation*, trans. Bridie Andrews, ebook ed. (New York: Columbia University Press, 2018), ch. 13.

2. David H. T. Wong, *Escape to Gold Mountain: A Graphic History of the Chinese in North America*, ebook ed. (Vancouver, BC: Arsenal Pulp Press, 2012); Venit Shelton, *Herbs and Roots*, 221.

3. "Kam Wah Chung," *Oregon Experience* (PBS, January 13, 2010), https://www.opb .org/television/programs/oregonexperience/segment/kam-wah-chung/.

4. Venit Shelton, *Herbs and Roots*, 81.

5. Venit Shelton, *Herbs and Roots*, 119, 129; Jodi Varon, "Ing Hay ('Doc Hay') (1862–1952)," *Oregon Encyclopedia*, accessed May 25, 2020, https:// oregonencyclopedia.org/articles/ing_doc_hay_1862_1952_/#.Xsv-RBNKg1I; Alan M. Kraut, *Silent Travelers: Germs, Genes, and the Immigrant Menace* (New York: Basic Books, 1994), 268.

6. Venit Shelton, *Herbs and Roots*, 218; Unschuld, *Traditional Chinese Medicine*, ch.15.

7. Venit Shelton, *Herbs and Roots*, 13.

## CHAPTER 16. THE "CURE" THAT WASN'T

1. Robert Taylor, *Saranac: America's Magic Mountain* (Boston: Houghton Mifflin Harcourt, 1986), 31, 75; Katherine Ott, *Fevered Lives: Tuberculosis in American Culture since 1870* (Cambridge, MA: Harvard University Press, 1999), 7; George Rosen, *A History of Public Health*, rev. exp. ed. (Baltimore: Johns Hopkins University Press, 2015), 78, 225.

2. "Wall Text, Main Exhibit" (Saranac Lake Laboratory Museum, Saranac Lake, New York).

3. Amy L. Fairchild, *Science at the Borders: Immigrant Inspection and the Shaping of the Modern Industrial Labor Force* (Baltimore: Johns Hopkins University Press, 2003), 167, 173.

4. Thomas Dormandy, *The White Death: A History of Tuberculosis* (New York: New York University Press, 2000), 78.

5. "Wall Text, Main Exhibit" (Saranac Lake); Gill Paul, *A History of Medicine in 50 Objects* (Buffalo, NY: Firefly Books, 2016), 104.

6. Paul, *A History of Medicine in 50 Objects*, 105; Ott, *Fevered Lives*, 94.

7. Rosen, *A History of Public Health*, 224, 232; Ott, *Fevered Lives*, 120.

8. "History," *Trudeau Institute*, accessed June 8, 2019. https://www.trudeauinstitute.org/history; Dormandy, *The White Death*, 387; Ott, *Fevered Lives*, 8.

## CHAPTER 17. COCAINE THE MEDICINE AND THE DRUG

1. Steven B. Karch, *A Brief History of Cocaine: From Inca Monarchs to Cali Cartels: 500 Years of Cocaine Dealing*, 2nd ed. (Boca Raton: Taylor & Francis, 2006), 32.

2. Karch, *A Brief History of Cocaine*, 5, 32, 56.

3. Joseph F. Spillane, *Cocaine: From Medical Marvel to Modern Menace in the United States, 1884–1920* (Baltimore: Johns Hopkins University Press, 2000), 14–19, 136, http://archive.org/details/cocainefrommedic00spil.

4. Robert M. Middleton and Michael B. Kirkpatrick, "Clinical Use of Cocaine," *Drug Safety* 9, no. 3 (September 1, 1993): 212–17, http://doi.org/10.2165/00002018-199309030-00006; Timothy Hickman, "The Double Meaning of Addiction: Habitual Narcotic Use and the Logic of Professionalizing Medical Authority in the United States, 1900–1920," in *Altering American Consciousness: The History of Alcohol and Drug Use in the United States, 1800–2000*, ed. Sarah Tracy and Caroline Acker (Amherst, MA: University of Massachusetts Press, 2004), 187.

5. Spillane, *Cocaine*, 119, 162; Hickman, "The Double Meaning of Addiction," 197.

6. Spillane, *Cocaine*, 14–19, 136; Susan Speaker, "Demons for the Twentieth Century: The Rhetoric of Drug Reform, 1920–1940," in *Altering American Consciousness: The History of Alcohol and Drug Use in the United States, 1800–2000*, ed. Sarah Tracy and Caroline Acker (Amherst, MA: University of Massachusetts Press, 2004), 212.

7. Frank H. Gawin and Everett H. Ellinwood, "Cocaine and Other Stimulants," *New England Journal of Medicine* 318, no. 18 (May 5, 1988): 1173–82, http://doi.org/10.1056/NEJM198805053181806.

8. Spillane, *Cocaine*, 159; Yngvild Olsen and Joshua M. Sharfstein, *The Opioid Epidemic: What Everyone Needs to Know* (Oxford: Oxford University Press, 2019), 103; Dorothy Roberts, *Killing the Black Body: Race, Reproduction, and the Meaning of Liberty* (New York: Vintage Books, 1997), 157.

9. Spillane, *Cocaine*, 159.

## CHAPTER 18. DON PEDRITO, A LEGENDARY HEALER

1. Eliseo Torres, *Healing with Herbs and Rituals: A Mexican Tradition*, ed. Timothy L. Sawyer (Albuquerque: University of New Mexico Press, 2006), 36.

2. Brett Hendrickson, *Border Medicine: A Transcultural History of Mexican American Curanderismo* (New York: NYU Press, 2014).

3. Ruth Dodson, "The Healer of Los Olmos," in *The Healer of Los Olmos and Other Mexican Lore*, Publications of the Texas Folklore Society, XXIV (Dallas: Southern Methodist University Press, 1951), 9, 12, 13, 40, http://archive.org/details/TheHealerOfLosOlmos; Torres, *Healing with Herbs and Rituals*, 41.

4. Dodson, "The Healer of Los Olmos," 17; Torres, *Healing with Herbs and Rituals*, 39–40.

5. Dodson, "The Healer of Los Olmos," 57; Hesham R. El-Seedi, "Antimicrobial Activity and Chemical Composition of Essential Oil of Eupatorium Glutinosum (Lam.)," *Natural Product Communications* 1, no. 8 (August 1, 2006), http://doi.org/10.1177/1934578X0600100811.

6. Dodson, "The Healer of Los Olmos," 13; "The Aztec Healer," *Milwaukee Daily Sentinel*, April 24, 1894, Gale Nineteenth Century U.S. Newspapers; Thomas Meade Harwell, *Studies in Texan Folklore—Rio Grande Valley: Twelve Folklore Studies with Introductions, Commentaries & a Bounty of Notes* (New York: Edwin Mellen Press, 1997), 60.

7. Harwell, *Studies in Texan Folklore*, 73; Torres, *Healing with Herbs and Rituals*, 38.

## CHAPTER 19. A WOODEN LEG IN A MECHANIZED WORLD

1. Kim E. Nielsen, *A Disability History of the United States* (Boston: Beacon Press, 2013), 85; Jennifer Davis McDaid, "'How a One-Legged Rebel Lives': Confederate Veterans and Artificial Limbs in Virginia," in *Artificial Parts, Practical Lives: Modern Histories of Prosthetics*, ed. Katherine Ott et al. (New York: NYU Press, 2002), 119–21.

2. Nielsen, *A Disability History of the United States*, 125; *The Conductor and Brakeman*, vol. 22 (Order of Railway Conductors and Brakemen, 1905), https:// books.google.com/books/about/The_Conductor_and_Brakeman .html?id=3Z4nQw3TGbwC.

3. Amy L. Fairchild, *Science at the Borders: Immigrant Inspection and the Shaping of the Modern Industrial Labor Force* (Baltimore: Johns Hopkins University Press, 2003), 33; Nielsen, *A Disability History of the United States*, 89, 108.

4. Davis McDaid, "How a One-Legged Rebel Lives," 127.

5. Steven Kurzman, "'There's No Language for This': Communication and Alignment in Contemporary Prosthetics," in *Artificial Parts, Practical Lives: Modern Histories of Prosthetics* (New York: NYU Press, 2002), 238.

6. Walter J. Sylvia, "U.S. City Directories, 1822–1995—AncestryLibrary.Com," in *Charleston, South Carolina, City Directory, 1916* (U.S. City Directories, 1822–1995— AncestryLibrary.com), accessed May 10, 2020, https://search.ancestrylibrary.com/ cgi-bin/sse.dll?indiv=1&dbid=2469&h=955193218&tid=&pid=&usePUB=true& _phsrc=FO022&_phstart=successSource; Nielsen, *A Disability History of the United States*, 127–29.

7. Kurzman, "There's No Language for This," 238.

## CHAPTER 20. A COMMUNITY DOCTOR'S LEGACY

1. Quoted in Joe Starita, *A Warrior of the People: How Susan La Flesche Overcame Racial and Gender Inequality to Become America's First Indian Doctor* (New York: St. Martin's Press, 2016), 47.

2. Starita, *A Warrior of the People*, 37.

3. Christine M. Lesiak and Princella RedCorn, *Medicine Woman* (PBS), accessed January 6, 2020, https://www.pbs.org/video/medicine-woman-full-episode/; David S. Jones, *Rationalizing Epidemics: Meanings and Uses of American Indian Mortality since 1600*, ill. ed. (Cambridge, MA: Harvard University Press, 2004), 119; Walter Brooks, "Native American Cultures, History Highlighted," *University of Nebraska Medical Center*, accessed January 2, 2020, https://www.unmc.edu/news.cfm?match=682.

4. Georgina Ferry, "Susan La Flesche Picotte: A Doctor Who Spanned Two Cultures," *The Lancet* 393, no. 10173 (February 23, 2019): 734, http://doi .org/10.1016/S0140-6736(19)30363-0.

5. Lesiak and RedCorn, *Medicine Woman*; Jones, *Rationalizing Epidemics*, 148.

6. Lesiak and RedCorn, *Medicine Woman*; Jones, *Rationalizing Epidemics*, 148.

7. Christopher M. Finan, *Drunks: The Story of Alcoholism and the Birth of Recovery*, reprint ed. (Boston: Beacon Press, 2018), 19; National Trust for Historic Preservation, "History Divided: Dr. Susan LaFlesche Picotte's Legacy in Three Buildings," *Saving Places*, accessed January 6, 2020, https://savingplaces.org/stories/history-divided-dr-susan-laflesche-picottes-legacy-in-three-buildings.

8. National Trust for Historic Preservation, "History Divided."

9. Lesiak and RedCorn, *Medicine Woman*.

10. "Preserving the Legacy of Dr. Susan La Flesche Picotte—Healing History," *DrSusanCenter.Org*, January 9, 2019, https://www.drsusancenter.org/2019/01/09/preserving-the-legacy-of-dr-susan-la-flesche-picotte-healing-history/; "Trailblazing Tribal Hospital Lands on 'Most Endangered Historic Places' List," *Indianz*, accessed January 26, 2020, https://www.indianz.com/News/2018/06/26/historic-indian-hospital-lands-on-most-e.asp.

## CHAPTER 21. CARVILLE, THE "LOUISIANA LEPER HOME"

1. Marcia Gaudet, *Carville: Remembering Leprosy in America* (Jackson: University Press of Mississippi, 2004), 11.

2. Quoted in Michelle T. Moran, *Colonizing Leprosy: Imperialism and the Politics of Public Health in the United States*, new ed. (Chapel Hill, NC: The University of North Carolina Press, 2007), 30.

3. Elizabeth Schexnyder, *Audio Tour: Carville: The National Leprosarium* (National Hansen's Disease Museum), accessed June 15, 2019, https://neworleanshistorical.org/tours/show/55.

4. José P. Ramirez Jr., *Squint: My Journey with Leprosy* (Jackson: University Press of Mississippi, 2009), 35.

5. Sally Squires, "Julia Rivera Elwood, 58," *The Washington Post*, November 16, 1997, https://www.washingtonpost.com/archive/politics/1997/11/16/julia-rivera-elwood-58/ff06aed1-d886-4824-92e6-e704d598d3a0/?utm_term=.2ef73f89e794; Schexnyder, *Carville Audio Tour*.

6. Gaudet, *Carville*, 175.

7. Betty Martin, *Miracle at Carville* (Garden City, NY: Doubleday & Company, Inc., 1950), 191.

8. Gaudet, *Carville*, 160; Schexnyder, *Carville Audio Tour*.

## CHAPTER 22. THE PROFESSIONAL NURSE ONLY

1. M. Patricia Donahue, *Nursing, The Finest Art: An Illustrated History*, 3rd ed. (Maryland Heights, MO: Mosby, 2010), 140, 188.

2. Narcy Recker, *An Institution of Organized Kindness* (Sioux Falls, SD: Sioux Valley Hospital, 1996), 1–3.

3. Recker, *An Institution of Organized Kindness*, 5; Donahue, *Nursing*, 161; Adda Eldredge, "The Responsibility of the Hospital to the Training School," *The American Journal of Nursing* 19, no. 5 (1919): 350, 352, http://doi.org/10.2307/3405568.

4. Recker, *An Institution of Organized Kindness*, 11.

5. Recker, *An Institution of Organized Kindness*, 7–8, 11; Donahue, *Nursing*, 146.

6. Kenneth M. Ludmerer, *Learning to Heal* (New York: Basic Books, 1988), 5.

7. W. H. Taft, "A Distinct Call to Women," *Ladies Home Journal* 35, no 5 (September 1917), quoted in Donahue, *Nursing*, 194.

8. S. Lillian Clayton and Anna C. Jamme, "Recruiting for the New Nursing Army," *The American Journal of Nursing* 17, no. 12 (1917): 1199, http://doi.org/10.2307/3405980.

## CHAPTER 23. THE PANDEMIC OF THE CENTURY: THE 1918 FLU

1. Gina Bari Kolata, *Flu: The Story of the Great Influenza Pandemic of 1918 and the Search for the Virus That Caused It*, ebook ed. (New York: Touchstone, 2001) ch. 1; John C. Acker, *Thru the War with Our Outfit: Being a Historical Narrative of the 107th Ammunition Train* (Sturgeon Bay, WI: Door County Publishing Co., 1920), 83, http://archive.org/details/thruwarwithourou00acke.

2. Jeremy Brown, *Influenza: The Hundred-Year Hunt to Cure the 1918 Spanish Flu Pandemic*, ebook ed. (New York: Atria Books, 2018), ch. 3.

3. Kolata, *Flu*, ch. 1; Mark Honigsbaum, "Why the 1918 Spanish Flu Defied Both Memory and Imagination," *Wellcome Collection*, accessed June 27, 2020, https://wellcomecollection.org/articles/W7TfGRAAAP5F0eKS.

4. Brown, *Influenza*, ch. 1.

5. Vanessa Northington Gamble, "'There Wasn't a Lot of Comforts in Those Days:' African Americans, Public Health, and the 1918 Influenza Epidemic," *Public Health Reports (1974–)* 125 (2010): 114–22.

6. Brown, *Influenza*, ch. 3.

## CHAPTER 24. THE BUBONIC PLAGUE MEETS BACTERIOLOGY

1. Paula Summerly, "Bowie, Anna Mary," in *The Handbook of Texas Online* (Texas State Historical Association), accessed May 18, 2020, https://tshaonline.org/handbook/online/articles/fbowi.

2. Myron Echenberg, "Pestis Redux: The Initial Years of the Third Bubonic Plague Pandemic, 1894–1901," *Journal of World History* 13, no. 2 (Fall 2002): 431.

3. Gail Jarrow, *Bubonic Panic: When Plague Invaded America*, ebook ed. (New York: Calkins Creek, 2016), chs. 4–5.

4. *Pacific Medical and Surgical Journal* 19 (1876): 36–37, quoted in Joan Trauner, "The Chinese as Medical Scapegoats in San Francisco, 1870–1905," *California History* 57, no. 1 (Spring 1978): 73, http://doi.org/10.2307/25157817.

5. Jarrow, *Bubonic Panic*, ch. 7.

6. Paula Summerly, "Bubonic Plague, Galveston (1920)," in *The Handbook of Texas Online* (Texas State Historical Association), accessed May 4, 2020, https://tshaonline.org/handbook/online/articles/smbub; Summerly, "Bowie, Anna Mary."

## CHAPTER 25. SAFE, SIMPLE, SURE? THE POWER OF X-RAYS

1. Richard Mould, "The Early History of X-Rays in Medicine for Therapy and Diagnosis," in *X-Rays: The First Hundred Years*, ed. Alan Michette and Slawka Pfauntsch (Chichester, NY: John Wiley & Sons, 1996), 25, http://archive.org/details/xraysfirsthundre0000unse.

2. Seth Turner, "The Thwaites X-Ray Machine: An Early Shock-Proof Dental X-Ray Unit" (Ann Arbor, MI: Sindecuse Museum of Dentistry, 2007), 10.

3. Mould, "The Early History of X-Rays," 36; "Giving of 'Ray' Treatments Brings Arrest of Dentist," *Grand Rapids Herald*, August 1, 1945.

4. Rebecca Herzig, "In the Name of Science: Suffering, Sacrifice, and the Formation of American Roentgenology," *American Quarterly* 53, no. 4 (December 2001): 563–66; Shannon O'Dell, personal communication, April 2020.

5. Mould, "The Early History of X-Rays," 34–38; Jacalyn Duffin and Charles R. R. Hayter, "Baring the Sole: The Rise and Fall of the Shoe-Fitting Fluoroscope," *Isis* 91, no. 2 (2000): 260–82.

6. William Bynum and Helen Bynum, *Great Discoveries in Medicine* (New York: Thames & Hudson, 2011), 121.

## CHAPTER 26. "ARE YOU PLAYING THE HEALTH GAME?"

1. George Rosen, *A History of Public Health*, enl. and exp. ed. (Baltimore: Johns Hopkins University Press, 1993), 359.

2. R. Alton Lee, *From Snake Oil to Medicine: Pioneering Public Health*, Healing Society: Disease, Medicine, and History (Westport, CT: Praeger Publishers, 2007), 53; James N. Giglio, "Voluntarism and Public Policy between World War I and the New Deal: Herbert Hoover and the American Child Health Association," *Presidential Studies Quarterly* 13, no. 3 (1983): 431.

3. Rosen, *A History of Public Health*, 355; "County Nurse Is Now Doing Duty," *The Evening Kansan-Republican*, August 5, 1921, Newspapers.com.

4. Alan M. Kraut, *Silent Travelers: Germs, Genes, and the Immigrant Menace* (New York: Basic Books, 1994) 62, 232, 236; Amy L. Fairchild, *Science at the Borders: Immigrant Inspection and the Shaping of the Modern Industrial Labor Force* (Baltimore: Johns Hopkins University Press, 2003), 42, 64.

5. Giglio, "Voluntarism and Public Policy," 430–32; Kraut, *Silent Travelers*, 237.

6. Giglio, "Voluntarism and Public Policy," 431; "CHO-CHO," *The Journal of Education* 90, no. 1 (1919): 13; Frank Watson, "The Contributions of American Social Agencies to Social Progress and Democracy," *The Journal of Social Forces* 1, no. 2 (January 1923): 87–90.

7. Steven B. Karch, *A Brief History of Cocaine: From Inca Monarchs to Cali Cartels: 500 Years of Cocaine Dealing*, 2nd ed. (Boca Raton: CRC/Taylor & Francis, 2006), 106; Kraut, *Silent Travelers*, 242.

## CHAPTER 27. THE PROBLEM WITH "GOOD" GENES

1. Adam Cohen, *Imbeciles: The Supreme Court, American Eugenics, and the Sterilization of Carrie Buck* (New York: Penguin Books, 2017), 61.

2. Steven Selden, *Inheriting Shame: The Story of Eugenics and Racism in America* (New York: Teachers College Press, 1999), 25, 30, 33, 35.

3. Kim E. Nielsen, *A Disability History of the United States* (Boston: Beacon Press, 2013), 101, 107.

4. Nielsen, *A Disability History of the United States*, 112.

5. Allan Chase, *The Legacy of Malthus: The Social Costs of the New Scientific Racism* (New York: Knopf, distributed by Random House, 1977), 74; Selden, *Inheriting Shame*, 2–3, 13.

6. Harriet A. Washington, *Medical Apartheid: The Dark History of Medical Experimentation on Black Americans from Colonial Times to the Present*, reprint (New York: Anchor, 2008), 191–92; Chase, *The Legacy of Malthus*, 210.

7. Selden, *Inheriting Shame*, 97.

8. Quoted in Amy L. Fairchild, *Science at the Borders: Immigrant Inspection and the Shaping of the Modern Industrial Labor Force* (Baltimore: Johns Hopkins University Press, 2003), 167, 169, 204–5.

9. Nielsen, *A Disability History of the United States*, 102; Cohen, *Imbeciles*, 317.

10. Washington, *Medical Apartheid,* 190–99; Selden, *Inheriting Shame*, xv.

## CHAPTER 28. MACHINERY AND MACHINATIONS

1. Austin C. Lescarboura, "Our Abrams Verdict," *Scientific American* 131, no. 3 (1924): 160.

2. Nancy Roth, "Good Vibrations: Abrams's Oscilloclast and the Instrumental Cure," *Medical Instrumentation* 15, no. 6 (December 1981).

3. Carolyn Thomas de la Peña, *The Body Electric: How Strange Machines Built the Modern American* (Austin: NYU Press, 2005); Lescarboura, "Our Abrams Verdict," 158.

4. Austin C. Lescarboura, "Our Abrams Investigation—VI," *Scientific American* 130, no. 3 (1924): 160.

5. Morris Fishbein, *Fads and Quackery in Healing: An Analysis of the Foibles of the Healing Cults* (New York: Covici Friede, 1932), 148, http://hdl.handle.net/2027/mdp.39015055447836; Austin C. Lescarboura, "Our Abrams Investigation—XI," *Scientific American* 131, no. 2 (1924): 142; Richard Van Vleck, "The Electronic Reactions of Albert Abrams," *American Artifacts*, accessed August 28, 2019, http://www.americanartifacts.com/smma/abrams/abrams.htm.

6. Lescarboura, "Our Abrams Verdict," 161.

## CHAPTER 29. DIABETES: A FATAL DISEASE BECOMES CHRONIC

1. Caroline Cox, *The Fight to Survive: A Young Girl, Diabetes, and the Discovery of Insulin* (New York: Kaplan Publishing, 2009), xii, 40.

2. Michael Bliss, *The Discovery of Insulin* (Chicago: University of Chicago Press, 1982), 22, 37.

3. Michael Bliss, *The Making of Modern Medicine: Turning Points in the Treatment of Disease* (Chicago: University of Chicago Press, 2011), 77.

4. Bliss, *The Making of Modern Medicine*, 79, 83.

5. Nadia Al-Samarrie, "The History of Diabetes," *Diabetes Health*, January 1, 2015, https://www.diabeteshealth.com/the-history-of-diabetes/.

6. Darby Herkert et al., "Cost-Related Insulin Underuse among Patients with Diabetes," *Journal of the American Medical Association Internal Medicine* 179, no. 1 (January 2019): 112–13.

## CHAPTER 30. THE TOOLS OF A CONTESTED TRADE: A MIDWIFE'S KIT

1. Octavia Davis, "Janie Clara Breckinridge [Interview]," *I Ain't Lying [Zine]*, Spring 1981, 1985.32.1, Mississippi Department of Archives & History.

2. Carolyn Conant Van Blarcom, *Getting Ready to Be a Mother: A Little Book of Information and Advice for the Young Woman Who Is Looking Forward to Motherhood* (New York: The MacMillan Company, 1922), 84, http://hdl.handle.net/2027/uc1.b3846025.

3. Judy Barrett Litoff, *American Midwives: 1860 to the Present*, reprint ed. (Westport, CT: Praeger, 1978), 55.

4. James H. Ferguson, "Mississippi Midwives," *Journal of the History of Medicine and Allied Sciences* 5, no. 1 (1950): 85–95; Davis, "Janie Clara Breckinridge [Interview]," 4.

5. Litoff, *American Midwives*, 36; Laura Ettinger, *Nurse-Midwifery: The Birth of a New American Profession* (Columbus, OH: Ohio State University Press, 2006), 8.

6. Litoff, *American Midwives*, 57; Charlotte G. Borst, *Catching Babies: The Professionalization of Childbirth, 1870–1920*, reprint ed. (Boston: Harvard University Press, 2014), 132, http://doi.org/10.4159/harvard.9780674733480.

7. Marie Jenkins Schwartz, *Birthing a Slave: Motherhood and Medicine in the Antebellum South* (Cambridge, MA: Harvard University Press, 2006), 10; Litoff *American Midwives*, 33; Borst, *Catching Babies*, 153.

8. Litoff, *American Midwives*, 40; Ettinger, *Nurse-Midwifery*, 5, 45, 72.

9. Ettinger, *Nurse-Midwifery*, 188.

10. Allison A. Vanderbilt and Marcie S. Wright, "Infant Mortality: A Call to Action Overcoming Health Disparities in the United States," *Medical Education Online* 18, no. 1 (January 1, 2013): 22503, http://doi.org/10.3402/meo.v18i0.22503.

## CHAPTER 31. SIPPING ON THE SUNSHINE VITAMIN

1. Catherine Price, *Vitamania: Our Obsessive Quest for Nutritional Perfection* (New York: Penguin Press, 2015), 43–45, 47, 67.

2. Frances Rachel Frankenburg, *Vitamin Discoveries and Disasters: History, Science, and Controversies* (Santa Barbara, CA: Praeger, 2009), 96, 101, 106.

3. Library of Congress Copyright Office, *Catalog of Copyright Entries 1936 Pamphlets, Leaflets, Etc.*, vol. 33 (US Government Printing Office, 1936), 326, http://archive.org/details/catalogofcopyri331li.

4. "Retro Ad of the Week: Schlitz Beer, 1936—Beverage Advertising," June 28, 2013, https://mascola.com/insights/beverage-advertising-retro-ad-of-the-week-schlitz-beer-1936/; "Schlitz 'Sunshine Vitamin D Beer Can,'" *Wisconsin Historical Society*, October 19, 2012, https://www.wisconsinhistory.org/Records/Article/CS2859.

5. Price, *Vitamania*, 69, 89.

6. Price, *Vitamania*, 73, 109.

## CHAPTER 32. PREEMIE CARE BEYOND THE WORLD'S FAIR

1. "Incubator for Baby," *The Plattsmouth Journal*, January 12, 1933, https://nebnewspapers.unl.edu/lccn/2016670206/1933-01-12/ed-1/seq-2/.

2. *Official Guidebook to the Trans-Mississippi International Exposition* (Omaha: 1898).

3. Dawn Raffel, *The Strange Case of Dr. Couney: How a Mysterious European Showman Saved Thousands of American Babies* (New York: Blue Rider Press, 2018), 57, 114.

4. "Dr. Adolph Lorenz on Physically Unfit Children," *Nebraska State Medical Journal* 22, no. 6 (June 1937): 239.

5. Raffel, *The Strange Case of Dr. Couney*, 171.

6. "Incubator for Baby," *The Plattsmouth Journal*; James C. Olson and Ronald C. Naugle, *History of Nebraska*, 3rd ed., (Lincoln: University of Nebraska Press, 1997), 293.

7. "6037-3 - Incubator, Infant; Nebraska Dept. of Health, 1938–1939," *History Nebraska Collections Catalog*, accessed July 6, 2019, https://nebraskahistory.pastperfectonline.com/webobject/F3E8FF74-26E6-4474-95A3-315194719570; "Report of Madison Five Counties Medical Society Meeting," *Nebraska State Medical Journal* 16, no. 19 (October 1931): 413; Raffel, *The Strange Case of Dr. Couney*, 189, 219.

8. "U.S., Social Security Applications and Claims Index, 1936–2007—AncestryLibrary.Com," accessed July 4, 2019.

## CHAPTER 33. THE PENICILLIN REVOLUTION

1. Robert Bud, *Penicillin: Triumph and Tragedy* (Oxford: Oxford University Press, 2009), 25–27.

2. Gladys L. Hobby, *Penicillin: Meeting the Challenge* (New Haven: Yale University Press, 1985), 247.

3. Bud, *Penicillin*, 15–17.

4. Hobby, *Penicillin*, 83, 96.

5. Eric Lax, *The Mold in Dr. Florey's Coat: The Story of the Penicillin Miracle* (New York: Holt Paperbacks, 2005), 155.

6. Lax, *The Mold in Dr. Florey's Coat*, 3; Hobby, *Penicillin*, 80; Bud, *Penicillin*, 35.

7. Lax, *The Mold in Dr. Florey's Coat*, 2.

8. Ramanan Laxminarayan et al., *Extending the Cure: Policy Responses to the Growing Threat of Antibiotic Resistance* (London: Earthscan, 2007), 12.

## CHAPTER 34. BLOOD TRANSFUSION COMES OF AGE

1. Susan E. Lederer, "Bloodlines: Blood Types, Identity, and Association in Twentieth-Century America," *The Journal of the Royal Anthropological Institute* (2013): S119.

2. Cherie Winner, *Circulating Life: Blood Transfusion from Ancient Superstition to Modern Medicine* (Minneapolis, MN: Twenty-First Century Books, 2007), 45; Lederer, "Bloodlines," S120.

3. William H. Schneider, "Blood Transfusion between the Wars," *Journal of the History of Medicine and Allied Sciences* 58, no. 2 (2003): 194.

4. Charles Dillon, "Free as Water," *The Science News-Letter* 33, no. 3 (1938): 42, http://doi.org/10.2307/3914547; Lederer, "Bloodlines," 127.

5. Winner, *Circulating Life*, 52–53; "Too Much Fuss over Blood Transfusions," *The Science News-Letter* 33, no. 6 (1938): 87, http://doi.org/10.2307/3915098.

6. Winner, *Circulating Life*, 59–61; Lederer, "Bloodlines," 125–26.

## CHAPTER 35. INSURING AND ENSURING HEALTH

1. Donna Jones, "Mother/Daughter Team—The Mother's Story," n.d., Rosie the Riveter WWII Home Front National Historic Park, https://museum.nps.gov/ParkObjdet.aspx?rID=RORI%20%20%20%202313%26db%3Dobjects%26dir%3DCR%20AAWEB%26page%3D1; "National Historical Park," Richmond General Plan 2030 (Richmond, CA: City of Richmond Planning and Building Services Department, 2012), 5–6, http://www.ci.richmond.ca.us/DocumentCenter/View/8820/150-National-Historical-Park?bidId=.

2. Christy Ford Chapin, "Ensuring America's Health: Publicly Constructing the Private Health Insurance Industry, 1945–1970," *Enterprise & Society* 13, no. 4 (December 2012): 732.

3. "National Historical Park," Richmond General Plan 2030, 6; Leon Applebaum, "The Development of Voluntary Health Insurance in the United States," *The Journal*

*of Insurance* 28, no. 3 (1961): 26, http://doi.org/10.2307/250372; Morris F. Collen, Bryan Culp, and Tom Debley, "Rosie the Riveter's Wartime Medical Records," *The Permanente Journal* 12, no. 3 (2008): 85–87.

4. Steven Brill, *America's Bitter Pill: Money, Politics, Backroom Deals, and the Fight to Fix Our Broken Healthcare System*, ebook ed. (New York: Random House Trade Paperbacks, 2015), ch. 2.

5. Chapin, "Ensuring America's Health," 734–35.

6. Chapin, "Ensuring America's Health," 730; Jones, "Mother/Daughter Team—The Mother's Story."

## CHAPTER 36. NURSING AT WAR

1. Mattie Donnell Hicks, Oral History, interview by Hermann Trojanowski, transcript, February 25, 1999, Martha Blakeney Hodges Special Collections and University Archives, The University of North Carolina at Greensboro, 7, http://libcdm1.uncg.edu/cdm/singleitem/collection/WVHP/id/4218.

2. Hicks, Oral History, 9.

3. "Social Advances," *The Department of Defense 60th Anniversary of the Korean War Commemoration*, accessed August 3, 2019, http://www.koreanwar60.com/social-advances/; Hicks, Oral History, 5.

4. U.S. Army Center of Military History, "The Army Nurse Corps," accessed August 3, 2019, https://history.army.mil/books/wwii/72-14/72-14.HTM; Diane Burke Fessler, *No Time for Fear: Voices of American Military Nurses in World War II* (East Lansing, MI: Michigan State University Press, 1997), 5; Hicks, Oral History, 10, 15.

## CHAPTER 37. THE SCIENCE AND POLITICS OF INHALING DUST

1. Wendy Richardson, "'The Curse of Our Trade': Occupational Disease in a Vermont Granite Town," *Proceedings of the Vermont Historical Society* 60, no. 1 (1992): 7.

2. Richardson, "The Curse of Our Trade," 13.

3. Richardson, "The Curse of Our Trade," 13.

4. Richardson, "The Curse of Our Trade," 6; Beris Penrose, "'So Now They Have Some Human Guinea Pigs': Aluminium Therapy and Occupational Silicosis," *Health and History* 9, no. 1 (2007): 56–79; Lorin E. Kerr, "Black Lung," *Journal of Public*

*Health Policy* 1, no. 1 (1980): 50–63, 52, http://doi.org/10.2307/3342357; Alan M. Kraut, *Silent Travelers: Germs, Genes, and the Immigrant Menace* (New York: Basic Books, 1994), 177.

5. "Fighting Silicosis: Dust Control in the Granite Industry, 1937," *The Green Mountain Chronicles* 89 (1988), https://vermonthistory.org/fighting-silicosis-dust-control-in-granite-industry-1937; David Rosner and Gerald Markowitz, "Workers, Industry, and the Control of Information: Silicosis and the Industrial Hygiene Foundation," *Journal of Public Health Policy* 16, no. 1 (1995): 32, http://doi.org/10.2307/3342976; Nelson Haas, "Understanding Workers' Compensation, Part I: History of Workers' Compensation in the United States and Vermont," *The Vermont Medical Society*, July 2011, http://www.vtmd.org/workerscomppart1; Penrose, "So Now They Have Some Human Guinea Pigs," 58.

6. George Rosen, *A History of Public Health*, rev. exp. ed. (Baltimore: Johns Hopkins University Press, 2015), 32, 36; Kraut, *Silent Travelers*, 169.

7. Penrose, "So Now They Have Some Human Guinea Pigs," 56; Harry B. Ashe, "Silicosis and Dust Control: Vermont's Granite Industry," *Public Health Reports (1896–1970)* 70, no. 10 (1955): 983–85, http://doi.org/10.2307/4589257; Kerr, "Black Lung," 52.

8. Kerr, "Black Lung," 55–56.

## CHAPTER 38. HEALTH UPLIFTED, HEALTH UPENDED

1. Sandra Quinn and Stephen Thomas, "The National Negro Health Week, 1915 to 1951: A Descriptive Account," *Minority Health Today* 2, no. 3 (April 2001): 44–45, https://www.researchgate.net/publication/277215643_The_National_Negro_Health_Week_1915_to_1951_A_Descriptive_Account.

2. Quinn and Thomas, "The National Negro Health Week," 44–48.

3. *National Negro Health Week. Annual Observance* (United States Public Health Service, 1923), 4, https://books.google.com/books?id=yd8KAQAAIAAJ&dq.

4. Fred Gray, *The Tuskegee Syphilis Study: An Insiders' Account of the Shocking Medical Experiment Conducted by Government Doctors against African American Men*, ebook ed. (Montgomery, AL: NewSouth Books, 2003), ch. 4; James H. Jones, *Bad Blood: The Tuskegee Syphilis Experiment, New and Expanded Edition* (New York: Free Press, 1993), 4.

5. Jones, *Bad Blood*, 4–6, 73.

6.  Harriet A. Washington, *Medical Apartheid: The Dark History of Medical Experimentation on Black Americans from Colonial Times to the Present*, reprint ed. (New York: Anchor, 2008), 160, 168–69; Jones, *Bad Blood*, 7, 189–90, 196, 202.

7.  Lois Snyder and Paul S. Mueller, "Research in the Physician's Office: Navigating the Ethical Minefield," *The Hastings Center Report* 38, no. 2 (2008): 23; Jones, *Bad Blood*, 204, 213–14; Gray, *The Tuskegee Syphilis Study*, ch. 14.

9.  Quinn and Thomas, "The National Negro Health Week," 48; Jones, *Bad Blood*, 220; April Dembosky, "No, the Tuskegee Study Is Not the Top Reason Some Black Americans Question the COVID-19 Vaccine," *KQED*, February 25, 2021, https://www.kqed.org/news/11861810/no-the-tuskegee-study-is-not-the-top-reason-some-black-americans-question-the-covid-19-vaccine; Washington, *Medical Apartheid*, 160.

## CHAPTER 39. DDT: THE DOUBLE-EDGED SWORD

1.  James McWilliams, *American Pests: The Losing War on Insects from Colonial Times to DDT* (New York: Columbia University Press, 2008), 35, 90; George Rosen, *A History of Public Health*, rev. exp. ed. (Baltimore: Johns Hopkins University Press, 2015), 298.

2.  McWilliams, *American Pests*, 129; Elena Conis, "Beyond Silent Spring: An Alternate History of DDT," *Science History Institute*, February 14, 2017, https://www.sciencehistory.org/distillations/beyond-silent-spring-an-alternate-history-of-ddt; David Kinkela, *DDT and the American Century: Global Health, Environmental Politics, and the Pesticide That Changed the World*, reprint ed. (Chapel Hill, NC: The University of North Carolina Press, 2013), 7.

3.  Conis, "Beyond Silent Spring"; McWilliams, *American Pests*, 199, 202.

4.  Rachel Carson, *Silent Spring* (Boston: Houghton Mifflin, 1962), 173.

5.  McWilliams, *American Pests*, 197.

6.  Jonathan Gornall, "To Eradicate Malaria, Bring Back DDT," *Asia Times*, September 21, 2019, sec. opinion, https://www.asiatimes.com/2019/09/opinion/to-eradicate-malaria-bring-back-ddt/; World Health Organization, "The Use of DDT in Malaria Vector Control: WHO Position Statement," revised 2011, https://apps.who.int/iris/bitstream/handle/10665/69945/WHO_HTM_GMP_2011_eng.pdf.

## CHAPTER 40. THE IRON LUNG AND THE POLIO EPIDEMICS

1. Martha Mason and Charlie Cornwell, *Breath: Life in the Rhythm of an Iron Lung* (Asheboro, NC: John F. Blair, 2003), 182.

2. Daniel J. Wilson, *Polio* (Santa Barbara, CA: ABC-CLIO, 2009), 3; Julie K. Silver and Daniel J. Wilson, *Polio Voices: An Oral History from the American Polio Epidemics and Worldwide Eradication Efforts* (Westport, CT: Praeger, 2007), 38.

3. Kathryn Black, *In the Shadow of Polio: A Personal and Social History* (Cambridge, MA: Da Capo Press, 1997), 72.

4. Black, *In the Shadow of Polio*, 67; "Trial on Patent Respirator Suit Scheduled Today," *The Harvard Crimson*, November 6, 1934, https://www.thecrimson.com/article/1934/11/6/trial-on-patent-respirator-suit-scheduled/; Quote in Daniel J. Wilson, *Living with Polio: The Epidemic and Its Survivors*, ill. ed. (Chicago: University of Chicago Press, 2008), 44.

5. Silver and Wilson, *Polio Voices*, 29, 35.

6. Silver and Wilson, *Polio Voices*, 148; Bernard Seytre and Mary Shaffer, *The Death of a Disease: A History of the Eradication of Poliomyelitis* (New Brunswick, NJ: Rutgers University Press, 2005), 42.

7. Tara Haelle, *Vaccination Investigation: The History and Science of Vaccines* (Minneapolis: Twenty-First Century Books, 2018), 56.

8. Seytre and Shaffer, *The Death of a Disease*, 70.

9. "Youngstown Polio Vaccine Immunization Volunteer Photograph," *Ohio Memory Collection*, accessed September 26, 2018, http://www.ohiomemory.org/cdm/ref/collection/p267401coll36/id/24967; Haelle, *Vaccination Investigation*, 79.

## CHAPTER 41. TWO ERAS OF CHANGE IN PHARMACY

1. John P. Swann, "The Evolution of the American Pharmaceutical Industry," *Pharmacy in History* 37, no. 2 (1995): 81; Stephen Hall, "The Upjohn Pharmacy in Disneyland," *Points: The Blog of the Alcohol & Drugs History Society*, November 19, 2019, https://pointsadhs.com/2019/11/19/the-upjohn-pharmacy-in-disneyland/; "ADventure in Disneyland!" *Upjohn News*, 1955, reproduced at http://www.upjohn.net/disneyland/disney/disney.htm.

2. Swann, "The Evolution of the American Pharmaceutical Industry," 77, 95.

3. William H. Helfand and David L. Cowen, "Evolution of Pharmaceutical Oral Dosage Forms," *Pharmacy in History* 25, no. 1 (1983): 5; Swann, "The Evolution of the American Pharmaceutical Industry," 79–80.

4. "In Soda Revival, Fizzy Taste Bubbles Up from the Past," *NPR.Org*, accessed June 22, 2020, https://www.npr.org/2011/09/01/140093866/in-soda-revival-fizzy-taste -bubbles-up-from-the-past.

5. Thomas Hager, *Ten Drugs: How Plants, Powders, and Pills Have Shaped the History of Medicine*, ebook ed. (New York: Abrams Press, 2019), ch. 9.

6. John Parascandola, "Industrial Research Comes of Age: The American Pharmaceutical Industry, 1920–1940," *Pharmacy in History* 27, no. 1 (1985): 14; James Le Fanu, *The Rise and Fall of Modern Medicine: Revised Edition*, ebook ed. (New York: Basic Books, 2012), ch. 3; George Urdang, "The Antibiotics and Pharmacy," *Journal of the History of Medicine and Allied Sciences* 6, no. 3 (1951): 405.

7. Hager, *Ten Drugs*, ch. 9.

## CHAPTER 42. MORE THAN A METAPHOR: THE STRAITJACKET

1. William Bynum and Helen Bynum, "Object Lessons: The Straitjacket," *The Lancet* 387 (April 16, 2016): 1607; Marylynne Diggs, "Romantic Friends or a 'Different Race of Creatures'? The Representation of Lesbian Pathology in Nineteenth-Century America." *Feminist Studies* 21, no. 2 (1995): 317–40. http://doi.org/10.2307/3178264.

2. Christopher M. Finan, *Drunks: The Story of Alcoholism and the Birth of Recovery*, reprint ed. (Boston: Beacon Press, 2018), 85, 154.

3. Mike Jay, *This Way Madness Lies* (New York: Thames & Hudson, 2016), 95, 187–88; Diane L. Goeres-Gardner, *Inside Oregon State Hospital: A History of Tragedy and Triumph* (Charleston: The History Press, 2013), 112.

4. George Rosen, *A History of Public Health*, rev. exp. ed. (Baltimore: Johns Hopkins University Press, 2015), 469.

5. Goeres-Gardner, *Inside Oregon State Hospital*, 105; Jay, *This Way Madness Lies*, 161.

6. Goeres-Gardner, *Inside Oregon State Hospital*, 92, 142.

7. Jay, *This Way Madness Lies*, 174.

8. Jay, *This Way Madness Lies*, 176–77, 181, 199.

9. "Jailing People with Mental Illness," *NAMI: National Alliance on Mental Illness*, accessed January 9, 2021, https://www.nami.org/Advocacy/Policy-Priorities/Divert -from-Justice-Involvement/Jailing-People-with-Mental-Illness; Treatment Advocacy Center, "The Treatment of Persons with Mental Illness in Prisons and Jails: A State Survey," 2014, www.TACReports.org/treatment-behind-bars.

## CHAPTER 43. CHANGING WAYS OF LOOKING AT THE GUT

1. Basil I. Hirschowitz, "Development and Application of Endoscopy," *Gastroenterology* 104, no. 2 (February 1, 1993): 337, http://doi.org/10.5555/ uri:pii:001650859390399W.

2. Hirschowitz, "Development and Application of Endoscopy," 337–38; Jonathan D. Kaunitz, "The Fruits of Fiber: The Invention of the Flexible Fiberoptic Gastroscope," *Digestive Diseases and Sciences* 59, no. 11 (November 2014): 2616, http://doi .org/10.1007/s10620-014-3339-4; Annetine C. Gelijns, Nathan Rosenberg, and Holly Dawkins, *From the Scalpel to the Scope: Endoscopic Innovations in Gastroenterology, Gynecology, and Surgery* (Washington, DC: National Academies Press, 1995), 7, https://www.ncbi.nlm.nih.gov/books/NBK232053/.

3. Basil I. Hirschowitz, "A Personal History of the Fiberscope," *Gastroenterology* 76, no. 4 (April 1, 1979): 865–66, http://doi.org/10.1016/S0016-5085(79)80190-0.

4. Hirschowitz, "A Personal History of the Fiberscope," 868.

5. Hank Black, "The Enlightening Endoscope," *University of Alabama at Birmingham Magazine*, accessed May 30, 2019, https://www.uab.edu/uabmagazine/ hirschowitz; Irvin M. Modlin, Mark Kidd, and Kevin D. Lye, "From the Lumen to the Laparoscope," *Archives of Surgery* 139, no. 10 (October 2004): 1110, http:// doi.org/10.1001/archsurg.139.10.1110; Hirschowitz, "A Personal History of the Fiberscope," 868.

## CHAPTER 44. THE PILL'S NEW ERA OF CHOICE (FOR SOME)

1. National Center for Health Statistics, Centers for Disease Control and Prevention, "FastStats–Contraceptive Use," November 21, 2019, https://www.cdc.gov/nchs/ fastats/contraceptive.htm.

2. Gabriela Soto Laveaga, *Jungle Laboratories: Mexican Peasants, National Projects, and the Making of the Pill* (Durham, NC: Duke University Press Books, 2009), 2, 13, 125.

3. Elaine Tyler May, *America and the Pill: A History of Promise, Peril, and Liberation*, reprint ed. (New York: Basic Books, 2011), 27.

4. Katherine Andrews, "The Dark History of Forced Sterilization of Latina Women," *University of Pittsburgh Panoramas*, October 30, 2017, https://www .panoramas.pitt.edu/health-and-society/dark-history-forced-sterilization-latina -women; Pamela Verma Liao and Janet Dollin, "Half a Century of the Oral Contraceptive Pill," *Canadian Family Physician* 58, no. 12 (December 2012): e757– 60; Andrea Tone, *Devices and Desires: A History of Contraceptives in America* (New York: Hill and Wang, 2002), 143, 223; May, *America and the Pill*, 30.

5. Charlotte G. Borst and Kathleen W. Jones, "As Patients and Healers: The History of Women and Medicine," *OAH Magazine of History* 19, no. 5 (2005): 25.

6. Tone, *Devices and Desires*, 248, 250.

7. Tone, *Devices and Desires*, 248, 250; William J. Curran, "Package Inserts for Patients: Informed Consent in the 1980s," *New England Journal of Medicine* 305, no. 26 (December 24, 1981): 1564–66, http://doi.org/10.1056/NEJM198112243052605.

8. Wendy Kline, "'Please Include This in Your Book': Readers Respond to *Our Bodies, Ourselves*," *Bulletin of the History of Medicine* 79, no. 1 (2005): 81–110, 86, 100; Susan M. Reverby, "Feminism & Health," *Health and History* 4, no. 1 (2002): 5–19, http://doi.org/10.2307/40111418, 11.

9. Dorothy Roberts, *Killing the Black Body: Race, Reproduction, and the Meaning of Liberty* (New York: Vintage, 1997), 134; Reverby, "Feminism & Health," 13.

10. Jimmy Wilkinson Meyer, "Oral Contraceptive Pill," *Dittrick Medical History Center*, accessed November 30, 2019, https://artsci.case.edu/dittrick/online -exhibits/history-of-birth-control/contraception-in-america-1950-present-day/oral -contraceptive-pill/; May, *America and the Pill*, 158; Tone, *Devices and Desires*, 291.

## CHAPTER 45. SMOKING UNDER SCRUTINY

1. Alton Ochsner, "My First Recognition of the Relationship of Smoking and Lung Cancer," *Preventive Medicine* 2 (1973): 611; Michael DeBakey, "Carcinoma of the Lung and Tobacco Smoking: A Historical Perspective," *The Ochsner Journal* 1, no. 3 (July 1999): 106.

2. Iain Gately, *Tobacco: A Cultural History of How an Exotic Plant Seduced Civilization*, ebook ed. (New York: Grove Press, 2007), chs. 10–12, 14.

3. DeBakey, "Carcinoma of the Lung and Tobacco Smoking," 106; Catalin Marian et al., "Reconciling Human Smoking Behavior and Machine Smoking Patterns: Implications for Understanding Smoking Behavior and the Impact on Laboratory Studies," *Cancer Epidemiology, Biomarkers & Prevention* 18, no. 12 (December 2009), https://cebp.aacrjournals.org/content/18/12/3305.long.

4. Marian et al., "Reconciling Human Smoking Behavior and Machine Smoking Patterns," 3307–8.

5. Mark Parascandola, "Two Approaches to Etiology: The Debate over Smoking and Lung Cancer in the 1950s," *Endeavour* 28, no. 2 (June 2004): 81–82.

6. Surgeon General's Advisory Committee on Smoking and Health, *Smoking and Health* (Washington, DC: US Dept. of Health, Education, and Welfare, Public Health Service, 1964), 14, 58, http://archive.org/details/smokinghealthrep00unit.

7. Austin Bradford Hill, "The Environment and Disease: Association or Causation?," *Proceedings of the Royal Society of Medicine* 58, no. 5 (May 1965): 295–300; Parascandola, "Two Approaches to Etiology," 84.

8. Ochsner, "My First Recognition of the Relationship of Smoking and Lung Cancer," 614.

9. Centers for Disease Control and Prevention, "Achievements in Public Health, 1900–1999: Tobacco Use -- United States, 1900–1999," *Morbidity and Mortality Weekly Report* 48, no. 43 (November 5, 1999): 986–93.

## CHAPTER 46. ED ROBERTS AND THE INDEPENDENT LIVING MOVEMENT

1. Edward Roberts, "When Others Speak for You, You Lose," *Edward V. Roberts Papers, The Bancroft Library: University of California, Berkeley*, accessed June 6, 2019, https://oac.cdlib.org/ark:/13030/hb3j49n6hw/?brand=oac4.

2. Edward Roberts, "The Emergence of the Disabled Civil Rights Movement," *Edward V. Roberts Papers, The Bancroft Library: University of California, Berkeley*, accessed June 6, 2019, https://oac.cdlib.org/ark:/13030/hb6m3nb1nw/?brand=oac4.

3. Kitty Cone, "Short History of the 504 Sit-In," *Disability Rights Education & Defense Fund*, accessed January 4, 2020, https://dredf.org/504-sit-in-20th-anniversary/short-history-of-the-504-sit-in/.

4. Deborah Little, "Identity, Efficiency and Disability Rights," *Disability Studies Quarterly* 30, no. 1 (November 18, 2009), http://doi.org/10.18061/dsq.v30i1.1013.

5. Christine Kelly, "Wrestling with Group Identity: Disability Activism and Direct Funding," *Disability Studies Quarterly* 30, no. 3/4 (August 26, 2010): 3, 9, http://doi .org/10.18061/dsq.v30i3/4.1279; *Ed Roberts and Judy Heumann in 1984 Interview* (Stockholm, Sweden, 1984), https://vimeo.com/29471050.

6. Victoria Dawson, "Ed Roberts' Wheelchair Records a Story of Obstacles Overcome," *Smithsonian*, accessed June 6, 2019, https://www.smithsonianmag. com/smithsonian-institution/ed-roberts-wheelchair-records-story-obstacles-overcome-180954531/.

## CHAPTER 47. BYPASSING THE HEART

1. James W. Blatchford, "Ludwig Rehn: The First Successful Cardiorrhaphy," *The Annals of Thoracic Surgery* 39, no. 5 (May 1985): 492, http://doi.org/10.1016/S0003 -4975(10)61972-8.

2. G. Wayne Miller, *King of Hearts: The True Story of the Maverick Who Pioneered Open Heart Surgery* (New York: Broadway Books, 2002), 81.

3. Miller, *King of Hearts*, 171; M. W. Lim, "The History of Extracorporeal Oxygenators," *Anaesthesia* 61, no. 10 (2006): 984, https://doi.org/10.1111/j.1365-2044.2006.04781.x.

4. "Black Hospital Movement in Alabama," *Encyclopedia of Alabama*, accessed June 22, 2019, http://www.encyclopediaofalabama.org/article/h-2410; Denton A. Cooley and O. H. Frazier, "The Past 50 Years of Cardiovascular Surgery," *Circulation* 102, no. suppl_4 (November 14, 2000): iv–87, http://doi.org/10.1161/circ.102.suppl_4.IV-87; Thomas Morris, *The Matter of the Heart* (New York: Thomas Dunne Books, 2018), 214.

## CHAPTER 48. FALSE HOPELESSNESS OR FALSE HOPE: THE EARLY YEARS OF AIDS

1. UNAIDS, "Global HIV & AIDS Statistics—Fact Sheet," accessed July 5, 2021, https://www.unaids.org/en/resources/fact-sheet. "Denying Science," *Nature Medicine* 12, no. 4 (April 2006): 369, http://doi.org/10.1038/nm0406-369.

2. Jonathan Engel, *The Epidemic: A Global History of AIDS* (New York: Smithsonian, 2006); Alan M. Kraut, *Silent Travelers: Germs, Genes, and the Immigrant Menace* (New York: Basic Books, 1994), 261; Nishant Shahani, "How to Survive the Whitewashing of AIDS: Global Pasts, Transnational Futures," *QED: A Journal in GLBTQ Worldmaking* 3, no. 1 (2016): 8, 20, 25, http://doi.org/10.14321/qed.3.1.0001.

3. Martin Delaney, PBS Frontline interview with Martin Delaney, 2004, https://www.pbs.org/wgbh/pages/frontline/aids/interviews/delaney.html.

4. Joseph Palca, "International Doubts about a Kenyan Cure," *Science* 250, no. 4978 (1990): 200; Jennifer J. Furin, "'You Have to Be Your Own Doctor': Sociocultural Influences on Alternative Therapy Use among Gay Men with AIDS in West Hollywood," *Medical Anthropology Quarterly* 11, no. 4 (1997): 499.

5. Delaney, PBS Frontline interview; Ronald Bayer and Gerald Oppenheimer, *AIDS Doctors: Voices from the Epidemic: An Oral History* (New York: Oxford University Press, 2000), 165; Dallas Buyer's Club, *NEW Source*, October 1991, University of North Texas Libraries, https://texashistory.unt.edu/ark:/67531/metadc271488/m1/5/; Dylan Matthews, "What 'Dallas Buyers Club' Got Wrong about the AIDS Crisis," *Washington Post*, accessed July 28, 2020, https://www.washingtonpost.com/news/wonk/wp/2013/12/10/what-dallas-buyers-club-got-wrong-about-the-aids-crisis/.

## CHAPTER 49. SEPTEMBER 11 AND EMERGENCY RESPONSE

1. Teresa McCallion, "EMS Providers Recall 9/11," *Journal of Emergency Medical Services* 36, no. 9 (September 1, 2011), https://www.jems.com/2011/08/31/ems-providers-recall-911/.

2. Ryan Corbett Bell, *The Ambulance: A History*, reprint ed. (Jefferson, NC: McFarland & Company, 2012), 4–6, 21, 40.

3. Bell, *The Ambulance*, 56, 71, 79, 135.

4. Bell, *The Ambulance*, 129, 258, 278, 305, 317.

5. Susan Hagen and Mary Carouba, *Women at Ground Zero: Stories of Courage and Compassion* (Indianapolis: Alpha, 2002), xv.

6. Benjamin Badillo, World Trade Center Task Force Interview, interview by Paul Radenberg, transcript, January 24, 2002, https://static01.nyt.com/packages/pdf/nyregion/20050812_WTC_GRAPHIC/9110495.PDF; Edward Martinez, World Trade Center Task Force Interview, interview by Paul Radenberg, transcript, January 24, 2002, https://static01.nyt.com/packages/pdf/nyregion/20050812_WTC_GRAPHIC/9110494.PDF.

## CHAPTER 50. SAVING LIVES AMID THE OPIOID CRISIS

1. Jay Olstad, "Montevideo Police Save Overdosing Woman with Naloxone," *KARE11 News* (September 20, 2016), https://www.kare11.com/article/news/montevideo-police-save-overdosing-woman-with-naloxone/89-322418080.

2. David E. Newton, *The Opioid Crisis: A Reference Handbook* (Santa Barbara, CA: ABC-CLIO, 2018), 16–26.

3. Kavita M. Babu, Jeffrey Brent, and David N. Juurlink, "Prevention of Opioid Overdose," *New England Journal of Medicine* 380, no. 23 (June 6, 2019): 2246–55, http://doi.org/10.1056/NEJMra1807054; National Institute on Drug Abuse, "Opioid Overdose Crisis," January 22, 2019, https://www.drugabuse.gov/drugs-abuse/opioids/opioid-overdose-crisis; Jon Collins, "Here's Why Minnesota Has a Big Problem with Opioid Overdoses," *MPR News* (April 18, 2016), https://www.mprnews.org/story/2016/04/18/opioid-overdose-epidemic-explained.

4. Pat O'Hare, "From Local to Global: A Short History of Harm Reduction," in *The History and Principles of Harm Reduction: Between Public Health & Social Change* (Paris: Médecins du Monde, 2013), https://issuu.com/medecinsdumonde/docs/mdm_rdr_en_bd; Yngvild Olsen and Joshua M. Sharfstein, *The Opioid Epidemic: What Everyone Needs to Know* (Oxford: Oxford University Press, 2019), 234.

5. Michael Lemanski, *A History of Addiction & Recovery in the United States: Traditional Treatments and Effective Alternatives* (Tucson, AZ: See Sharp Press, 2001), 53–55, 65; Christopher M. Finan, *Drunks: The Story of Alcoholism and the Birth of Recovery*, reprint ed. (Boston: Beacon Press, 2018), 92–93.

6. Newton, *The Opioid Crisis*, 107–12; Olsen and Sharfstein, *The Opioid Epidemic*, 76.

7. Olstad, "Montevideo Police Save Overdosing Woman with Naloxone."

# Bibliography

"6037-3 - Incubator, Infant; Nebraska Dept. of Health, 1938–1939." *History Nebraska Collections Catalog.* Accessed July 6, 2019. https://nebraskahistory .pastperfectonline.com/webobject/F3E8FF74-26E6-4474-95A3-315194719570.

Abrams, Herbert K. "A Short History of Occupational Health." *Journal of Public Health Policy* 22, no. 1 (2001): 34–80. http://doi.org/10.2307/3343553.

Acker, John C. *Thru the War with Our Outfit: Being a Historical Narrative of the 107th Ammunition Train.* Sturgeon Bay, WI: Door County Publishing Co., 1920. http://archive.org/details/thruwarwithourou00acke.

"ADventure in Disneyland!" *Upjohn News*, 1955. http://www.upjohn.net/disneyland/ disney/disney.htm.

Ainsworth, Claire. "Sex Redefined." *Nature News* 518, no. 7539 (February 19, 2015): 288. http://doi.org/10.1038/518288a.

Al-Samarrie, Nadia. "The History of Diabetes." *Diabetes Health*, January 1, 2015. https://www.diabeteshealth.com/the-history-of-diabetes/.

American Dental Association. "History of Dentistry Timeline." Accessed July 21, 2019. https://www.ada.org/en/about-the-ada/ada-history-and-presidents-of-the -ada/ada-history-of-dentistry-timeline.

Andrews, Katherine. "The Dark History of Forced Sterilization of Latina Women." *University of Pittsburgh Panoramas*, October 30, 2017. https://www.panoramas .pitt.edu/health-and-society/dark-history-forced-sterilization-latina-women.

Applebaum, Leon. "The Development of Voluntary Health Insurance in the United States." *The Journal of Insurance* 28, no. 3 (1961): 25–33. http://doi .org/10.2307/250372.

Ashe, Harry B. "Silicosis and Dust Control: Vermont's Granite Industry." *Public Health Reports (1896–1970)* 70, no. 10 (1955): 983–85. http://doi .org/10.2307/4589257.

Babu, Kavita M., Jeffrey Brent, and David N. Juurlink. "Prevention of Opioid Overdose." *New England Journal of Medicine* 380, no. 23 (June 6, 2019): 2246–55. http://doi.org/10.1056/NEJMra1807054.

Badillo, Benjamin. World Trade Center Task Force Interview. Interview by Paul Radenberg. Transcript, January 24, 2002. https://static01.nyt.com/packages/pdf/ nyregion/20050812_WTC_GRAPHIC/9110495.PDF.

Bale, Tracy L., and C. Neill Epperson. "Sex as a Biological Variable: Who, What, When, Why, and How." *Neuropsychopharmacology* 42, no. 2 (January 2017): 386–96. http://doi.org/10.1038/npp.2016.215.

Barkley, Archibald. *Kentucky's Pioneer Lithotomists.* Cincinnati: C. J. Krehbiel & Company, 1913. http://archive.org/details/kentuckyspioneer00bark.

Bayer, Ronald, and Gerald Oppenheimer. *AIDS Doctors: Voices from the Epidemic: An Oral History.* New York: Oxford University Press, 2000.

Bell, Ryan Corbett. *The Ambulance: A History.* Reprint ed. Jefferson, NC: McFarland & Company, 2012.

Bigelow, Henry Jacob. "Insensibility during Surgical Operations Produced by Inhalation." *The Boston Medical and Surgical Journal* 35, no. 16 (November 18, 1846): 311–17.

Black, Hank. "The Enlightening Endoscope." *University of Alabama at Birmingham Magazine.* Accessed May 30, 2019. https://www.uab.edu/uabmagazine/hirschowitz.

"Black Hospital Movement in Alabama." *Encyclopedia of Alabama.* Accessed June 22, 2019. http://www.encyclopediaofalabama.org/article/h-2410.

Black, Kathryn. *In the Shadow of Polio: A Personal and Social History.* Cambridge, MA: Da Capo Press, 1997.

Blatchford, James W. "Ludwig Rehn: The First Successful Cardiorrhaphy." *The Annals of Thoracic Surgery* 39, no. 5 (May 1985): 492–95. http://doi.org/10.1016/S0003 -4975(10)61972-8.

*Ed Roberts and Judy Heumann in 1984 Interview.* Stockholm, Sweden, 1984. https://vimeo.com/29471050.

Ehrenreich, Barbara, and Deirdre English. *For Her Own Good: Two Centuries of the Experts' Advice to Women.* 2nd ed. New York: Anchor, 2005.

Eldredge, Adda. "The Responsibility of the Hospital to the Training School." *The American Journal of Nursing* 19, no. 5 (1919). http://doi.org/10.2307/3405568.

El-Seedi, Hesham R. "Antimicrobial Activity and Chemical Composition of Essential Oil of Eupatorium Glutinosum (Lam.)." *Natural Product Communications* 1, no. 8 (August 1, 2006). http://doi.org/10.1177/1934578X0600100811.

Engel, Jonathan. *The Epidemic: A Global History of AIDS.* New York: Smithsonian, 2006.

Eschner, Kat. "This American Doctor Pioneered Abdominal Surgery by Operating on Enslaved Women." *Smithsonian Magazine.* Accessed February 27, 2020. https://www.smithsonianmag.com/history/father-abdominal-surgery-practiced-enslaved-women-180967589/.

Ettinger, Laura. *Nurse-Midwifery: The Birth of a New American Profession.* Columbus, OH: Ohio State University Press, 2006.

Fairchild, Amy L. *Science at the Borders: Immigrant Inspection and the Shaping of the Modern Industrial Labor Force.* Baltimore: Johns Hopkins University Press, 2003.

Fallouji, M. A. "History of Surgery of the Abdominal Cavity. Arabic Contributions." *International Surgery* 78, no. 3 (September 1993): 236–38.

Fenn, Elizabeth A. *Pox Americana: The Great Smallpox Epidemic of 1775–82.* New York: Hill and Wang, 2002.

Fenster, J. M. *Ether Day: The Strange Tale of America's Greatest Medical Discovery and the Haunted Men Who Made It.* New York: Harper Perennial, 2002.

Ferguson, James H. "Mississippi Midwives." *Journal of the History of Medicine and Allied Sciences* 5, no. 1 (1950): 85–95.

Ferry, Georgina. "Susan La Flesche Picotte: A Doctor Who Spanned Two Cultures." *The Lancet* 393, no. 10173 (February 23, 2019): 734. http://doi.org/10.1016/S0140-6736(19)30363-0.

Fessler, Diane Burke. *No Time for Fear: Voices of American Military Nurses in World War II.* East Lansing, MI: Michigan State University Press, 1997.

"Fighting Silicosis: Dust Control in the Granite Industry, 1937." *The Green Mountain Chronicles* 89 (1988). https://vermonthistory.org/fighting-silicosis-dust-control-in -granite-industry-1937.

Fildes, Valerie A. *Breasts, Bottles and Babies: A History of Infant Feeding.* Edinburgh: Edinburgh University Press, 1986.

Finan, Christopher M. *Drunks: The Story of Alcoholism and the Birth of Recovery.* Reprint ed. Boston: Beacon Press, 2018.

Fischman, Stuart L. "The History of Oral Hygiene Products: How Far Have We Come in 6000 Years?" *Periodontology 2000* 15, no. 1 (November 1997): 7–14. http://doi.org/10.1111/j.1600-0757.1997.tb00099.x.

Fishbein, Morris. *Fads and Quackery in Healing: An Analysis of the Foibles of the Healing Cults.* New York: Covici Friede, 1932. http://hdl.handle.net/2027/ mdp.39015055447836.

Fitzharris, Lindsey. *The Butchering Art: Joseph Lister's Quest to Transform the Grisly World of Victorian Medicine.* New York: Farrar, Straus and Giroux, 2017.

Flagg, J. F. "The Inhalation of an Ethereal Vapor to Prevent Sensibility to Pain during Surgical Operations." *Boston Medical and Surgical Journal* (November 23, 1846).

Frankenburg, Frances Rachel. *Vitamin Discoveries and Disasters: History, Science, and Controversies.* Santa Barbara, CA: Praeger, 2009.

Furin, Jennifer J. "'You Have to Be Your Own Doctor': Sociocultural Influences on Alternative Therapy Use among Gay Men with AIDS in West Hollywood." *Medical Anthropology Quarterly* 11, no. 4 (1997).

Gamble, Vanessa Northington. "'There Wasn't a Lot of Comforts in Those Days:' African Americans, Public Health, and the 1918 Influenza Epidemic." *Public Health Reports (1974–)* 125 (2010): 114–22.

Gately, Iain. *Tobacco: A Cultural History of How an Exotic Plant Seduced Civilization.* Ebook ed. New York: Grove Press, 2007.

Gaudet, Marcia. *Carville: Remembering Leprosy in America.* Jackson: University Press of Mississippi, 2004.

Gawin, Frank H., and Everett H. Ellinwood. "Cocaine and Other Stimulants." *New England Journal of Medicine* 318, no. 18 (May 5, 1988): 1173–82. http://doi .org/10.1056/NEJM198805053181806.

Gehred, Kathryn. "Did George Washington's False Teeth Come from His Slaves?: A Look at the Evidence, the Responses to That Evidence, and the Limitations of History." *Washington's Quill, The Washington Papers, University of Virginia*, October 19, 2016. http://gwpapers.virginia.edu/george-washingtons-false-teeth -come-slaves-look-evidence-responses-evidence-limitations-history/.

Gelijns, Annetine C., Nathan Rosenberg, and Holly Dawkins. *From the Scalpel to the Scope: Endoscopic Innovations in Gastroenterology, Gynecology, and Surgery.* Washington, DC: National Academies Press, 1995. https://www.ncbi.nlm.nih.gov/ books/NBK232053/.

Giglio, James N. "Voluntarism and Public Policy between World War I and the New Deal: Herbert Hoover and the American Child Health Association." *Presidential Studies Quarterly* 13, no. 3 (1983): 430–52.

Gilje, Paul A., and Howard B. Rock. "'Sweep O! Sweep O!': African-American Chimney Sweeps and Citizenship in the New Nation." *The William and Mary Quarterly* 51, no. 3 (1994): 507–38. http://doi.org/10.2307/2947440.

"Giving of 'Ray' Treatments Brings Arrest of Dentist." *Grand Rapids Herald.* August 1, 1945.

Goeres-Gardner, Diane L. *Inside Oregon State Hospital: A History of Tragedy and Triumph.* Charleston: The History Press, 2013.

Goldberg, Johanna. "Did Corsets Harm Women's Health?" *Books, Health and History: The New York Academy of Medicine Blog,* May 29, 2015. https:// nyamcenterforhistory.org/2015/05/29/did-corsets-harm-womens-health/.

Gornall, Jonathan. "To Eradicate Malaria, Bring Back DDT." *Asia Times,* September 21, 2019, sec. Opinion. https://www.asiatimes.com/2019/09/opinion/to-eradicate -malaria-bring-back-ddt/.

Gould, A. B. "Charles T. Jackson's Claim to the Discovery of Etherization." In *Anaesthesia,* edited by Joseph Rupreht, Marius Jan van Lieburg, John Alfred Lee, and Wilhelm Erdmann, 384–87. Berlin, Heidelberg: Springer, 1985. http://doi .org/10.1007/978-3-642-69636-7_81.

Gray, Fred. *The Tuskegee Syphilis Study: An Insiders' Account of the Shocking Medical Experiment Conducted by Government Doctors against African American Men.* Ebook ed. Montgomery, AL: NewSouth Books, 2003.

Haas, Nelson. "Understanding Workers' Compensation, Part I: History of Workers' Compensation in the United States and Vermont." *The Vermont Medical Society*, July 2011. http://www.vtmd.org/workerscomppart1.

Haelle, Tara. *Vaccination Investigation: The History and Science of Vaccines.* Minneapolis: Twenty-First Century Books, 2018.

Hagen, Susan, and Mary Carouba. *Women at Ground Zero: Stories of Courage and Compassion.* Indianapolis: Alpha, 2002.

Hager, Thomas. *Ten Drugs: How Plants, Powders, and Pills Have Shaped the History of Medicine.* New York: Abrams Press, 2019.

Hall, Stephen. "The Upjohn Pharmacy in Disneyland." *Points: The Blog of the Alcohol & Drugs History Society*, November 19, 2019. https://pointsadhs.com/2019/11/19/the-upjohn-pharmacy-in-disneyland/.

Haller, John S. *The Physician and Sexuality in Victorian America.* New York: W. W. Norton, 1974. http://archive.org/details/physiciansexuali0000unse.

Haridas, Rajesh P. "Horace Wells' Demonstration of Nitrous Oxide in Boston." *Anesthesiology: The Journal of the American Society of Anesthesiologists* 119, no. 5 (November 1, 2013): 1014–22. http://doi.org/10.1097/ALN.0b013e3182a771ea.

Harkness, Laura. "The History of Enteral Nutrition Therapy: From Raw Eggs and Nasal Tubes to Purified Amino Acids and Early Postoperative Jejunal Delivery." *Journal of the American Dietetic Association* 102, no. 3 (March 1, 2002): 399–404. http://doi.org/10.1016/S0002-8223(02)90092-1.

Harwell, Thomas Meade. *Studies in Texan Folklore—Rio Grande Valley: Twelve Folklore Studies with Introductions, Commentaries & a Bounty of Notes. Lore 1.* New York: Edwin Mellen Press, 1997.

Helfand, William H., and David L. Cowen. "Evolution of Pharmaceutical Oral Dosage Forms." *Pharmacy in History* 25, no. 1 (1983).

Hendrickson, Brett. *Border Medicine: A Transcultural History of Mexican American Curanderismo.* New York: NYU Press, 2014.

Herkert, Darby, et al. "Cost-Related Insulin Underuse among Patients with Diabetes." *Journal of the American Medical Association Internal Medicine* 179, no. 1 (January 2019): 112–13.

Herndl, Diane Price. "The Invisible (Invalid) Woman: African-American Women, Illness, and Nineteenth-Century Narrative." In *Women and Health in America*, edited by Judith Walzer Leavitt, 2nd ed. Madison, WI: The University of Wisconsin Press, 1984.

Herzig, Rebecca. "In the Name of Science: Suffering, Sacrifice, and the Formation of American Roentgenology." *American Quarterly* 53, no. 4 (December 2001): 563–89.

Hickman, Timothy. "The Double Meaning of Addiction: Habitual Narcotic Use and the Logic of Professionalizing Medical Authority in the United States, 1900–1920." In *Altering American Consciousness: The History of Alcohol and Drug Use in the United States, 1800–2000*, edited by Sarah Tracy and Caroline Acker, 182–202. Amherst, MA: University of Massachusetts Press, 2004.

Hicks, Mattie Donnell. Oral History. Interview by Herman Trojanowski. Transcript, February 25, 1999. Martha Blakeney Hodges Special Collections and University Archives, The University of North Carolina at Greensboro. http://libcdm1.uncg .edu/cdm/singleitem/collection/WVHP/id/4218.

Hill, Austin Bradford. "The Environment and Disease: Association or Causation?" *Proceedings of the Royal Society of Medicine* 58, no. 5 (May 1965): 295–300.

Hirschowitz, Basil I. "A Personal History of the Fiberscope." *Gastroenterology* 76, no. 4 (April 1, 1979): 864–69. http://doi.org/10.1016/S0016-5085(79)80190-0.

———. "Development and Application of Endoscopy." *Gastroenterology* 104, no. 2 (February 1, 1993): 337–42. http://doi.org/10.5555/uri:pii:001650859390399W.

"History." *Trudeau Institute*. Accessed June 8, 2019. https://www.trudeauinstitute.org/ history.

Hobby, Gladys L. *Penicillin: Meeting the Challenge*. New Haven: Yale University Press, 1985.

Hoffman, Kelly M., et al. "Racial Bias in Pain Assessment and Treatment Recommendations, and False Beliefs about Biological Differences between Blacks and Whites." *Proceedings of the National Academy of Sciences of the United States of America* 113, no. 16 (2016): 4296–4301.

Honigsbaum, Mark. "Why the 1918 Spanish Flu Defied Both Memory and Imagination." *Wellcome Collection*. Accessed June 27, 2020. https:// wellcomecollection.org/articles/W7TfGRAAAP5F0eKS.

*Hostetter's Illustrated United States Almanac, for the Year 1868.* Pittsburgh, PA: Hostetter and Smith, 1868. http://archive.org/details/hostettersillust1868amer.

Humphreys, Margaret. *Marrow of Tragedy: The Health Crisis of the American Civil War.* Baltimore: Johns Hopkins University Press, 2013.

"In Soda Revival, Fizzy Taste Bubbles Up from the Past." *NPR.* Accessed June 22, 2020. https://www.npr.org/2011/09/01/140093866/in-soda-revival-fizzy-taste -bubbles-up-from-the-past.

"Incubator for Baby." *The Plattsmouth Journal,* January 12, 1933. Nebraska Historical Society.

Institute of Medicine (US) Committee on Understanding and Eliminating Racial and Ethnic Disparities in Health Care. "Executive Summary." In *Unequal Treatment: Confronting Racial and Ethnic Disparities in Health Care,* edited by Brian D. Smedley, Adrienne Y. Stith, and Alan R. Nelson. Washington, DC: National Academies Press, 2003. https://www.ncbi.nlm.nih.gov/books/NBK220355/.

Izuo, Masaru. "Medical History: Seishu Hanaoka and His Success in Breast Cancer Surgery under General Anesthesia Two Hundred Years Ago." *Breast Cancer* 11, no. 4 (November 1, 2004): 319–24. http://doi.org/10.1007/BF02968037.

"Jailing People with Mental Illness." *NAMI: National Alliance on Mental Illness.* Accessed January 9, 2021. https://www.nami.org/Advocacy/Policy-Priorities/ Divert-from-Justice-Involvement/Jailing-People-with-Mental-Illness.

Janik, Erika. *Marketplace of the Marvelous: The Strange Origins of Modern Medicine.* Reprint ed. Boston: Beacon Press, 2015.

Jantos, Marek, and Hosen Kiat. "Prayer as Medicine: How Much Have We Learned?" *The Medical Journal of Australia* 186, no. 10 (May 21, 2007): S51. http://doi .org/10.5694/j.1326-5377.2007.tb01041.x.

Jarrow, Gail. *Bubonic Panic: When Plague Invaded America.* Ebook ed. New York: Calkins Creek, 2016.

Jay, Mike. *This Way Madness Lies.* New York: Thames & Hudson, 2016.

Jefferson, Thomas. Letter to Benjamin Waterhouse, December 1, 1801. Benjamin Waterhouse papers, Box: 01, Folder: 24 Identifier: H MS c16. Countway Library of Medicine. https://hollisarchives.lib.harvard.edu/repositories/14/archival _objects/1910488.

Jones, David S. *Rationalizing Epidemics: Meanings and Uses of American Indian Mortality since 1600*. Ill. ed. Cambridge, MA: Harvard University Press, 2004.

Jones, Donna. "Mother/Daughter Team—The Mother's Story," n.d. Rosie the Riveter WWII Home Front National Historic Park. https://museum.nps.gov/ParkObjdet .aspx?rID=RORI%20%20%20%202313%26db%3Dobjects%26dir%3DCR%20 AAWEB%26page%3D1.

Jones, James H. *Bad Blood: The Tuskegee Syphilis Experiment, New and Expanded Edition*. New York: Free Press, 1993.

"Kam Wah Chung." *Oregon Experience*. PBS, January 13, 2010. https://www.opb.org/ television/programs/oregonexperience/segment/kam-wah-chung/.

Karch, Steven B. *A Brief History of Cocaine: From Inca Monarchs to Cali Cartels: 500 Years of Cocaine Dealing*. 2nd ed. Boca Raton: Taylor & Francis, 2006.

Kaunitz, Jonathan D. "The Fruits of Fiber: The Invention of the Flexible Fiberoptic Gastroscope." *Digestive Diseases and Sciences* 59, no. 11 (November 2014): 2616–18. http://doi.org/10.1007/s10620-014-3339-4.

Kelly, Christine. "Wrestling with Group Identity: Disability Activism and Direct Funding." *Disability Studies Quarterly* 30, no. 3/4 (August 26, 2010). http://doi .org/10.18061/dsq.v30i3/4.1279.

Kerr, Lorin E. "Black Lung." *Journal of Public Health Policy* 1, no. 1 (1980): 50–63. http://doi.org/10.2307/3342357.

Kinkela, David. *DDT and the American Century: Global Health, Environmental Politics, and the Pesticide That Changed the World*. Reprint ed. Chapel Hill: The University of North Carolina Press, 2013.

Kline, Wendy. "'Please Include This in Your Book': Readers Respond to *Our Bodies, Ourselves*." *Bulletin of the History of Medicine* 79, no. 1 (2005): 81–110.

Kolata, Gina Bari. *Flu: The Story of the Great Influenza Pandemic of 1918 and the Search for the Virus That Caused It*. Ebook ed. New York: Touchstone, 2001.

Kotar, S. L., and J. E. Gessler. *Smallpox: A History*. Jefferson, NC: McFarland, 2013.

Kraut, Alan M. *Silent Travelers: Germs, Genes, and the Immigrant Menace*. New York: Basic Books, 1994.

Kurlansky, Mark. *Milk!: A 10,000-Year Food Fracas*. New York: Bloomsbury Publishing, 2018.

Kurzman, Steven. "'There's No Language for This': Communication and Alignment in Contemporary Prosthetics." In *Artificial Parts, Practical Lives: Modern Histories of Prosthetics*. New York: NYU Press, 2002.

Lagay, Faith. "The Legacy of Humoral Medicine." *AMA Journal of Ethics* 4, no. 7 (July 1, 2002). http://doi.org/10.1001/virtualmentor.2002.4.7.mhst1-0207.

Laveaga, Gabriela Soto. *Jungle Laboratories: Mexican Peasants, National Projects, and the Making of the Pill*. Durham, NC: Duke University Press Books, 2009.

Lax, Eric. *The Mold in Dr. Florey's Coat: The Story of the Penicillin Miracle*. New York: Holt Paperbacks, 2005.

Laxminarayan, Ramanan, et al. *Extending the Cure: Policy Responses to the Growing Threat of Antibiotic Resistance*. London: Earthscan, 2007.

Lederer, Susan E. "Bloodlines: Blood Types, Identity, and Association in Twentieth-Century America." *The Journal of the Royal Anthropological Institute* (2013): S118–29.

Lee, R. Alton. *From Snake Oil to Medicine: Pioneering Public Health*. Healing Society: Disease, Medicine, and History. Westport, CT: Praeger Publishers, 2007.

Le Fanu, James. *The Rise and Fall of Modern Medicine: Revised Edition*. Ebook ed. New York: Basic Books, 2012.

Legan, Marshall Scott. "Hydropathy in America: A Nineteenth Century Panacea." *Bulletin of the History of Medicine* 45, no. 3 (1971): 267–80.

Lemanski, Michael. *A History of Addiction & Recovery in the United States: Traditional Treatments and Effective Alternatives*. Tucson, AZ: See Sharp Press, 2001.

Lescarboura, Austin C. "Our Abrams Investigation—VI." *Scientific American* 130, no. 3 (1924): 159–215.

———. "Our Abrams Investigation—XI." *Scientific American* 131, no. 2 (1924).

———. "Our Abrams Verdict." *Scientific American* 131, no. 3 (1924): 158–60.

Lesiak, Christine M., and Princella RedCorn. *Medicine Woman*. PBS. Accessed January 6, 2020. https://www.pbs.org/video/medicine-woman-full-episode/.

Liao, Pamela Verma, and Janet Dollin. "Half a Century of the Oral Contraceptive Pill." *Canadian Family Physician* 58, no. 12 (December 2012): e757–60.

Library of Congress Copyright Office. *Catalog of Copyright Entries 1936 Pamphlets, Leaflets, Etc.* Vol. 33. US Government Printing Office, 1936. http://archive.org/details/catalogofcopyri331li.

Lim, M. W. "The History of Extracorporeal Oxygenators." *Anaesthesia* 61, no. 10 (2006): 984–95. https://doi.org/10.1111/j.1365-2044.2006.04781.x.

Lister, Joseph. "On the Antiseptic Principle in the Practice of Surgery." *The British Medical Journal* 2, no. 351 (1867): 246–48.

Litoff, Judy Barrett. *American Midwives: 1860 to the Present.* Reprint ed. Westport, CT: Praeger, 1978.

Little, Deborah. "Identity, Efficiency and Disability Rights." *Disability Studies Quarterly* 30, no. 1 (November 18, 2009). http://doi.org/10.18061/dsq.v30i1.1013.

Ludmerer, Kenneth M. *Learning to Heal.* New York: Basic Books, 1988.

———. *Time to Heal: American Medical Education from the Turn of the Century to the Era of Managed Care.* Rev. ed. New York; Oxford: Oxford University Press, 2005.

Madrigal, Alexis C. "Disposable America." *The Atlantic*, June 21, 2018. https://www.theatlantic.com/technology/archive/2018/06/disposable-america/563204/.

Mann, Barbara Alice. *The Tainted Gift: The Disease Method of Frontier Expansion.* Ill. ed. Santa Barbara, CA: Praeger, 2009.

Marian, Catalin, et al. "Reconciling Human Smoking Behavior and Machine Smoking Patterns: Implications for Understanding Smoking Behavior and the Impact on Laboratory Studies." *Cancer Epidemiology, Biomarkers & Prevention* 18, no. 12 (December 2009). https://cebp.aacrjournals.org/content/18/12/3305.long.

Martin, Betty. *Miracle at Carville.* Garden City, NY: Doubleday & Company, Inc., 1950.

Martinez, Edward. World Trade Center Task Force Interview. Interview by Paul Radenberg. Transcript, January 24, 2002. https://static01.nyt.com/packages/pdf/nyregion/20050812_WTC_GRAPHIC/9110494.PDF.

Mason, Martha, and Charlie Cornwell. *Breath: Life in the Rhythm of an Iron Lung.* Asheboro, NC: John F. Blair, 2003.

Matthews, Dylan. "What 'Dallas Buyers Club' Got Wrong about the AIDS Crisis." *Washington Post.* Accessed July 28, 2020. https://www.washingtonpost.com/news/wonk/wp/2013/12/10/what-dallas-buyers-club-got-wrong-about-the-aids-crisis/.

May, Elaine Tyler. *America and the Pill: A History of Promise, Peril, and Liberation.* Reprint ed. New York: Basic Books, 2011.

McCallion, Teresa. "EMS Providers Recall 9/11." *Journal of Emergency Medical Services* 36, no. 9 (September 1, 2011). https://www.jems.com/2011/08/31/ems -providers-recall-911/.

McCamish, Mark, Gustavo Bounous, and Maureen Geraghty. "History of Enteral Feeding: Past and Present Perspectives." In *Clinical Nutrition: Enteral and Tube Feeding* by John L. Rombeau and Rolando Rolandelli, 1–11. Philadelphia: W. B. Saunders Company, 1997.

McWilliams, James. *American Pests: The Losing War on Insects from Colonial Times to DDT.* New York: Columbia University Press, 2008.

Middleton, Robert M., and Michael B. Kirkpatrick. "Clinical Use of Cocaine." *Drug Safety* 9, no. 3 (September 1, 1993): 212–17. http://doi.org/10.2165/00002018 -199309030-00006.

Miller, G. Wayne. *King of Hearts: The True Story of the Maverick Who Pioneered Open Heart Surgery.* New York: Broadway Books, 2002.

Modlin, Irvin M., Mark Kidd, and Kevin D. Lye. "From the Lumen to the Laparoscope." *Archives of Surgery* 139, no. 10 (October 2004): 1110–26. http://doi .org/10.1001/archsurg.139.10.1110.

Moran, Michelle T. *Colonizing Leprosy: Imperialism and the Politics of Public Health in the United States.* New ed. Chapel Hill, NC: The University of North Carolina Press, 2007.

Morris, Thomas. *The Matter of the Heart: A History of the Heart in Eleven Operations.* New York: Thomas Dunne Books, 2018.

Mould, Richard. "The Early History of X-Rays in Medicine for Therapy and Diagnosis." In *X-Rays: The First Hundred Years*, edited by Alan Michette and Slawka Pfauntsch. Chichester, NY: John Wiley & Sons, 1996. http://archive.org/ details/xraysfirsthundre0000unse.

Mullaly, John. *The Milk Trade in New York and Vicinity: Giving an Account of the Sale of Pure and Adulterated Milk.* New York: Fowlers and Wells, 1853. https:// books.google.com/books/about/The_Milk_Trade_of_New_York_and_Vicinity .html?id=KXIZAAAAYAAJ.

National Center for Health Statistics, Centers for Disease Control and Prevention. "FastStats - Contraceptive Use," November 21, 2019. https://www.cdc.gov/nchs/fastats/contraceptive.htm.

"National Historical Park." Richmond General Plan 2030. Richmond, CA: City of Richmond Planning and Building Services Department, 2012. http://www.ci.richmond.ca.us/DocumentCenter/View/8820/150-National-Historical-Park?bidId=.

National Institute on Drug Abuse. "Opioid Overdose Crisis." January 22, 2019. https://www.drugabuse.gov/drugs-abuse/opioids/opioid-overdose-crisis.

*National Negro Health Week. Annual Observance.* United States Public Health Service, 1923. https://books.google.com/books?id=yd8KAQAAIAAJ&dq.

National Trust for Historic Preservation. "History Divided: Dr. Susan LaFlesche Picotte's Legacy in Three Buildings." *Saving Places.* Accessed January 6, 2020. https://savingplaces.org/stories/history-divided-dr-susan-laflesche-picottes-legacy-in-three-buildings.

Newton, David E. *The Opioid Crisis: A Reference Handbook.* Santa Barbara, CA: ABC-CLIO, 2018.

Nielsen, Kim E. *A Disability History of the United States.* Boston: Beacon Press, 2013.

Ochsner, Alton. "My First Recognition of the Relationship of Smoking and Lung Cancer." *Preventive Medicine* 2 (1973): 611–14.

O'Dell, Shannon. Personal communication. April 2020.

*Official Guidebook to the Trans-Mississippi International Exposition.* Omaha: 1898.

Offit, Paul. *Bad Faith: When Religious Belief Undermines Modern Medicine.* New York: Basic Books, 2015.

O'Hare, Pat. "From Local to Global: A Short History of Harm Reduction." In *The History and Principles of Harm Reduction: Between Public Health & Social Change.* Paris: Médecins du Monde, 2013. https://issuu.com/medecinsdumonde/docs/mdm_rdr_en_bd.

Olsen, Yngvild, and Joshua M. Sharfstein. *The Opioid Epidemic: What Everyone Needs to Know.* Oxford: Oxford University Press, 2019.

Olson, James C., and Ronald C. Naugle. *History of Nebraska.* 3rd ed. Lincoln: University of Nebraska Press, 1997.

Olson, James S. *Bathsheba's Breast: Women, Cancer, and History*. Rev. ed. Baltimore: Johns Hopkins University Press, 2005.

Olstad, Jay. "Montevideo Police Save Overdosing Woman with Naloxone." *KARE11 News*, September 20, 2016. https://www.kare11.com/article/news/montevideo -police-save-overdosing-woman-with-naloxone/89-322418080.

Ott, Katherine. *Fevered Lives: Tuberculosis in American Culture since 1870*. Cambridge, MA: Harvard University Press, 1999.

Palca, Joseph. "International Doubts about a Kenyan Cure." *Science* 250, no. 4978 (1990): 200.

Parascandola, John. "Industrial Research Comes of Age: The American Pharmaceutical Industry, 1920–1940." *Pharmacy in History* 27, no. 1 (1985): 12–21.

Parascandola, Mark. "Two Approaches to Etiology: The Debate over Smoking and Lung Cancer in the 1950s." *Endeavour* 28, no. 2 (June 2004): 81–86.

Paul, Gill. *A History of Medicine in 50 Objects*. Buffalo, NY: Firefly Books, 2016.

Peña, Carolyn Thomas de la. *The Body Electric: How Strange Machines Built the Modern American*. Austin, TX: NYU Press, 2005.

Penrose, Beris. "'So Now They Have Some Human Guinea Pigs': Aluminium Therapy and Occupational Silicosis." *Health and History* 9, no. 1 (2007): 56–79. http://doi.org/10.2307/40111558.

Phillips, George Lewis. *American Chimney Sweeps: An Historical Account of a Once Important Trade*. Trenton: Past Times Press, 1957.

"Preserving the Legacy of Dr. Susan La Flesche Picotte—Healing History." *DrSusanCenter.Org*, January 9, 2019. https://www.drsusancenter.org/2019/01/09/ preserving-the-legacy-of-dr-susan-la-flesche-picotte-healing-history/.

Price, Catherine. *Vitamania: Our Obsessive Quest for Nutritional Perfection*. New York: Penguin Press, 2015.

Quinn, Sandra, and Stephen Thomas. "The National Negro Health Week, 1915 to 1951: A Descriptive Account." *Minority Health Today* 2, no. 3 (April 2001).

Raffel, Dawn. *The Strange Case of Dr. Couney: How a Mysterious European Showman Saved Thousands of American Babies*. New York: Blue Rider Press, 2018.

Ramirez, José P., Jr. *Squint: My Journey with Leprosy*. Jackson: University Press of Mississippi, 2009.

Recker, Narcy. *An Institution of Organized Kindness*. Sioux Falls, SD: Sioux Valley Hospital, 1996.

Redman, Samuel J. *Bone Rooms: From Scientific Racism to Human Prehistory in Museums*. Cambridge, MA: Harvard University Press, 2016.

"Report of Madison Five Counties Medical Society Meeting." *Nebraska State Medical Journal* 16, no. 19 (October 1931): 413.

"Retro Ad of the Week: Schlitz Beer, 1936—Beverage Advertising," June 28, 2013. https://mascola.com/insights/beverage-advertising-retro-ad-of-the-week-schlitz -beer-1936/.

Reverby, Susan M. "Feminism & Health." *Health and History* 4, no. 1 (2002): 5–19. http://doi.org/10.2307/40111418.

Richardson, Wendy. "'The Curse of Our Trade': Occupational Disease in a Vermont Granite Town." *Proceedings of the Vermont Historical Society* 60, no. 1 (1992): 5–28.

Roberts, Dorothy. *Killing the Black Body: Race, Reproduction, and the Meaning of Liberty*. New York: Vintage Books, 1997.

Roberts, Edward. "The Emergence of the Disabled Civil Rights Movement." *Edward V. Roberts Papers, The Bancroft Library. University of California, Berkeley*. Accessed June 6, 2019. https://oac.cdlib.org/ark:/13030/hb6m3nb1nw/?brand=oac4.

———. "When Others Speak for You, You Lose." *Edward V. Roberts Papers, The Bancroft Library. University of California, Berkeley*. Accessed June 6, 2019. https:// oac.cdlib.org/ark:/13030/hb3j49n6hw/?brand=oac4.

Rosen, George. *A History of Public Health*. Rev. exp. ed. Baltimore: Johns Hopkins University Press, 2015.

Rosner, David, and Gerald Markowitz. "Workers, Industry, and the Control of Information: Silicosis and the Industrial Hygiene Foundation." *Journal of Public Health Policy* 16, no. 1 (1995): 29–58. http://doi.org/10.2307/3342976.

Roth, Nancy. "Good Vibrations: Abrams's Oscilloclast and the Instrumental Cure." *Medical Instrumentation* 15, no. 6 (December 1981).

Schachner, August. *Ephraim McDowell, "Father of Ovariotomy": His Life and His Work*. Reprinted from *The Johns Hopkins Hospital Bulletin* 24, no. 267 (May 1913). http://archive.org/details/b30619658.

———. *Ephraim McDowell, "Father of Ovariotomy" and Founder of Abdominal Surgery, with an Appendix on Jane Todd Crawford*. Philadelphia, London: J. B. Lippincott Company, 1921. http://archive.org/details/ephraimmcdowellf00schaiala.

Schexnyder, Elizabeth. *Audio Tour: Carville: The National Leprosarium*. National Hansen's Disease Museum. Accessed June 15, 2019. https://neworleanshistorical.org/tours/show/55.

"Schlitz 'Sunshine Vitamin D Beer Can.'" *Wisconsin Historical Society*, October 19, 2012. https://www.wisconsinhistory.org/Records/Article/CS2859.

Schneider, William H. "Blood Transfusion between the Wars." *Journal of the History of Medicine and Allied Sciences* 58, no. 2 (2003): 187–224.

Schroeder-Lein, Glenna R. *The Encyclopedia of Civil War Medicine*. New York: Routledge, 2008.

Schwartz, Marie Jenkins. *Birthing a Slave: Motherhood and Medicine in the Antebellum South*. Cambridge, MA: Harvard University Press, 2006.

Schwarz, Gerhart. "Society, Physicians, and the Corset." *Bulletin of the New York Academy of Medicine* 55, no. 6 (June 1979): 551–90.

Selden, Steven. *Inheriting Shame: The Story of Eugenics and Racism in America*. New York: Teachers College Press, 1999.

Seytre, Bernard, and Mary Shaffer. *The Death of a Disease: A History of the Eradication of Poliomyelitis*. New Brunswick, NJ: Rutgers University Press, 2005.

Shahani, Nishant. "How to Survive the Whitewashing of AIDS: Global Pasts, Transnational Futures." *QED: A Journal in GLBTQ Worldmaking* 3, no. 1 (2016): 1–33. http://doi.org/10.14321/qed.3.1.0001.

Silver, Julie K., and Daniel Wilson. *Polio Voices: An Oral History from the American Polio Epidemics and Worldwide Eradication Efforts*. Westport, CT: Praeger, 2007.

Smith-Rosenberg, Carroll, and Charles E. Rosenberg. "The Female Animal: Medical and Biological Views of Woman and Her Role in Nineteenth Century America." In *Women and Health in America*, edited by Judith Walzer Leavitt, 2nd ed. Madison, WI: The University of Wisconsin Press, 1984.

Snyder, Lois, and Paul S. Mueller. "Research in the Physician's Office: Navigating the Ethical Minefield." *The Hastings Center Report* 38, no. 2 (2008): 23–25.

"Social Advances." *The Department of Defense 60th Anniversary of the Korean War Commemoration.* Accessed August 3, 2019. http://www.koreanwar60.com/social -advances/.

Speaker, Susan. "Demons for the Twentieth Century: The Rhetoric of Drug Reform, 1920–1940." In *Altering American Consciousness: The History of Alcohol and Drug Use in the United States, 1800–2000*, edited by Sarah Tracy and Caroline Acker, 203–24. Amherst, MA: University of Massachusetts Press, 2004.

Spillane, Joseph F. *Cocaine: From Medical Marvel to Modern Menace in the United States, 1884–1920.* Baltimore: Johns Hopkins University Press, 2000. http://archive .org/details/cocainefrommedic00spil.

Squires, Sally. "Julia Rivera Elwood, 58." *The Washington Post*, November 16, 1997. https://www.washingtonpost.com/archive/politics/1997/11/16/julia-rivera -elwood-58/ff06aed1-d886-4824-92e6-e704d598d3a0/?utm_term=.2ef73f89e794.

Starita, Joe. *A Warrior of the People: How Susan La Flesche Overcame Racial and Gender Inequality to Become America's First Indian Doctor.* New York: St. Martin's Press, 2016.

Steele, Valerie. *The Corset: A Cultural History.* New Haven, CT: Yale University Press, 2003.

Stryker, Susan. *Transgender History: The Roots of Today's Revolution.* Berkeley: Seal Press, 2017.

Stryker, William. *Record of Officers and Men of New Jersey in the Civil War, 1861–1865.* Vol. 1. Trenton, NJ: John L. Murphy, Steam Book and Job Printer, 1876. http://slic.njstatelib.org/slic_files/searchable_publications/civilwar/ NJCWn267.html.

Summerly, Paula. "Bowie, Anna Mary." In *The Handbook of Texas Online*. Texas State Historical Association. Accessed May 18, 2020. https://tshaonline.org/handbook/ online/articles/fbowi.

———. "Bubonic Plague, Galveston (1920)." In *The Handbook of Texas Online*. Texas State Historical Association. Accessed May 4, 2020. https://tshaonline.org/ handbook/online/articles/smbub.

Surgeon General's Advisory Committee on Smoking and Health. *Smoking and Health*. Washington, DC: U.S. Dept. of Health, Education, and Welfare, Public Health Service, 1964. http://archive.org/details/smokinghealthrep00unit.

Swann, John P. "The Evolution of the American Pharmaceutical Industry." *Pharmacy in History* 37, no. 2 (1995): 76–86.

Sylvia, Walter J. "U.S. City Directories, 1822–1995—AncestryLibrary.Com." In *Charleston, South Carolina, City Directory, 1916*. U.S. City Directories, 1822–1995—AncestryLibrary.com. Accessed May 10, 2020. https://search.ancestrylibrary.com/cgi-bin/sse.dll?indiv=1&dbid=2469&h=955193218&tid=&pid=&usePUB=true&_phsrc=FOo22&_phstart=successSource.

TallBear, Kim. *Native American DNA: Tribal Belonging and the False Promise of Genetic Science*. Minneapolis: University of Minnesota Press, 2013.

Taylor, Robert. *Saranac: America's Magic Mountain*. Boston: Houghton Mifflin Harcourt, 1986.

"The Aztec Healer." *Milwaukee Daily Sentinel*, April 24, 1894. Gale Nineteenth Century U.S. Newspapers.

*The Conductor and Brakeman*. Vol. 22. Order of Railway Conductors and Brakemen, 1905. https://books.google.com/books/about/The_Conductor_and_Brakeman.html?id=3Z4nQw3TGbwC.

*The Industrial Advance of Rochester: A Historical, Statistical & Descriptive Review*. Philadelphia: National Publishing Company, 1884. https://books.google.com/books/about/The_Industrial_Advance_of_Rochester.html?id=VSEaAAAAYAAJ.

Tone, Andrea. *Devices and Desires: A History of Contraceptives in America*. New York: Hill and Wang, 2002.

"Too Much Fuss over Blood Transfusions." *The Science News-Letter* 33, no. 6 (1938). http://doi.org/10.2307/3915098.

Torres, Eliseo. *Healing with Herbs and Rituals: A Mexican Tradition*. Edited by Timothy L. Sawyer. Albuquerque: University of New Mexico Press, 2006.

"Trailblazing Tribal Hospital Lands on 'Most Endangered Historic Places' List." *Indianz*. Accessed January 26, 2020. https://www.indianz.com/News/2018/06/26/historic-indian-hospital-lands-on-most-e.asp.

Trauner, Joan. "The Chinese as Medical Scapegoats in San Francisco, 1870–1905." *California History* 57, no. 1 (Spring 1978): 70–87. http://doi.org/10.2307/25157817.

Treatment Advocacy Center. "The Treatment of Persons with Mental Illness in Prisons and Jails: A State Survey," 2014. TACReports.org/treatment-behind-bars.

"Trial on Patent Respirator Suit Scheduled Today." *The Harvard Crimson*. November 6, 1934. https://www.thecrimson.com/article/1934/11/6/trial-on-patent-respirator-suit-scheduled.

Turner, Seth. "The Thwaites X-Ray Machine: An Early Shock-Proof Dental X-Ray Unit." Ann Arbor, MI: Sindecuse Museum of Dentistry, 2007.

UNAIDS. "Global HIV & AIDS Statistics—Fact Sheet." Accessed July 5, 2021. https://www.unaids.org/en/resources/fact-sheet.

Unschuld, Paul. *Traditional Chinese Medicine: Heritage and Adaptation*, translated by Bridie Andrews. Ebook ed. New York: Columbia University Press, 2018.

Urdang, George. "The Antibiotics and Pharmacy." *Journal of the History of Medicine and Allied Sciences* 6, no. 3 (1951): 388–405.

U.S. Army Center of Military History. "The Army Nurse Corps." Accessed August 3, 2019. https://history.army.mil/books/wwii/72-14/72-14.HTM.

U.S. National Park Service. "The Ray House—Wilson's Creek National Battlefield." Accessed October 6, 2019. https://www.nps.gov/wicr/learn/historyculture/the-ray-house.htm.

"U.S., Social Security Applications and Claims Index, 1936–2007—AncestryLibrary. Com." Accessed July 4, 2019.

Van Blarcom, Carolyn Conant. *Getting Ready to Be a Mother: A Little Book of Information and Advice for the Young Woman Who Is Looking Forward to Motherhood*. New York: The MacMillan Company, 1922. http://hdl.handle.net/2027/uc1.b3846025.

Van Vleck, Richard. "The Electronic Reactions of Albert Abrams." *American Artifacts*. Accessed August 28, 2019. http://www.americanartifacts.com/smma/abrams/abrams.htm.

Vanderbilt, Allison A., and Marcie S. Wright. "Infant Mortality: A Call to Action Overcoming Health Disparities in the United States." *Medical Education Online* 18, no. 1 (January 1, 2013): 22503. http://doi.org/10.3402/meo.v18i0.22503.

Varon, Jodi. "Ing Hay ('Doc Hay') (1862–1952)." *Oregon Encyclopedia*, accessed May 25, 2020. https://oregonencyclopedia.org/articles/ing_doc_hay_1862_1952_/#.Xsv-RBNKg1I.

Venit Shelton, Tamara. *Herbs and Roots: A History of Chinese Doctors in the American Medical Marketplace*. New Haven, CT: Yale University Press, 2019.

Vertinsky, Patricia A. *The Eternally Wounded Woman: Women, Doctors, and Exercise in the Late Nineteenth Century*, Illini Books. Urbana, IL: University of Illinois Press, 1994.

"Virtual Tour." *McDowell House Museum Website*. Accessed March 8, 2020. http://www.mcdowellhouse.com/virtual-tour/.

Vyas, Ritva, et al. "Squamous Cell Carcinoma of the Scrotum: A Look beyond the Chimneystacks." *World Journal of Clinical Cases: WJCC* 2, no. 11 (November 16, 2014): 654–60. http:doi.org/10.12998/wjcc.v2.i11.654.

"W-615A-D Mount Vernon Fact Sheet." Mount Vernon Ladies' Association, May 20, 2019.

Waldron, H. A. "A Brief History of Scrotal Cancer." *British Journal of Industrial Medicine* 40, no. 4 (1983): 390–401.

Wallace, W. Clay. "Remarks on the Inhalation of Ether Previous to Surgical Operations." *Boston Medical and Surgical Journal* (n.d.): 435–36.

"Wall Text, Main Exhibit." Saranac Lake Laboratory Museum, Saranac Lake, New York.

Warren, John Collins. "Inhalation of an Etheral Vapor for the Prevention of Pain in Surgical Operations." *Boston Medical and Surgical Journal* (December 3, 1846).

Washburn, Frederic. "Remarks on the History of the Old Surgical Amphitheatre." *The Boston Medical and Surgical Journal* 195, no. 26 (December 23, 1926): 1193–94. http:/.doi.org/10.1056/NEJM192612231952602.

Washington, George. *The Writings of George Washington from the Original Manuscript Sources, 1745–1799*. Washington, DC: United States George Washington Bicentennial Commission, 1931. http://archive.org/details/writingsofgeorge28wash.

Washington, Harriet A. *Medical Apartheid: The Dark History of Medical Experimentation on Black Americans from Colonial Times to the Present*. Reprint. New York: Anchor, 2008.

Waterhouse, Benjamin. Letter to John Coakley Lettsom, November 5, 1801. Harvard University Libraries. https://hollisarchives.lib.harvard.edu/repositories/14/archival_objects/1910494.

Watson, Frank. "The Contributions of American Social Agencies to Social Progress and Democracy." *The Journal of Social Forces* 1, no. 2 (January 1923): 87–90.

Weinberger, Bernhard Wolf. *An Introduction to the History of Dentistry*. Vol. 2. 2 vols. St. Louis: C. V. Mosby Co., 1948. https://catalog.hathitrust.org/Record/001571139.

Wertz, Richard W., and Dorothy C. Wertz. *Lying-In: A History of Childbirth in America*. New York: Free Press, 1977.

Wilkinson Meyer, Jimmy. "Oral Contraceptive Pill." *Dittrick Medical History Center*. Accessed November 30, 2019. https://artsci.case.edu/dittrick/online-exhibits/history-of-birth-control/contraception-in-america-1950-present-day/oral-contraceptive-pill/.

Wilson, Daniel J. *Living with Polio: The Epidemic and Its Survivors*. Ill. ed. Chicago: University of Chicago Press, 2008.

———. *Polio*. Santa Barbara, CA: ABC-CLIO, 2009.

Winner, Cherie. *Circulating Life: Blood Transfusion from Ancient Superstition to Modern Medicine*. Minneapolis, MN: Twenty-First Century Books, 2007.

Wong, David H. T. *Escape to Gold Mountain: A Graphic History of the Chinese in North America*. Ebook ed. Vancouver, BC: Arsenal Pulp Press, 2012.

World Health Organization. "Smallpox." Accessed December 8, 2019. https://www.who.int/health-topics/smallpox#tab=tab_1.

———. "The Use of DDT in Malaria Vector Control: WHO Position Statement." Revised 2011. https://apps.who.int/iris/bitstream/handle/10665/69945/WHO_HTM_GMP_2011_eng.pdf.

Young, James Harvey. *The Toadstool Millionaires: A Social History of Patent Medicines in America before Federal Regulation*. Princeton, NJ: Princeton University Press, 1961. http://archive.org/details/toadstoolmillion00youn.

"Youngstown Polio Vaccine Immunization Volunteer Photograph." *Ohio Memory Collection*. Accessed September 26, 2018. http://www.ohiomemory.org/cdm/ref/collection/p267401coll36/id/24967.

# Index

Page references for figures are italicized.

# About the Author

**Tegan Kehoe** is a public historian specializing in healthcare and science. She does exhibits and education at the Russell Museum of Medical History and Innovation at Massachusetts General Hospital in Boston. Her exhibits have ranged from a temporary exhibit for an innovation festival that used xylophones to explain how anesthesia affects the brain, to a display of the personal items belonging to a WWI nurse.

Kehoe writes about scientific and social history and topics related to museums and archives, and she edited a newsletter column on medical museums for three years. She received her MA in History and Museum Studies from Tufts University. In her free time, she is a knitter and nature enthusiast, and is involved in an audio drama group, where she has an unintentional pattern of writing about nineteenth-century medical ideas and experiments, having written adaptations of Poe's *The Premature Burial* and Stevenson's *Jekyll and Hyde.*